CHINA AND ITS NEIGHBOURHOOD

Perspectives from India and Vietnam

CHINA AND ITS NEIGHBOURHOOD

Perspectives from India and Vietnam

Editors

Jabin T. Jacob and Hoang The Anh

PENTAGON PRESS

China and Its Neighbourhood: Perspectives from India and Vietnam

Editors: Jabin T. Jacob and Hoang The Anh

First Published in 2017

ISBN 978-93-86618-14-6

Disclaimer: The views expressed in this book are those of the authors and do not necessarily reflect those of the Institute of Chinese Studies, Delhi, or the Vietnam Academy of Social Sciences, Hanoi.

Published by

PENTAGON PRESS
206, Peacock Lane, Shahpur Jat
New Delhi-110049
Phones: 011-64706243, 26491568
Telefax: 011-26490600
email: rajan@pentagonpress.in
website: www.pentagonpress.in

Printed at Aegean Offset Printers, Greater Noida, U.P.

Contents

Indian Preface

The Institute of Chinese Studies (ICS) is pleased to bring out this joint volume on China and its neighbourhood with our partners in the Vietnam Academy of Social Sciences (VASS). Our relationship has progressed rapidly in the few years since we signed an MoU with the Institute for Indian and Southwest Asian Studies of the VASS first, followed by another one with its Institute of Chinese Studies in Hanoi. The ICS values this partnership and the regular interactions between our scholars as an important component imparting strength and vitality to the larger India-Vietnam relationship.

Our two countries have a multifaceted and strategic relationship, anchored in history and shared interests and perceptions. We have much in common in terms of development goals and aspirations as well as challenges in our foreign and security policies. While India and Vietnam seek cooperative and constructive relations with China, they also share certain anxieties with respect to their common neighbour. It is natural and important for our two sides to come together in order to understand each other's perspectives on the world's second-largest economy as well as a rising political and military power.

India and Vietnam both have territorial differences with China and yet this is not the only important aspect of our respective bilateral ties with China today or even the most defining one. Our respective economic ties with China are growing and increasingly creating dynamics of their own with larger questions and issues being raised about the direction and nature of globalisation and multilateral institutional arrangements.

Both India and Vietnam are agreed that the world should no longer have place for hegemonic behaviour. Both of us prefer a multipolar Asia. Both of us have vital stakes in maritime security, including freedom of navigation and commerce and peaceful settlement of maritime disputes in accordance with international law. Indeed, our strong bilateral ties are based on mutual trust and convergence of views on various regional and international issues. Vietnam is a strong pillar of India's Act East Policy. In India, there is respect and admiration for the courage, resolve and achievements of the Vietnamese people.

Surely then, there is much to learn and discuss among Indian and Vietnamese scholars as well as government officials as we seek to nurture a comprehensive strategic partnership between our two countries. However, Indo-Vietnamese ties also have yet to progress sufficiently beyond the government and academic and think-tank circles. Without deeper and more extensive involvement of ordinary people in both countries, the relationship cannot grow, diversify and strengthen itself in sync with its vast potential. The fact that this volume is being produced in both the English and Vietnamese languages is a small step in that direction.

Let me take this opportunity to recall the work of former ICS Director, Prof. Alka Acharya, my senior colleagues at the Institute, and colleagues across various institutions in New Delhi who have participated in our discussions and delegation visits to Vietnam in strengthening the ICS' ties with the VASS. I also take this opportunity to thank our colleagues in the VASS, including President Prof. Nguyen Quang Thuan, a scholar of China himself, and especially its Institute of Chinese Studies, for their great enthusiasm for our deliberations and their warm hospitality on our many visits to Hanoi.

Finally, let me thank the contributors to this volume and particularly the editors, Jabin T. Jacob and Hoang The Anh, for their hard work over a whole year in putting this work together and bringing out what I am sure will be an important and widely referenced book on Indian and Vietnamese analyses of China's foreign and security policies.

Ambassador Ashok K. Kantha (retd)

Director, Institute of Chinese Studies, Delhi

Vietnamese Preface

In recent years, along with the strategic adjustments and transforming development model in China after the 18th National Congress of the Communist Party of China, the country has focused on promoting its relations with its neighbours as part of its overall global strategy. Among these, China has strengthened its openness and foreign economic cooperation, fostered free trade talks, built cross-border economic zones, promoted regional economic integration and established interconnectivity with neighbouring countries. In order to create a breakthrough in diplomacy with the neighbouring countries, China has been concentrating on the implementation of the 'Belt and Road' initiative, establishing economic belts and corridors along parts of the old Silk Road.

Yet, the relationship between China and some of its neighbours also has some problems, such as territorial disputes, including over islands, asymmetrical economic relations, unbalanced political relations and so on. These lead to a variety of perspectives on analysing and evaluating the current situation of relations between China and its neighbours. Therefore, sharing perspectives among scholars of neighbouring countries on relations with China is a necessity.

Vietnam and India are neighbours of China and both have vicissitudes in their relationship with China. In the context of China's powerful rise with many unpredictable factors of the regional and the global situation at present, how to maintain effective cooperation with China while avoiding the economic, security and political risks and challenges it poses is a question that both countries have in common.

Therefore, within the cooperation framework between the Institute of Chinese Studies, Vietnam Academy of Social Sciences and the Institute of

Chinese Studies, New Delhi, India, Vietnamese and Indian scholars have shared their perspectives on the relationship with China in this book.

This volume analyses and assesses the impact of China's foreign strategic adjustment affecting security and politics in the ASEAN region, including bilateral relations between China and neighbouring countries such as China-Vietnam relations, China-India, China-Cambodia, and China's ties with Mongolia and Pakistan. It also covers the impact of regional geopolitics and geo-economics such as from FTAs, the Greater Mekong Subregion framework and the American factor, among others.

This is a joint book and has involved many Vietnamese and Indian social scientists with different approaches and independent perspectives which do not, of course, represent those of their organisations. Their arguments may cause controversy and have shortcomings, but we look forward to receiving feedback and comments from the readers.

On the occasion of publishing this book, we sincerely thank Prof. Nguyen Quang Thuan, President of the Vietnam Academy of Social Sciences and former Director-General of the Institute of Chinese Studies and Prof. Alka Acharya, former Director of the Institute of China Studies, Delhi for proposing the idea and supporting this joint research between the two institutes. We also express our thanks to the Social Sciences Publishing House, Hanoi for editing and publishing this book in Vietnamese.

Nguyen Xuan Cuong, PhD

Director-General, Institute of Chinese Studies, Hanoi

Foreword

China's stated foreign policy is one of seeking a friendly neighbourhood. This is because it needs a friendly neighbourhood to achieve its goal of *xiaokang shehui* (小康社会) or a moderately well-off society in an all-round way. If one were to translate this, it will indicate China growing to the level of a middle-level power, a goal set out in the early years of this millennium. This goal has now transformed into the two centenary goals of 2021 and 2049 representing the hundredth anniversaries of the founding of the Communist Party of China and the People's Republic of China, respectively.

For China to achieve its goals, it needs a friendly neighbourhood. But its actions in the past few years convey a different sense. Its relations with Japan, which were never cordial, remain tense while those with South Korea, which were looking up, have taken a step back because of the deployment of the Terminal High Altitude Air Defence System in that country by the United States early in 2017. China-North Korea relations also have never been as low as they are now. The claimants in the South China Sea area are not too happy either with China. One can view China's relations with all its neighbours barring Pakistan in the same light. In the latest instance, in mid-2017, Indian and Chinese forces engaged in two-month long standoff in the Doklam territory of Bhutan when the Chinese started illegal construction in the area.

Amongst the Southeast Asian nations, Vietnam stands out as one country, which has stood up to China better than any other involved in the South China Sea dispute. Vietnam-China relations have been tumultuous at best. Though starting in the first century BC, it was a relationship that was like a see-saw always. Marriages took place between the Chinese and Vietnamese and the Vietnamese writ would run till present-day Guangxi and Guangdong at times. Coming to the more recent past, when the China-USSR rift took place, China offered assistance to Vietnam, provided the latter did not accept Soviet aid. The 2 August 1964 Gulf of Tonkin incident between the *USS Maddox* and Vietnamese patrol boats of the 135 Torpedo Squadron was a precursor to the Vietnam War. During that American war in Vietnam, China and Vietnam put aside their differences only to revive the animosity later. The bitter war that the Chinese fought with Vietnam in 1979 based on the 'teach a lesson' theory saw thousands of casualties on both sides.

China-Vietnam relations have many facets and many of them resemble the India-China relationship. The first of these is on the political plane. At the leadership level the relations seem to be reasonable. This also resembles India-China relations at the leadership level that existed before the Doklam incident. Communist parties of both the countries maintain good contacts and relations. The second aspect is the economic relationship. The present trade between Vietnam and China stood at US$66 billion in 2015. This is similar to the trade figures between India and China. However, Vietnam had a trade deficit of US$32 billion in 2015 while India has a trade deficit with China of approximately US$51 billion. The reason for this can be found by looking closely at the basket of items that are being traded between them. China has invested approximately US$11 billion in Vietnam. The FDI from China into India between April 2000 and December 2016 was however, just US$1.6 billion. During the May 2017 visit of Vietnamese President Tran Dai Quang to China, he said that the trade between the two countries was before long expected to increase to US$100 billion. Similar goals exist also for India-China trade.

The third similarity is in the defence relationship. Military-to-military level bonhomie between Vietnam and China is not at the optimum level. There is a deep-rooted suspicion on both sides about each other. This is also true for the relationship between the Indian and Chinese armed forces. Vietnam also bore the brunt of Chinese action in 1974 when China forcibly secured the Paracel Islands killing 70 South Vietnamese soldiers and capturing 58 prisoners of war. Similarly, the 1962 India–China war has left deep scars in the minds of the Indian people.

A number of factors mentioned above reveal a similarity between India-China and Vietnam-China relations. Therefore, it is not rocket science to expect that close India-Vietnam relations are a natural result of this triangular relationship. For a fair amount of time, the shadow of China has loomed large over India-Vietnam relations. But cultural and economic ties between the two countries date back to the second century AD. In contemporary times, India conveyed its opposition to US actions in the Vietnam War and supported Vietnam in its war with Cambodia. The relationship between these two countries has been growing. Indian Prime Minister, Narendra Modi's visit to Vietnam in September 2016 has facilitated a further growth of this friendship. The extension of a US$500 million credit line for defence purposes and US$5 million for a software technology park have further cemented this relationship. Trade between India and Vietnam is expected to reach the US$15 billion mark by 2020 from US$7 billion in 2015.

It is against this background that the Institute of Chinese Studies in India and the Institute of Chinese Studies of the Vietnam Academy of Social Sciences, Hanoi, have brought out this volume. It is a timely and contextual effort that puts in perspective Vietnam-China relations as well as China's relations with other countries and the regional geopolitical environment. Each author has very lucidly covered their brief and presented several issues that need to be studied carefully also for furthering India-Vietnam relations.

Lt. Gen. S. L. Narasimhan (retd)

Member, National Security Advisory Board, India

Acknowledgments

Jabin T. Jacob would like to thank his colleagues at the Institute of Chinese Studies, Delhi, including former Director, Prof. Alka Acharya, for their encouragement and support in seeing this volume to fruition. In particular, he would like to thank Naina Singh for her editorial and research assistance. Hoang The Anh would like to thank his colleagues in the International Cooperation Department and the Institute for Indian and Southwest Asian Studies of the Vietnam Academy of Social Sciences for their support and help in translations and editing of the Vietnamese papers.

List of Contributors

Anushree Chakraborty, PhD, Assistant Professor of Political Science, Vidyasgar College, Calcutta University, Kolkata

Aravind Yelery, PhD, Assistant Director, Institute of Chinese Studies, Delhi

Atul Kumar, PhD, Lecturer in International Politics, University of Queensland, Brisbane, Australia

Bui Thi Thu Hien, PhD, Deputy Director, Center for East Sea Studies,Institute of Chinese Studies, Vietnam Academy of Social Sciences, Hanoi

Debashis Chakraborty, PhD, Assistant Professor of Economics, Indian Institute of Foreign Trade, Kolkata & Associate Editor, *Foreign Trade Review*

Hoang The Anh, PhD, Vice Director-General, Institute of Chinese Studies, Vietnam Academy of Social Sciences, Hanoi & Editor-in-Chief, *Chinese Studies Review*

Jabin T. Jacob, PhD, Fellow, Institute of Chinese Studies, Delhi & Associate Editor, *China Report*

Kush Kumar Gayasen, Assistant Professor of Political Science, Janki Devi Memorial College, University of Delhi

Mirza Zulfiqur Rahman, Senior Research Fellow, Department of Humanities and Social Sciences, Indian Institute of Technology, Guwahati, Assam

Nguyen Huy Hoang, PhD, Associate Professor, Director General, Institute for Southeast Asian Studies, Vietnam Academy of Social Sciences, Hanoi

Nguyen Thi Phuong Hoa, PhD, Head, Department of Vietnam-China Relations Studies, Institute of Chinese Studies, Vietnam Academy of Social Sciences, Hanoi & Deputy Editor-in-Chief, *Chinese Studies Review*

Nguyen Xuan Trung, PhD, Director, Institute for Indian and Southwest Asian Studies & Associate Professor, Graduate Academy of Social Sciences, Vietnam Academy of Social Sciences, Hanoi

Panchali Saikia, Scientific Officer-Social Science, International Water Management Institute, New Delhi

Pham Cao Cuong, PhD, Vice-Director-General, Institute of American Studies, Vietnam Academy of Social Sciences, Hanoi

1

Introduction: China as a Common Concern

Jabin T. Jacob and Hoang The Anh

This volume is an outcome of the growing interactions between the Institute of Chinese Studies, Delhi and counterparts in the Vietnam Academy of Social Sciences and specifically, the Vietnam Institute of Indian and Southwest Asian Studies and the Vietnam Institute of Chinese Studies in Hanoi. These ties have been built up over recent years to complement and strengthen the bilateral relationship between the two countries.

In India, Vietnam has the image of an uncompromising bulwark against China and almost any discussion of India's external options vis-à-vis China is not complete without bringing Vietnam into the picture. Hanoi meanwhile, sees India as a big neighbour to China and that while the relationship between the two countries has had its ups and downs in history, New Delhi now seems to be both cooperating and competing with China. India's experience of dealing with China holds lessons for Vietnam.

And yet, the actual capacity on Vietnam within the Indian government and academic institutions in the country has been practically non-existent. Take the number of Vietnamese speakers in India for example. The Ministry of External Affairs according to its latest Annual Report (2015-16) has four officers with 'proficiency' in the language (Ministry of External Affairs, Government of India 2016) while no recognised Indian academic institution appears to offer

Vietnamese language courses. Institutionalised scholarly interactions between India and Vietnam have remained strangely limited. It is no wonder, therefore, that despite talk, there is actually very little understanding of how Vietnam deals with China, except perhaps in the military domain. However, as the only other socialist nation besides China to both successfully retain power in the ruling communist party's hands and promote economic development, and which has used China as a model, Vietnam's ties with its northern neighbour are more complex than Indian analysts generally understand or are able to communicate to audiences in India.

In effect, Vietnam has a very realistic understanding of its limitations and continuing interests with respect to China, despite whatever other tensions might occur over the East Sea/South China Sea and increasingly, over their economic ties. If New Delhi is to be a serious player in East Asia under the ambit of the Act East Policy, it is important that it recognises these dynamics in not just Sino-Vietnamese ties but in China's other bilateral relations in the region. Indeed, as the essays in this volume will make clear, these dynamics are of considerable strategic import and if even the relationship between Vietnam and China are so complex and multi-layered as to prevent the former from tilting too strongly against the latter, one can imagine how still weaker countries fare in their relations with Beijing.

This volume is an attempt in developing a more nuanced understanding of China's ties with its neighbours. It is not designed to be a historical work but is contextualised against the backdrop of developments of the last three years or so as the East Sea/South China Sea disputes flared and new and competing ideas of multilateral regional economic arrangements have arisen and sometimes fallen in the form of the Trans-Pacific Partnership (TPP) and the Regional Comprehensive Economic Partnership (RCEP).

Therefore, this book too, focuses on a few key areas, covering in the main the military and economic dimensions from a strategic perspective. At the same time, there is also the attempt to situate Vietnam-China relations against the wider canvas of the interactions between the two national communist parties on the one hand and in the sub-regional multilateral organisations on the other. The first of these gives a somewhat unique dimension of interactions between the two socialist countries while the latter is important, given how China has used sub-regional initiatives especially in Southeast Asia, as a way of marking its presence in the region and, as is increasingly evident, to undermine the centrality of the ASEAN. In addition, one might also note the stress on studying China's bilateral relationships in the Vietnamese chapters in the volume.

Structure of the Book

The book is divided into 13 chapters with this Introduction followed by a chapter on interactions between the Communist Party of China (CPC) and the Communist Party of Vietnam (CPV) by **Jabin T. Jacob**. Sino-Vietnamese communist party-to-communist party ties are a model of successful management. These party-to-party ties constitute an important anchor of the relationship and perhaps explain why despite all else, the relationship refuses to go off-kilter. And yet, it is not the case that the Chinese pull their punches. It is a characteristic of China's rise in recent years that Deng Xiaoping's dictum to China's leaders to 'hide our capacities and bide our time; be good at maintaining a low profile; and never claim leadership'[1] is no longer practised. And China has consistently refused to compromise on the East Sea/South China Sea issues, openly accusing the Vietnamese of being aggressive and falling prey to Western machinations.

And yet, despite clashes at sea between the two sides and the worst anti-Chinese riots in Vietnam in decades taking place in the last few years, channels of communication between the two party leaderships remain open. Several members of the CPC Politburo Standing Committee including both Xi Jinping and Li Keqiang have visited Vietnam or received leaders from their neighbour. The Vietnamese for their part have exercised caution in their ties, understanding well their dependence on the Chinese in the economic realm. The Vietnamese perhaps do not seek a comprehensive victory on each and every matter vis-à-vis the Chinese—merely holding the latter in check on a few key issues would be good enough—as they seek greater room for manoeuvre by slowly increasing the gamut and range of their bilateral cooperation with other countries. Indeed, Beijing itself is well aware of this reality and as a result, the Sino-Vietnamese relationship will be a constant balancing act as each side tries to push the envelope. For outsiders watching, the conclusion must be that it will be impossible to expect either side, least of all the Vietnamese, to go all out in its opposition to the other, leavened as the relationship is by the intimate ties between the two communist parties.

The third chapter by **Nguyen Huy Hoang** also uses the CPC as a starting point looking at the impact of its 18th Party Congress in 2012 on the subsequent evolution of policies towards the ASEAN. In fact, he calls it a 'new Southeast Asia policy' that has attempted to address political and security concerns in the region over China, while Beijing simultaneously also tries to bind these countries ever more closely to itself. Hoang is clear in stating that the Chinese objective 'is to maintain and expand its influence, to narrow and gradually repel American influence in Southeast Asia, and to implement China's ambitions in the East Sea of Vietnam as well as to expand space for the development of the Chinese economy'. Clearly, the Southeast Asian nations are under no illusions as far as the Chinese foreign and security policies are concerned. What is evident however, is also the lack of room for manoeuvre that these countries have, given the reality of China's economic might, the distance of the US from the region, especially now perhaps under the confusing foreign policy of Donald Trump as well as the lack of any other regional powers capable of challenging China's dominance. These realities are reflected in the concluding section of the chapter that outlines the potential futures in the China-ASEAN relationship. It will be interesting to watch how China's Southeast Asia policy develops post-the 19th Party Congress later in 2017.

Bui Thi Thu Hien does a deep dive into the development of Vietnam-China relations post-normalisation, using the East Sea/South China Sea issue as a prism. What comes through very clearly is the level of Vietnamese resentment and concern over China's actions in this regard. In particular, the Chinese decision to up the ante on the bilateral maritime dispute by moving the Haiyang Shiyou 981 oil rig into the continental shelf and exclusive economic zone of Vietnam, seems to have become something of a watershed moment in bilateral ties, given the reactions among the ordinary Vietnamese as well as within the Vietnamese leadership, thus making progress towards positive ties particularly difficult. Hien's recommendations such as the need for the media on both sides to report honestly and accurately, to conclude a Code of Conduct as soon as possible, as well as for better treatment of each other's fishermen, themselves suggest the serious difficulties that the relationship is facing.

This then leads us to the next three chapters with their greater focus on the geopolitical dimension of China-Vietnam ties. India figures prominently in each case. In the fifth chapter by **Kush Kumar Gayasen**, the angle is a Sino-Indian one as he assesses the place of Vietnam in the maritime interactions between the two Asian giants. India's growing corpus of maritime strategy documents increasingly look at the East Sea/South China Sea as part of India's area of interest, even if only secondary to the Indian Ocean. It is of course, natural that India's relations with Vietnam are being viewed through the prism of tensions in the Sino-Indian relationship broadly and the Sino-Vietnamese maritime disputes specifically.

Against this backdrop, Gayasen examines the relevance of Vietnam for India's strategic interests in Southeast Asia in general and to balance China's maritime power in particular. He argues that the growing India-Vietnam equations in the strategic-military realm can be seen as the extension of India's own growing maritime power and its consistent, proactive maritime engagements towards Southeast Asia, and not as merely a reaction to China's own expanding maritime power.

In the sixth chapter, **Nguyen Thi Phuong Hoa** in his review of the US rebalancing strategy towards Asia highlights the growth in US-Vietnam relations fuelled clearly by common concerns over China. That these former adversaries should come together so quickly and in a substantive manner only highlights the impact that China's regional assertiveness has had on Vietnam's own regional calculations.

It is clear that Vietnam's growing ties with the US have prompted the Chinese to put some more focus on courting the Vietnamese, especially at the party-to-party level. However, the US rebalance has not had much impact on Vietnam's great economic dependence on China. If anything, Hoa states that the US rebalance has probably prompted Beijing to take an even harder line on the maritime disputes with Vietnam with more frequent intrusions into Vietnamese waters and the impeding and destruction of Vietnamese vessels and property. Thus, in the overall analysis, the US rebalance appears to have negatively impacted Vietnam-China relations.

The following chapter by **Atul Kumar** posits the intriguing possibility of Vietnam's addition as a member of the cooperative security framework of the Quadrilateral Security Dialogue comprising also the US, India, Japan and Australia. There is more than a hint here of the possibility also of Vietnam replacing Australia if need be, given the latter's less than fully enthusiastic approach to joint activity under the aegis of the Quad. Even leaving aside this particular aspect, Kumar argues that the inclusion of Vietnam in the Quad is essential for enhancing its cohesiveness and the quality of interaction between the members. Already, Vietnam's strategic relations with India, the US and Japan have grown significantly over the last decade. In addition to highlighting the deepening political and military ties between Vietnam and the three senior members of the Quad, Kumar also makes an economic case for Vietnam's inclusion in the Quad noting that it also enjoys close and growing economic ties to the US and Japan and not just with China.

The next three chapters go into greater detail on the economic dimensions with **Hoang The Anh** in the eighth chapter focusing on the development of Vietnam-China economic relations following the normalisation of bilateral ties. He provides the details of this relationship in trade and investments, which have grown by leaps and bounds while underlining Hanoi's concerns over the increasing and unsustainable trade deficit—a problem Indian policymakers too are confronted with in the India-China economic relationship—as well as concerns about the shoddy workmanship of Chinese contractors on various projects in Vietnam. The latter issue has, in fact, become a cause for substantial acrimony at the popular level in Vietnam. And yet, at the same time, Vietnam is aware of the opportunities created by China's rising labour costs and the greater disposable income of Chinese consumers. Its proximity to the Chinese market allows it to potentially benefit from the shift of industries, the flow of tourists and other such developments. That said, it will also be difficult to insulate the Vietnam-China economic relationship from the larger trends in their political and security ties.

Chapter 9 by **Debashis Chakraborty and Anushree Chakraborty** is once again an examination through an India-China angle, of their growing economic integration with ASEAN. Specifically, the authors look at the effects of the ASEAN-China and ASEAN-India FTAs on their respective trade balances coming to the conclusion that while both countries have deepened their trade relationships, the gains have been significantly more for China and relatively modest for India, with the latter also facing trade deficits with major economies in the region. Further, China is much more deeply integrated with the ASEAN economies than is India in terms of both trade and production networks.

From the point of view of the Vietnam factor, two of the authors' conclusions stand out. One, physical connectivity between China and the ASEAN markets plays a key role in maintaining the former's advantages. From India's point of view, the consistent failure of big-ticket physical connectivity projects between India and the rest of Southeast Asia to take off has severe economic costs. Two, without the advantages of scale and greater enterprise, Indian firms will not be able to expand their economic footprint in any manner significant enough to challenge, replace or compete with their larger Chinese counterparts in the ASEAN. What success Indian firms will enjoy as they expand their production networks will come at the cost of Japanese and South Korean firms based on a cost advantage. Again from a policy point of view, New Delhi must consider ways and means of encouraging and supporting Indian entrepreneurship and economic activity in Southeast Asia without which Vietnam's (and others') dependence and limitations vis-à-vis China are likely to continue. The Act East Policy therefore, has its work cut out.

Aravind Yelery's chapter on Vietnam's economic relations with India and China in the context of the proposed TPP and RCEP mega FTAs goes into greater detail about Vietnam's domestic economic conditions. He contextualises Vietnam's rise as the newest 'Asian tiger' before delving into the specifics of India-Vietnam and China-Vietnam trade. The differences are obvious and stark with China-Vietnam trade just under ten times the size of India-Vietnam trade in 2015 and expected to grow faster still. Equally significant, while Vietnam like India suffers from a huge trade deficit with China, it is also slowly gaining comparative advantage against China on labour, cost and accessibility to markets. Indeed, many Chinese companies are also shifting production to Vietnam on these grounds even as Vietnamese companies themselves ramp up their standards.

Despite the travails of the TPP, the CPV had shown its commitment by approving accession and allowing the matter to get to the National Assembly before it was put aside following the results of the US presidential elections in November 2016. As a potential member of both the RCEP and the TPP or whatever might replace the latter, Vietnam stands to gain from both. Despite the advantages of the RCEP, the Vietnamese will for political and economic reasons also prefer to diversify away from ASEAN and China. This has implications for the Chinese companies currently active in the Vietnamese economy. India meanwhile, which is both a non-member of the TPP and looks likely to have problems acceding to another China-led initiative in the form of the RCEP, will face even greater difficulties deepening its already weak presence in the Vietnamese economy. According to Yelery, the TPP and RCEP will bring about major changes in the way Vietnam interacts with both the Chinese and Indian economies.

In chapter 11, **Nguyen Xuan Trung** makes an interesting comparison of China's relations with Mongolia and Pakistan. It would appear that China's effort in each case is to fill the gaps in the bilateral relationship and to draw each country closer still. For instance, while the security relationship is the most important part of China-Pakistan ties, this is the weaker leg in the Sino-Mongolian relationship. As a result, China has pushed to fill the economic vacuum in the former through the China-Pakistan Economic Corridor while in the latter case, Beijing has tried to draw Mongolia into a closer political and security embrace through the Shanghai Cooperation Organization and other China-led regional organisations.

While China is the largest economic partner for both Mongolia and Pakistan, it is worth stressing that for China itself, its trade ties with both countries are insignificant in the context of its larger international trade. However, as Trung points out, both countries are heavily dependent on China, economically speaking, and this dependence is only likely to increase if they are unable to diversify their economic partners. To extend the point further, it would also appear that Pakistan is quite happy to continue a deepening relationship with China on all fronts and is only making small steps to diversify economically. Mongolia, on the other hand, is handicapped by its landlocked situation as was evident in 2016 when it came under economic sanctions by Beijing for having invited the Dalai Lama to visit and unable to bear the pain, soon apologised to China for its action (*The Indian Express* 2016).

The following chapter by **Pham Cao Cuong** focuses on the growing bilateral relationship between China and Cambodia, a relationship that has caused much angst and heartburn within the ASEAN; Cambodia has through its closeness to Beijing almost functioned as a proxy for it in the regional grouping, leading to division and stalemate. The chapter highlights how China has enmeshed the smaller country in a tight embrace through trade and economic and development aid. This is backed by close military cooperation, including frequent exchanges of visits of military officials that are particularly significant for Phnom Penh. In effect, Beijing has succeeded in using Cambodia as a 'counterweight' to Vietnam. Also of note in this chapter is the deep economic penetration of the Chinese companies in Cambodia, particularly in the infrastructure and extractive industries. The relationship appears to be one of extreme Cambodian dependence on China, but growing closer still.

Indian analysts and policymakers will be familiar with the problems of getting China to share hydrological data and engage in cooperative, non-threatening behaviour in the area of transboundary rivers, specifically, the Brahmaputra and the Sutlej. The final chapter on Sino-Vietnamese engagement on the Mekong River by **Panchali Saikia and Mirza Zulfiqur Rahman** is therefore an important addition to this volume and returns once again to the politics that animates the relationship. The 1995 Mekong Agreement, which established the Mekong River Commission (MRC) to manage the Mekong River, has been regarded as a milestone in international water resource management treaties among co-riparian countries, due to its emphasis on joint development of the river basin and its resources, ecological protection and a dynamic process of transboundary water allocation. The MRC has, however, been struggling in balancing varied interests within the basin and in persuading China, the upper riparian state, to address the priorities and concerns of the downstream countries.

China has consistently refused to accept any legal obligations and its priority in the Mekong has been driven by energy demand growth and dam development. Not surprisingly, at least from an Indian point of view, these moves appear to be strategic in nature lacking in normative commitment and are in marked contrast to the larger regional priorities of plugging gaps in the river basin development or addressing the concerns of lower riparian states. Saikia and Rahman analyse the trajectory of conflict and cooperation between China and the Lower Mekong countries of Thailand, Laos, Cambodia and Vietnam, and examine to what extent the current institutional regimes governing the transboundary river have been successful in contributing towards collective action and in addressing the interests, threat perceptions and concerns of the co-riparians. As the authors note, the most critical effects of the Chinese interventions upstream on the Mekong will be felt furthest downstream of the basin countries, namely, Vietnam. Vietnam's stress is on livelihood concerns tied to agricultural production, the sustainability and development of fisheries, and other important environment-related issues, but the two countries have yet to find a reliable and sustainable way forward to address these issues.

Any reader of this volume will be aware of some clear and visible differences between the approaches of the Indian and Vietnamese authors, including those of methodology and framing. This volume allows the Vietnamese authors to use a style and terminology that is uniquely Vietnamese – for instance, the use of the term 'East Sea' for what is internationally known as the South China Sea. We believe that volumes such as these must preserve these differences in approach and presentation in order to provide to the reader a better understanding of each country's/author's issues of concern and interest, even if the chapters represent the personal views of the authors and do not necessarily reflect the views of their particular institutions. The objective has been to communicate the focus of both Indian and Vietnamese thinking on China as well as a better sense of their worldviews.

Conclusion

The wide-ranging set of chapters in this volume highlight the complex nature of China-Vietnam relations. While anchored in a common modern lexicon of communism and revolutionary struggle, and now also of economic reform, these ties have nevertheless not been able to overcome centuries of mutual suspicion and differences based on history and nationalism. Despite the resolution of the land boundary dispute, these factors continue to find their expression in the territorial disputes in the East Sea/South China Sea. There are also newer manifestations in the form of tensions over trade deficits and other economic pressures from the Chinese as well as over the lack of Chinese flexibility or generosity on the Mekong River. The similarities to the India-China context are obvious.

In effect, therefore, Vietnam and China are engaged in a sometimes delicate balancing act to maintain stable political ties involving the two national ruling parties. But the Chinese are sometimes not shy of turning up the pressure on their smaller neighbours on the trade front, particularly in the case of the highly vulnerable (from a Vietnamese point of view) border trade. They have also been consistent in ignoring Vietnamese (and international) protestations and continued to reclaim, build on and militarise disputed features in the East Sea/South China Sea.

Against this backdrop, how relations between the two most successful communist regimes in the world – politically and economically speaking – will develop, remains to be seen. It would appear that the Vietnamese are extremely realist about their prospects in any case of all-out friction or conflict with the Chinese, whether economically or militarily. Hanoi will therefore, temper its activities and responses accordingly, even as it will like Beijing refuse to compromise on issues of sovereignty and its national interest. In part, this is also driven by the strong nationalist sentiment in Vietnam that will only take so much of an overbearing Chinese attitude and assertiveness. Nationalism also drives the Chinese as also an increasing sense of exceptionalism that make it less certain how Beijing will proceed with its plans for the region and in its ties with Vietnam or respond to what it perceives as provocations.

It is therefore, extremely essential for policymakers and strategic analysts in India to keep a close eye on the dynamics of the China-Vietnam relationship. There are both lessons to be learnt and cautionary tales here. New Delhi should have a realistic assessment of the lengths to which Vietnam will go in countering China's assertiveness in the region, given that it is the smaller country. At the same time, given Vietnamese history, there is also scope for calibrated measures to support Vietnam's national capacity. However, for this to not look like India trying to use Hanoi as a proxy against China, New Delhi will also need to commit more significantly to a closer, deeper relationship with Vietnam in the economic, political and cultural spheres that is not dependent on the China factor at all. Ultimately, the best guarantee of a Vietnam capable of holding its own in its relationship with the Chinese and balancing Chinese power in the region is a Vietnam that also develops balanced and mutually beneficial bilateral partnerships with other big countries such as India.

NOTES

1. The quote in full is '*lengjingguancha, wenzhuzhenjiao, chenzhuoyingfu, taoguangyanghui, shanyushouzhuo, juebudangtou, yousouzuowei*' (冷静观察,稳住阵脚,沉着应付,韬光养晦,善于守拙,决不当头, 有所作为) [Observe calmly; secure our position; cope with affairs calmly; hide our capacities and bide our time; be good at maintaining a low profile; never claim leadership; achieve something]

REFERENCES

Ministry of External Affairs, Government of India. 2016. *Annual Report 2015-2016*, Publications, 13 March, http://www.mea.gov.in/Uploads/PublicationDocs/26525_26525_External_Affairs_English_AR_2015-16_Final_compressed.pdf (accessed on 20 July 2017).

The Indian Express. 2016. 'Will Never Let in Dalai Lama Again: Mongolia', 21 December, http://indianexpress.com/article/world/will-never-let-in-dalai-lama-again-mongolia-4438654/ (accessed on 2 July 2017).

2

China-Vietnam Relations: In Steady State despite Tensions

Jabin T. Jacob

Given their deep historical linkages, China and Vietnam have a relationship that cannot simply be described as uniformly cooperative or conflictual at any given point of time. Vietnam appears to be a near permanent bulwark against China in Southeast Asia but it will not and cannot simultaneously be in a state of constant antagonism either. This chapter looks at how China and Vietnam have tried in recent years to deal with their bilateral disputes at the political level and suggests that there is frequently an element of rethinking and pulling back from extreme postures on both sides that ensures the relationship does not turn completely hostile or irretrievable. In this context, the relationship between the ruling communist parties is a significant factor.

Relationship Status: It's Complicated

The Sino-Vietnamese relationship is complex and multi-dimensional.[1] Even as clashes between the Vietnamese and Chinese continue, including between their naval vessels, in the disputed waters of the Paracels and Spratlys in the South China Sea,[2] bilateral trade has kept increasing from US$65.478 billion in 2013 to US$83.631 billion in 2014 to US$91.509 in 2015 (UN Comtrade Database 2016). And while tourism between the two countries has dropped as bilateral relations deteriorated (*Global Times* 2015c), regular interactions at the sub-national level continue (*Vietnam Breaking News* 2014; *Vietnam News Agency* 2014; *Vietnam Breaking News* 2015).[3] Nationalist eruptions are kept in check also by the memory of a common struggle against Western colonialism and imperialism. Despite strong nationalist tendencies on either side, like the Chinese, the Vietnamese too, emphasise people-to-people and cultural exchanges (*Xinhua* 2015f, i, k).

Party-to-party ties remain deep with regular bilateral visits (*Global Times* 2015a) and interactions focusing on the study of both theory and each other's experiences (*Xinhua* 2014f, g) and messages of felicitation on important anniversaries on either side (*Xinhua* 2015g, Thayer 2015). Top leaders have also met in third countries on the sidelines of various multilateral forums.[4] CPC General Secretary Xi Jinping and his counterpart in the Communist Party of Vietnam (CPV), Nguyen Phu Trong, marked the 65th anniversary of China-Vietnam diplomatic relations through a telephone conversation in February 2015 – the third year that the two have marked the occasion thus (*Xinhua* 2015i). Such regular telephone calls also take place between other officials on the two sides (*Xinhua* 2015f).[5] In April 2015, Trong made a formal visit to Beijing as part of the celebrations with a delegation that included 'about one third of Vietnam's politburo' (*Global Times* 2015b).

Xi has not only lauded the support extended by the two countries and peoples to each other (*Xinhua* 2015j), and their common adherence to the leadership of communist parties and the socialist path (*Xinhua* 2015c), but also called the relationship one of 'strategic importance' (*Xinhua* 2015i). Importantly, the Chinese leader has also used a phrase of comparatively recent vintage stating that the two had become part of 'a community of common destiny' (*Xinhua* 2015i). This phrase is now widely used as part of the discourse around China's 'one belt, one road' project—also referred to as the new Silk Road or the 'Belt and Road Initiative'—and especially also in the context of Sino-Southeast Asian ties, and possibly suggests a Chinese belief that the Vietnamese are an important factor in any major Chinese relationship with Southeast Asia.

China's Hard Line

Beijing's position on its territorial claims in the South China Seas is, however, uncompromising and Vietnam remains the most serious contestant that China faces in the dispute, being in possession of the maximum number of disputed islands. China's deployment of an oil drilling platform, the Haiyang Shiyou-981 (HS-981), in May 2014 in the waters Vietnam claimed as its own, led to clashes at sea between the two sides and the worst anti-Chinese riots in Vietnam in decades (Krishnan 2014).

Vietnam has been indirectly accused of becoming more aggressive vis-à-vis China (Shang 2014; Zhang H. 2014; Zhao 2014. See also Zhang J. 2014; *Xinhua* 2014a) and of falling victim to 'instigation from outside' (Wang 2015). On the eve of the CPV General Secretary's visit to China in April 2015, a *Xinhua* commentary specifically stated that, 'Some outsiders, for selfish reasons, are exploiting every possible excuse to sow discord between them, while a few in Vietnam's political circle have been deluded by external Pied Pipers and become accomplices' (Deng 2015).

While these are usually oblique references to the role of the United States,[6] China has also criticised Hanoi in the past for its ties to India, noting for example, that just a day after China and Vietnam had signed an agreement in 2011 on basic principles guiding the settlement of maritime issues between them, Vietnam's state-owned energy corporation signed a three-year agreement with India to exploit gas and oil in the disputed waters in the South China Sea, 'heedless of any objection from China' (*People's Daily* 2014; see also *Global Times* 2014).

With respect to the involvement of the ASEAN, Chinese commentators noted that in 2014, the Chairman's Statement at the 25th ASEAN Summit in Nay Pyi Taw on 13 November 2014, only mentioned that it was 'concerned over the situation in the South China Sea' (ASEAN 2014a)—a toning down from the expression of 'serious concerns over the ongoing developments in the South China Sea' that was included in the 24th Summit statement (ASEAN 2014a). This has been interpreted as proof of limits being imposed on Vietnam, among others, on criticising China (Xue 2014), implying in turn that Beijing had succeeded in convincing others in the grouping of its point of view. The Chairman's statement at the 26th ASEAN Summit however, had a separate section on the South China Sea issue and talked about 'serious concerns expressed by some Leaders on the land reclamation being undertaken in the South China Sea' (ASEAN 2015a)[7] and China in turn stated it was 'opposed to the actions of an "individual country" kidnapping the ASEAN' (cited in *Xinhua* 2015c). Beijing also noted that Vietnam and the Philippines had also undertaken large-scale reclamation work on islands and reefs in their control and so had violated Chinese sovereignty (*Xinhua* 2015a).

While acknowledging the differences between the two countries over the South China Sea territorial issues, Xi in his 2015 message to his Vietnamese counterpart also declared that it was 'in line with the fundamental interests of both sides and conducive to regional peace, stability and prosperity for the two sides to cement political mutual trust, boost win-win cooperation, strengthen guidance of public opinion, and properly handle differences' (*Xinhua* 2015i).[8] The references to guiding public opinion[9] and properly handling differences are probably intended to remind Hanoi to not allow a repeat of the riots earlier in 2014 against Chinese firms (*China Daily* 2014; see also *Sina.com* 2014; *Xinhua* 2014i). Chinese State Councillor Yang Jiechi in a telephone conversation with Vietnamese Deputy Prime Minister and Foreign Minister Pham Binh Minh in February 2015 was more specific, asking that Hanoi 'properly handle maritime issues' (*Xinhua* 2015f). In an earlier visit in mid-June 2014, even as the rig remained in position, Yang had gone so far as to say that his country would 'take all necessary measures' to protect its sovereignty and the HS-981 (*Xinhua* 2014e).

Similarly, during his visit to Vietnam in late December 2014, Chairman of the Chinese People's Political Consultative Conference and No. 4 on the Politburo Standing Committee, Yu Zhengsheng, called for the development of China-Vietnam relations 'in a correct path' (Ng 2014). This was preceded by Xi's call in August in a conversation with Le Hong Anh, the visiting special envoy of CPV General Secretary Nguyen Phu Trong for both sides to make "correct political decisions" to put ties on the right track (*Xinhua* 2014j). These statements can be interpreted as a renewed demand that Vietnam stick to the bilateral route in resolving disputes. Yu stressed that 'Megaphone diplomacy can only trigger volatility of public opinion, which should be avoided by both sides' (*Xinhua* 2014e). Elsewhere, China has accused the ASEAN's Vietnamese Secretary-General Le Luong Minh for his 'biased comments on the issue of the South China Sea'. Le had earlier declared that ASEAN claimants Brunei, Malaysia, the Philippines and Vietnam could not accept China's nine-dash claim line since it was not in accordance with international law (Parameswaran 2015).

Beijing Rethink?

Beijing has, however, not really helped its case by some of its actions. When the HS-981 first entered disputed waters, the Vietnamese tried desperately to get in touch with CPC authorities but the latter apparently did not take their calls. Yang Jiechi's June 2014 visit was received poorly by the Vietnamese for the aggressive tone he took with them (Hiebert 2016).

The Chinese probably now realise that their role in the South China Sea disputes has brought Vietnam and the Philippines together. In late November 2014, two Vietnamese navy warships visited Manila for the first time (*Reuters* 2014). Vietnam also made a submission to The Hague's Permanent Court of Arbitration on a case brought by the Philippines against China over territorial claims in the waters (Oanh and Diep 2014), which the Philippines said was 'helpful in terms of promoting the rule of law and in finding peaceful and nonviolent solutions to the South China Sea claims' (cited in Orendain 2014).

One Chinese commentator from the Chinese Academy of Social Sciences writing before the PCA award speculated that Vietnam was getting closer to the US and Japan, and that Hanoi was 'likely to continue with the legal moves' (cited in Ng 2014). A Western analyst has suggested that the balance of views on China within the CPV briefly tilted towards the hardliners on China in the wake of the HS-981 incident with a June 2014 meeting of the Party's Central Committee unanimously condemning the Chinese action (Abuza 2014). Further, in a message clearly aimed at China, the ASEAN foreign ministers meeting at Kota Kinabalu in Malaysia in late January 2015, agreed to 'intensify efforts towards achieving the full and effective implementation of the Declaration on the Conduct of Parties in the South China Sea and work vigorously towards the early conclusion of the Code of Conduct on the South China Sea' (*South China Morning Post* 2015).

The Chinese did not fail to pick up the signals and have tried to bring ties with Vietnam back on even keel. It is, in fact, a sign of the seriousness with which China views ties with its southern neighbour that it sent Yu to visit Vietnam at the end of 2014 (Thayer 2015). Given that Yu is also part of the so-called 'Iron Triangle' of those with a Shaanxi connection within the PBSC (along with Wang Qishan and Xi Jinping), his visit was possibly also meant to mark Xi's personal attention to improving ties with Vietnam. In fact, since Hanoi's furious diplomatic and military reaction to HS-981, the Chinese have at least until now, more or less limited provoking their southern neighbour. And even if, China's construction activities in the disputed territories continue – including another brief foray of the HS-981 in April 2016 (Yu 2016) – relations remain largely calm. The Chinese have pushed for greater stability in the relationship through a series of important visits to Vietnam by its leaders notably of Xi Jinping in November 2015 (*People's Daily* 2015) and before that of No. 7 on the CPC Politburo Standing Committee, Zhang Gaoli, in July that year (*China Daily* 2015). This had followed visits by Chinese Premier Li Keqiang in 2013 (*Xinhua* 2013b) and the above-mentioned visit of Yu Zhengsheng in 2014. In November 2016, No. 3 on the CPC Politburo and head of the National People's Congress of China, Zhang Dejiang, was the latest top Chinese leader to visit Vietnam (*VietnamNet* 2016a).

Later, during the CPV General Secretary's visit to Beijing in April 2015, a *Xinhua* commentary declared that 'Tension at sea is not the whole picture for the Sino-Vietnamese relationship. Past disputes have been calmed without damage to ties in the long term' (*Xinhua* 2015d). Xi Jinping himself suggested that the two countries 'control their disputes' so as to ensure their ties developed 'in a right track' and that both the two parties and the two nations increase their high-level interactions in order to find 'new solutions to their problems and new ideas to advance the bilateral relationship in a sustained way' (*Xinhua* 2015c).

The Trong visit was soon followed with a visit by Chinese State Councilor and Public Security Minister Guo Shengkun later in April 2015 (*Xinhua* 2015e). China has frequently expressed hopes that Vietnam can come around (*Xinhua* 2015b, c; Li 2014) to seeing the need for a bilateral resolution of the dispute away from reliance on either the ASEAN or outside powers. Chinese commentaries have also underlined the need for stability in Sino-Vietnamese ties in order to push its 'belt and road' initiative. As one commentary noted, 'China doesn't want territorial and maritime antagonism with Vietnam standing in the way of implementing these programs. Vietnam should be roped into this grand vision' (*Global Times* 2015a; see also *Xinhua* 2015h). To this end, Beijing has also tried the soft power approach by offering opportunities to Vietnam 'for personnel training and media swaps, to lay solid public opinion foundation' for the development of bilateral ties (*Xinhua* 2014e).

Vietnamese Caution

Vietnam has tried to improve relations with the United States as part of its efforts to expand its foreign policy options. There was the significant visit in July 2015 of CPV General Secretary Trong to Washington where American President Barack Obama received him in the Oval Office despite this not being strictly part of protocol as the former is not a head of state or of government

(Beatty and Cartillier 2015). Obama himself visited Hanoi the following year in May 2016 (*Yahoo! News* 2016). However, these visits were usually also preceded or followed by equally significant high-level visits between Vietnamese and Chinese leaders as mentioned in the previous section. In fact, in 2015, there were visits by three of Vietnam's top leaders – besides Trong, the then President Truong Tan Sang (Ministry of Foreign Affairs, the People's Republic of China 2015), and the then Chairman of the National Assembly Nguyen Sinh Hung, who also visited China (*Vietnam Pictorial* 2015).

With over US$40 billion in trade deficit with the Chinese in 2015 (UN Comtrade Database 2016), and a heavy dependence on China for the basic raw material for many of its manufactured products, there are also limits to how much Vietnam can antagonise Beijing. Already, there is much worry about the Chinese ability to set the terms and apply pressure using the trade lever including that of border trade (Ngo 2016). Therefore, it is not surprising that even as it is open to participating in the Chinese 'Belt and Road Initiative' and the Chinese plan for a Regional Comprehensive Economic Partnership trade grouping, Hanoi is actively considering joining the Trans-Pacific Partnership (TPP) led by the US as a way of reducing its dependence on its northern neighbour.

And yet, there are also divergent views within Vietnam to joining the American-led initiative. Thus despite the CPV already agreeing to join in January 2016, as late as September, the ratification of the TPP did not figure on the agenda of the Vietnamese parliament. One reason that was put out was that the government proposal was 'not completed'. In essence, however, this appeared to be a case of waiting for the results of the US elections in November, given the negative rhetoric in the US itself over going ahead with the TPP (*Bangkok Post* 2016). In the event, with the election of Donald Trump as president in the United States and his professed opposition to the trade deal, this Vietnamese hedge against China might not take off at all. In any case, it is worth noting that Chinese companies in anticipation of the TPP were already planning to move in greater numbers to Vietnam. This, in turn, only solidifies Vietnam's economic links with China (*Thanh Nien News* 2014).

Further, despite the conflict with China over the South China Sea, the Vietnamese have been open to receiving Chinese warships at their Cam Ranh Bay as in October 2016. This followed yet another visit to China by the Vietnamese Prime Minister Nguyen Xuan Phuc the previous month in

September when the two countries pledged to manage maritime differences and continue to promote bilateral ties. While the Vietnamese have been open to receiving other foreign navies at Cam Ranh Bay including the Americans who arrived just a few weeks prior to the Chinese—in their first visit since the normalisation of relations in 1995 (Vu 2016) – the limits of their hedging strategy is obvious in that they were also open to the visit of a power that was engaged in an ongoing conflict with them. The Vietnamese must also have closely observed how despite the Philippines victory in the PCA Arbitration on the South China Sea issue in July 2016 (Permanent Court of Arbitration 2016), the Chinese were quickly able to turn the Philippines under a new president to apparently sideline the PCA decision. The Philippines has gone so far as to sign several billion dollars worth of trade deals during the visit same month in October 2016 of its President to China (Blanchard 2016), and there is even talk of joint exploration with China for oil and gas in the South China Sea (Perlez 2016).

Nevertheless, it is important to note that as careful as Vietnam is about how it goes about its relationship with China, there are also differences at the political level between the two communist parties. As one analyst notes, the direction of the CPV's political reform is increasingly different from that of the CPC and that disagreements seem to be rising between the two communist parties on how to successfully pursue political reform (Yun 2016). Given how internal developments are panning out in China against the backdrop of a sense of destiny and assertiveness on the foreign policy front, the CPC might also not be too open to lessons from Vietnam and instead, seek to win the CPV over to its side of the doctrine.[10] However, the CPV is pushing forward more rapidly and boldly with political liberalisation than the CPC and an important aspect here is the separation of party and state, despite one-party rule (Yun 2016) that stands in contrast to how the CPC under Xi Jinping seems to be binding the two ever more closely together. Given how important it is to the CPC to be seen as providing a successful alternative to the Western political systems, the CPV's willingness to differ with the CPC also weakens this Chinese project and might be seen more than any action on the South China Sea maritime disputes as the ultimate Vietnamese resistance against the Chinese.

Conclusion

History and proximity together ensure that neither Beijing nor Hanoi can take each other for granted, even if China's economic growth and rapid military modernisation are beginning to fundamentally change ground realities. What other regional and external powers need to remember is that this change might not always be opposed by Vietnam. For instance, China's new 'belt and road' initiative—at least, as Beijing has portrayed it—is about economic development through infrastructure connectivity in a mutually beneficial and non-hegemonic manner. Even if this turns out to be mere rhetoric in the long term, Vietnam could certainly use more capital and infrastructure development expertise to boost its economic growth in the immediate term, and it is China, more than any other country, that is best placed to provide a large share of these. While anti-China voices might have dominated in the immediate aftermath of the HS-981 crisis, the two sides soon returned to their default position of exchanging high-level visits, including between the communist parties; an evidence of careful calibration on both sides.

There is thus, a tripwire of caution built into the Sino-Vietnamese relationship, perhaps the more so, on the Vietnamese side. When the two sides express the desire to 'jointly safeguard the right direction in developing bilateral ties' (*Xinhua* 2015j) or to 'jointly safeguard maritime peace and stability' (*Xinhua* 2015f), not only is each side trying to put the onus on the other to mend matters, it also agrees that no matter where the responsibility for the dispute lies, it too, must contribute its part to repairing ties.

If they could hold the Chinese to some sort of a stalemate on the disputes in the South China Sea, the Vietnamese will consider their battle won and be more open to Chinese trade and investments. Beijing too, might come around to accepting the need for a stalemate in the short term, in order to further soften Vietnamese resistance. For Hanoi though, the challenge will be to see how the economic exchanges with China do not shift the balance such that Vietnam will eventually find it disadvantageous to counter any future Chinese strengthening of claims on disputed territory.

NOTES

1. For a recent analysis of the history and development of this relationship, see Thayer (2016).
2. For clashes between fishing and coast guard vessels and on naval confrontations, see Dobell (2014), Abuza (2014) and *People's Daily* (2014). See also Chan (2014), *China Military Online* (2014).
3. The customs services of China's Yunnan and Vietnam's Lao Cai provinces also have regular bilateral delegation visits (Vietnam Ministry of Foreign Affairs 2014).
4. For example, the then Chinese President Hu Jintao and the Vietnamese President Truong

Tan Sang met at the September 2012 APEC forum in Vladivostok, Russia (*Xinhua* 2012). Premier Li Keqiang met with Vietnamese Prime Minister Nguyen Tan Dung in Milan in October 2013 (*Xinhua* 2013a). Chinese President Xi Jinping met with his counterpart at the November 2014 APEC summit in Beijing (*Xinhua* 2014f).

5. For the 66th anniversary in 2016, the two sides appear to have only 'cabled' messages (*VietnamNet* 2016b).
6. The US has also been directly named. For instance, see *Global Times* (2015a).
7. The 27th ASEAN Summit too had a separate section on the South China Sea issue but only talked about 'concerns' as opposed to 'serious concerns' (ASEAN 2015b). It had returned to 'seriously concerned' in 2016 (ASEAN 2016).
8. On guiding public opinion, see also *Xinhua* (2014e).
9. See also the Vietnamese Ambassador to China's statement in *Global Times* (2015c).
10. One Chinese commentary pointed out how some sections of the CPV had demanded that Vietnam 'abandon socialism and stop depending on China' while another opinion expressed was that more Chinese investment would help the CPV consolidate its rule (Ding 2016).

REFERENCES

Abuza, Zachary. 2014. 'Vietnam buckles under Chinese pressure, *Asia Times Online*, 29 July, http://www.atimes.com/atimes/Southeast_Asia/SEA-01-290714.html (accessed on 28 January 2015).

ASEAN. 2014a. 'Chairman's Statement of the 24th ASEAN Summit: "Moving forward in Unity to a Peaceful and Prosperous Community", Nay Pyi Taw, 11 May, http://www.asean.org/storage/images/documents/24thASEANSummit/24th%20ASEAN%20Summit%20Chairman%27s%20Statement.pdf (accessed on 25 November 2016).

ASEAN. 2014b. 'Chairman's Statement of the 25th ASEAN Summit: "Moving Forward in Unity to a Peaceful and Prosperous Community"', Nay Pyi Taw, 12 November, http://www.asean.org/wp-content/uploads/images/pdf/2014_upload/Chairman%20Statement%20of%20th%2025th%20ASEAN%20Summit.pdf (accessed on 25 November 2016).

ASEAN. 2015a. 'Chairman's Statement of the 26th ASEAN Summit: "Our People, Our Community, Our Vision"', Kuala Lumpur & Langkawi, 27 April, http://www.asean.org/storage/images/2015/april/26th_asean_summit/Chairman%20Statement%2026th%20ASEAN%20Summit_final.pdf (accessed on 25 November 2016).

ASEAN. 2015b. 'Chairman's Statement of the 27th ASEAN Summit: "Our People, Our Community, Our Vision"', Kuala Lumpur, 21 November, http://www.asean.org/wp-content/uploads/2015/12/Final-Chairmans-Statement-of-27th-ASEAN-Summit-25-November-2015.pdf (accessed on 25 November 2016).

ASEAN. 2016. 'Chairman's Statement of the 28th and 29th ASEAN Summits: Turning Vision Into Reality For A Dynamic ASEAN Community', Vientiane, 6-7 September 2016, http://asean.org/storage/2016/08/Final-Chairmans-Statement-of-the-28th-and-29th-ASEAN-Summits-rev-fin.pdf (accessed on 25 November 2016).

Bangkok Post. 2016. 'Vietnam delays TPP vote', 16 September, http://www.bangkokpost.com/news/asia/1087705/vietnam-delays-tpp-vote (accessed on 25 November 2016).

Beatty, Andrew and Jerome Cartillier. 2015. 'Obama to host head of Vietnam communist party', *Yahoo! News*, 3 July, https://www.yahoo.com/news/obama-host-head-vietnam-communist-party-132418818.html (accessed on 25 November 2016).

Blanchard, Ben. 2016. 'Duterte aligns Philippines with China, says U.S. has lost', *Reuters*, 20 October, http://www.reuters.com/article/us-china-philippines-idUSKCN12K0AS (accessed on 25 November 2016).

Chan, Minnie. 2014. 'PLA reports maritime drill near Vietnam simulating threat to oil rig', *South China Morning Post*, 24 August, http://www.scmp.com/news/china/article/1580189/pla-reports-maritime-drill-near-vietnam-simulating-threat-oil-rig (accessed on 28 January 2015).

China Daily. 2014. 'China urges Vietnam to implement remedies for riots', 25 August, http://www.chinadaily.com.cn/world/2014-08/25/content_18483809.htm (accessed on 28 January 2015).

China Daily. 2015. 'Chinese vice-premier voices confidence in relationship with Vietnam', 18 July, http://www.chinadaily.com.cn/world/2015-07/18/content_21321273.htm (accessed on 15 August 2015).

China Military Online. 2014. 'Commentary: Vietnam's submarine no way to scare China', 11 September, http://eng.chinamil.com.cn/news-channels/china-military-news/2014-09/11/content_6132748.htm (accessed on 28 January 2015).

Deng Yushan. 2015. 'No room for wedge in China-Vietnam relations', *Xinhua*, 7 April, http://news.xinhuanet.com/english/2015-04/07/c_134129188.htm (accessed on 7 April 2015).

Ding Gang. 2016. 'Chinese investment helps stabilize socialist rule in Vietnam', *Global Times*, 21 September, http://www.globaltimes.cn/content/1007543.shtml (accessed on 25 November 2016).

Dobell, Graeme. 2014. 'China's Dangerous South China Sea Strategy', *The National Interest*, 10 June, http://nationalinterest.org/blog/the-buzz/chinas-dangerous-south-china-sea-strategy-10636 (accessed on 28 January 2015).

Global Times. 2014. 'Hanoi Can't Rely on Favor of Others in Handling Ties with Beijing', 29 October, http://www.globaltimes.cn/content/888972.shtml (accessed on 28 January 2015).

Global Times. 2015a. 'Party-to-party ties bring Beijing, Hanoi closer', 9 April, http://www.globaltimes.cn/content/915939.shtml (accessed on 9 April 2015).

Global Times. 2015b. 'Sino-Vietnamese conflicts can be contained till solution found', 13 April, http://www.globaltimes.cn/content/916658.shtml (accessed on 15 April 2015).

Global Times. 2015c. 'Vietnam "will not cooperate" with any third country to contain China', 16 January, http://www.globaltimes.cn/content/902277.shtml (accessed on 28 January 2015).

Hiebert, Murray. 2016. 'With Eye on China, Obama Strengthens Ties With Vietnam', *Yale Global Online*, 24 May, http://yaleglobal.yale.edu/content/eye-china-obama-strengthens-ties-vietnam (accessed on 25 November 2016).

Krishnan, Ananth. 2014. 'Anti-China riots kill two, injure 100 in Vietnam', *The Hindu*, 16 May, http://www.thehindu.com/todays-paper/tp-international/antichina-riots-kill-two-injure-100-in-vietnam/article6014346.ece (accessed on 28 January 2015).

Li Li. 2014. 'China-Vietnam Ties Should Not Fall Victim To Territorial Row', *Xinhua*, 27 August, http://news.xinhuanet.com/english/china/2014-08/27/c_133590685.htm (accessed on 28 January 2015).

Ministry of Foreign Affairs, the People's Republic of China. 2015. 'Xi Jinping Meets with President Trýõng T¥n Sang of Viet Nam', 3 September, http://www.fmprc.gov.cn/mfa_eng/zxxx_662805/t1294756.shtml (accessed on 25 November 2016).

Ng, Teddy. 2014. 'Senior Chinese leader Yu Zhengsheng calls for "correct path" in relations with Vietnam', *South China Morning Post*, 27 December, http://www.scmp.com/news/china/article/1668632/senior-chinese-leader-yu-zhengsheng-calls-correct-path-relations-vietnam (accessed on 25 November 2016).

Ngo Xuan Binh. 2016. 'Challenges in Vietnam-China Trade and Investment Relations', *ICS Wednesday Seminar*, Institute of Chinese Studies, Delhi, 9 November 2016.

Oanh Ha and Diep Ngoc Pham, 'South China Sea Tensions Flare as Vietnam Files Stance to Court', *Bloomberg Business*, 12 December 2014, http://www.bloomberg.com/news/2014-12-12/south-china-sea-tensions-flare-as-vietnam-files-stance-to-court.html (accessed on 25 November 2016).

Orendain, Simone. 2014. 'Challenges Mount to Beijing's South China Sea Claims', *Voice of America*, 14 December, http://m.voanews.com/a/challenges-mount-to-beijng-south-china-sea-claims/2558448.html (accessed on 28 January 2015).

Parameswaran, Prashanth. 2015. 'China Blasts ASEAN Head for South China Sea Remarks', *The Diplomat*, 12 March, http://thediplomat.com/2015/03/china-blasts-asean-head-for-south-china-sea-remarks/ (accessed on 15 April 2015).

People's Daily. 2014. 'Vietnam must be sincere over maritime disputes', 31 October, http://en.people.cn/n/2014/1031/c98649-8802735.html (accessed on 28 January 2015).

People's Daily. 2015. 'Xi's Vietnam, Singapore trip to boost China-ASEAN ties', 31 October, http://en.people.cn/n/2015/1031/c90000-8969478.html (accessed on 1 November 2015).

Perlez, Jane. 2016. 'Rodrigo Duterte and Xi Jinxing agree to reopen South China Sea Talks', *The New York Times*, 19 October, http://www.nytimes.com/2016/10/21/world/asia/rodrigo-duterte-philippines-china-xi-jinping.html (accessed on 25 November 2016).

Permanent Court of Arbitration. 2016. The South China Sea Arbitration (The Republic of the Philippines v. The People's Republic of China), The Hague, 12 July, https://pca-cpa.org/wp-content/uploads/sites/175/2016/07/PH-CN-20160712-Press-Release-No-11-English.pdf (accessed on 25 November 2016).

Reuters. 2014. 'Vietnam warships visit Philippines amid South China Sea dispute', 25 November, http://www.reuters.com/article/2014/11/25/us-philippines-vietnam-southchinasea-idUSKCN0J90FO20141125 (accessed on 28 January 2015).

Shang Jun. 2014. 'A calm South China doesn't need US stoking flames of conflict', *Global Times*, 13 August, http://www.globaltimes.cn/content/876052.shtml (accessed on 28 January 2015).

Sina.com. 2014. 'Vietnam feels sorry over Chinese workers' casualties in mid-May riots: spokesperson', 25 August, http://english.sina.com/world/2014/0825/730618.html (accessed on 28 January 2015).

South China Morning Post. 2015. 'Asean seeks early conclusion of a maritime pact for South China Sea', 28 January, http://www.scmp.com/news/asia/article/1694444/asean-seeks-early-south-china-sea-pact (accessed on 28 January 2015).

Thanh Nien News. 2014. 'Vietnam will watch China eat its TPP lunch', 13 May, http://www.thanhniennews.com/business/vietnam-will-watch-china-eat-its-tpp-lunch-26247.html (accessed on 28 January 2015).

Thayer, Carl. 2015. 'China and Vietnam Eschew Megaphone Diplomacy', *The Diplomat*, 2 January, http://thediplomat.com/2015/01/china-and-vietnam-eschew-megaphone-diplomacy/ (accessed on 28 January 2015).

Thayer, Carlyle A. 2016. 'Vietnam's Strategy of "Cooperating and Struggling" With China Over Maritime Disputes in the South China Sea', *Journal of Asian Security and International Affairs*, Vol. 3, No. 2, 200-20.

UN Comtrade Database. 2016. https://comtrade.un.org/data/ (accessed on 25 November 2016).

Vietnam Breaking News. 2014. 'Party leader praises growing economic ties with China', 15 April, http://www.vietnambreakingnews.com/2014/04/party-leader-praises-growing-economic-ties-with-china/ (accessed on 15 April 2015).

Vietnam Breaking News. 2015. 'Vietnamese and Chinese units sign twinning agreement', 13 March, http://www.vietnambreakingnews.com/tag/lao-cai-international-border-gate/ (accessed on 7 April 2015).

Vietnam Ministry of Foreign Affairs. 2014. 'Vietnam-China borders customs services exchange visits', Vietnamese Diplomatic Missions, 20 October, http://www.vietnamembassy-bangladesh.org/en/vnemb.vn/tinkhac/ns081021102142?b_start:int=320 (accessed on 25 November 2016).

Vietnam News Agency. 2014. 'Dozens of economic deals struck at China-Vietnam border trade fair', 11 November, http://en.hanoi.vietnamplus.vn/Home/Dozens-of-economic-deals-struck-at-ChinaVietnam-border-trade-fair/201411/4140.vnplus (accessed on 25 November 2016).

Vietnam Pictorial. 2015. 'National Assembly Chairman Nguyen Sinh Hung's Visit to Promote the Vietnam-China Political Trust', 30 December, http://vietnam.vnanet.vn/english/national-assembly-chairman-nguyen-sinh-hungs-visit-to-promote-the-vietnam-china-political-trust/206974.html (accessed on 25 November 2016).

VietnamNet. 2016a. 'Chinese top legislator concludes official visit to Vietnam', 11 November, http://english.vietnamnet.vn/fms/government/166827/chinese-top-legislator-concludes-official-visit-to-vietnam.html (accessed on 25 November 2016).

VietnamNet. 2016b. 'Vietnamese, Chinese leaders exchange congratulatory messages', 18 January, http://english.vietnamnet.vn/fms/government/150213/vietnamese—chinese-leaders-exchange-congratulatory-messages.html (accessed on 25 November 2016).

Vu Trong Khanh. 2016. 'Chinese Warships to Dock in Vietnam', *The Wall Street Journal*, 19 October, http://www.wsj.com/articles/chinese-warships-to-dock-in-vietnam-1476878216 (accessed on 25 November 2016).

Wang Shang. 2014. 'Spotlight: What has really happened in South China Sea?', *Xinhua*, 15 December, http://news.xinhuanet.com/english/china/2014-12/15/c_133855804.htm (accessed on 30 April 2015).

Xinhua. 2012. 'Chinese, Vietnamese presidents meet on ties', 7 September, http://news.xinhuanet.com/english/china/2012-09/07/c_131833079.htm (accessed on 28 January 2015).

Xinhua. 2013a. 'China, Vietnam agree to deepen partnership along three tracks', 13 October, http://news.xinhuanet.com/english/china/2013-10/13/c_132795280.htm (accessed on 28 January 2015).

Xinhua. 2013b. 'Chinese premier arrives in Hanoi for Vietnam visit', 13 October, http://news.xinhuanet.com/english/china/2013-10/13/c_132794829.htm (accessed on 28 January 2015).

Xinhua. 2014a. 'Backgrounder: China's stands on South China Sea disputes', 15 December, http://news.xinhuanet.com/english/china/2014-12/15/c_133855926.htm (accessed on 28 January 2015).

Xinhua. 2014b. 'China Voice: Big-picture perspective needed for China-Vietnam ties', 28 August, http://news.xinhuanet.com/english/china/2014-08/28/c_133603760.htm (accessed on 28 January 2015).

Xinhua. 2014c. 'China-ASEAN expo creates new spaces for Vietnamese enterprises: FM', 19 September, http://www.globaltimes.cn/content/882330.shtml (accessed on 28 January 2015).

Xinhua. 2014d. 'China, Vietnam agree to properly handle sensitive bilateral issues', 18 June, http://news.xinhuanet.com/english/china/2014-06/18/c_133418102.htm (accessed on 28 January 2015).

Xinhua. 2014e. 'China, Vietnam agree to properly settle maritime disputes', 27 December, http://news.xinhuanet.com/english/china/2014-12/27/c_133881526.htm (accessed on 28 January 2015).

Xinhua. 2014f. 'China, Vietnam to handle maritime issues through dialogue, consultation', 10 November, http://news.xinhuanet.com/english/china/2014-11/10/c_133778527.htm (accessed on 28 January 2015).

Xinhua. 2014g. 'Chinese, Vietnamese Parties Hold 10th Theory Seminar', 4 November, http://news.xinhuanet.com/english/china/2014-11/04/c_127178393.htm (accessed on 28 January 2015).

Xinhua. 2014h. 'CPC to attend rule of law seminars in Vietnam, Laos', 28 October, http://news.xinhuanet.com/english/china/2014-10/28/c_133748044.htm (accessed on 28 January 2015).

Xinhua. 2014i. 'Vietnam's special envoy to visit China to cool down situation: spokesperson', 25 August, http://news.xinhuanet.com/english/china/2014-08/25/c_133582778.htm (accessed on 28 January 2015).

Xinhua. 2014j. 'Xi eyes mended China-Vietnam ties', 27 August, http://news.xinhuanet.com/english/china/2014-08/27/c_133590950.htm (accessed on 28 January 2015).

Xinhua. 2015a. 'China tells Philippines, Vietnam to cease intrusive action at sea', 29 April, http://news.xinhuanet.com/english/2015-04/29/c_134196716.htm (accessed on 30 April 2015).

Xinhua. 2015b. 'China voices "serious concern" over ASEAN statement on South China Sea', 28 April, http://news.xinhuanet.com/english/2015-04/28/c_134192958.htm (accessed on 30 April 2015).

Xinhua. 2015c. 'China, Vietnam pledge closer friendship, partnership', 7 April, http://news.xinhuanet.com/english/2015-04/07/c_134131246.htm (accessed on 30 April 2015).

Xinhua. 2015d. 'China, Vietnam should transcend disputes, seek cooperation', 8 April, http://en.people.cn/n/2015/0408/c90780-8875476.html (accessed on 30 April 2015).

Xinhua. 2015e. 'China, Vietnam to strengthen cooperation on securities: official', 17 April, http://news.xinhuanet.com/english/2015-04/17/c_134160171.htm (accessed on 30 April 2015).

Xinhua. 2015f. 'Chinese state councilor, Vietnamese deputy PM hold phone talks on ties', 13 February, http://news.xinhuanet.com/english/china/2015-02/13/c_127494569.htm (accessed on 30 April 2015).

Xinhua. 2015g. 'CPC congratulates the Vietnamese Communist Party on 85th anniversary', 3 February, http://news.xinhuanet.com/english/china/2015-02/03/c_133966672.htm (accessed on 30 April 2015).

Xinhua. 2015h. 'Maritime Silk Road offers new opportunity for China-Vietnam cooperation', 8 April, http://news.xinhuanet.com/english/2015-04/08/c_134133884.htm (accessed on 30 April 2015).

Xinhua. 2015i. 'Spotlight: China, Vietnam vow to deepen partnership', 11 February, http://news.xinhuanet.com/english/china/2015-02/11/c_127485474.htm (accessed on 30 April 2015).

Xinhua. 2015j. 'Vietnam hopes to further promote ties with China: official', 16 January 2015, http://news.xinhuanet.com/english/china/2015-01/16/c_127390942.htm (accessed on 30 April 2015).

Xue Zuxian. 2014. 'ASEAN-China relations go beyond disputes', *Global Times*, 17 November, http://www.globaltimes.cn/content/892219.shtml (accessed on 30 April 2015).

Yahoo! News. 2016. 'President Obama visits Vietnam', 24 May, https://www.yahoo.com/news/president-obama-visits-vietnam-215802322.html (accessed on 25 November 2016).

Yu, Jessica Macy. 2016. 'China rebuffs Vietnam criticism of oil rig move', *Reuters*, 8 April, http://www.reuters.com/article/us-southchinasea-china-vietnam-idUSKCN0X50WU (accessed on 25 November 2016).

Zhang Hong. 2014. 'Why is the US going in hard in the South China Sea disputes?', *People's Daily*, 13 August, http://en.people.cn/n/2014/0813/c90000-8768907.html (accessed on 25 November 2016).

Zhang Junshe. 2014. 'Who is breaking international rules, China or the US?', *People's Daily*, 15 August, http://en.people.cn/n/2014/0815/c90000-8770188.html (accessed on 28 January 2015).

Zhao Minghao. 2014. 'Do not let US stoke disputes', *China Daily*, 12 August, http://usa.chinadaily.com.cn/opinion/2014-08/12/content_18292970.htm (accessed on 28 January 2015).

3

China's Strategic Moves since the Communist Party of China's 18th National Congress: Impact on ASEAN Security and Politics

Nguyen Huy Hoang

Under the Chinese leadership of Xi Jinping and Li Keqiang, China is carrying out strategic adjustments and new development methods. These adjustments are reflected in the country's domestic and foreign policies in order to successfully implement the objectives set by the 18th National Congress of the Communist Party of China. For Southeast Asia, a region with a special importance in China's strategy of becoming a global power, Beijing's policies for the region have also been seen major adjustments. These adjustments were announced in a speech by the Chinese President Xi Jinping at the Parliament of Indonesia on 2 October 2013 (ASEAN-China Centre 2013), and formulated in the 2+7 Cooperation Framework initiated by the Premier Li Keqiang at the ASEAN-China Summit Meeting in Brunei in November of the same year (Ministry of Foreign Affairs of the People's Republic of China 2013a).

New Southeast Asia Policy

China's new Southeast Asian policy contains several important points. First, it seeks to promote the building of political trust with Southeast Asian countries and to bind ASEAN with China on all aspects. In the political sphere, it seeks to upgrade ASEAN-China relations from a 'strategic partnership' to the still closer 'community of shared destiny' while in the economic aspect, Beijing has sought to upgrade the ASEAN-China FTA, thereby making ASEAN more dependent on the Chinese economy, to physically connect ASEAN to China through the establishment of the Asian Infrastructure Investment Bank (AIIB) and the projects under it. In the area of military and defence, China has proposed a China-ASEAN defence ministerial meeting, paving the way for the institutionalisation of military and defence cooperation with ASEAN. China also suggested building the 21st Century Maritime Silk Road to facilitate its access to the important sea ports in Southeast Asia. Other objectives include building the social basis and exchanges necessary for ASEAN-China relations as well as to enhance bilateral relations with the important members of ASEAN such as Indonesia, Malaysia, Brunei, Vietnam and Thailand.

The purpose behind the policy adjustments by China is to maintain and expand its influence, to narrow and gradually repel American influence in Southeast Asia, and to implement China's ambitions in the East Sea of Vietnam[1] as well as to expand space for the development of the Chinese economy. To implement the above-mentioned policy since late 2013, China has conducted a series of activities related to Southeast Asia. What were these activities? How did these activities affect peace and security in Southeast Asia? Those are the main issues that will be discussed in this paper.

China's Implementation of the 2+7 Cooperation Framework since 2013

Promoting Strategic Trust with ASEAN Countries

As part of China's confidence-building strategy with the ASEAN, its leaders including Xi Jinping, Li Keqiang and Foreign Minister Wang Yi have always talked about the 'sincerity' of China in the development of its relations with ASEAN. Speaking at the Parliament of Indonesia on 2 October 2013, Xi declared 'China is committed to a relationship of sincerity and friendship with ASEAN countries and to enhance mutual political and strategic trust' (ASEAN-China Centre 2013). Li also affirmed the importance of ASEAN to China and that China considered the ASEAN as a priority in its foreign strategy towards neighbouring countries, in his speech at the 16th ASEAN-China

Summit in 2013 (Ministry of Foreign Affairs of the People's Republic of China 2013a).

Similar statements have also been reiterated by Wang Yi at the ASEAN-China Ministerial Meeting in Nay Pyi Taw in August 2014 where he stated that China and ASEAN countries shared common interests as well as a common destiny. No matter how the international situation evolved, he said, China would continue to take up ASEAN as a priority in its neighbourhood diplomacy. China firmly supported a more prosperous and stronger ASEAN and its centrality in regional cooperation, as well as the conclusion of ASEAN community-building in 2015. He continued to stress that China was committed to the path of peaceful development and that it pursued a policy of good-neighbourliness and friendship with its neighbours (*China Daily Europe* 2014).

Along with the above-mentioned statements, Chinese leaders have actively lobbied ASEAN to accept the idea of and to sign a treaty of good-neighbourliness, friendship and cooperation between China and ASEAN initiated by President Xi, when he spoke at the Indonesian Parliament in October 2013. Furthermore, at the 16th ASEAN-China Summit held in October 2013 in Brunei, Chinese Premier Li Keqiang stated 'we need to actively discuss the possibility of concluding a treaty on good-neighbourliness, friendship and cooperation between China and ASEAN countries. Good-neighbourliness and friendship are a treasure for China-ASEAN cooperation to which we all need to remain truly committed. The new Chinese government attaches great importance to ASEAN and takes ASEAN as a priority on its diplomatic agenda regarding the neighbourhood' (*China Daily Europe* 2014). In addition to the official statement, at the 17th ASEAN-China Summit meeting in Nay Pyi Taw in November 2014, Premier Li also conducted several exchanges of views with ASEAN leaders on strengthening political and security cooperation between ASEAN and China (Ministry of Foreign Affairs of the People's Republic of China 2014a)

The impatience of China in promoting discussion and the signing of the treaty on good-neighbourliness, friendship and cooperation between China and ASEAN is because '...if consensus could be reached and the treaty finally signed, it will provide legal and institutional safeguards for China-ASEAN strategic cooperation, and will become a banner guiding the development of China-ASEAN relations' (Ministry of Foreign Affairs of the People's Republic of China 2013a). The above-mentioned viewpoint by the heads of the Chinese government does not represent all of China's intentions behind the treaty proposal. What China really wants is that once the treaty is signed, it would create the legal basis for the construction of the ASEAN-China Community of Common Destiny. This Community, in its turn, will bind the future of ASEAN with China not only economically but also politically and for security purposes. ASEAN leaders are aware of China's intention. Talking to the *Straits Times* Le Luong Minh, the Secretary General of ASEAN, said that the proposal by China had to be studied carefully in advance. However, under the influence of China, at the special ASEAN-China Foreign Ministerial Meeting held in August 2014, ASEAN and China did discuss the possibility of signing the treaty on good-neighbourliness, friendship and cooperation between the ASEAN countries and China.

Another measure actively promoted by China in order to strengthen strategic trust with ASEAN was the initiative of organising the informal ASEAN-China Defence Ministerial meeting in China in 2015. In his speech at the 17th ASEAN-China Summit, Chinese Premier Li announced that China welcomed the ASEAN defence ministers participating at the meeting and suggested that the two sides could discuss setting up a defence hotline and conducting joint exercises, and continue to strengthen non-traditional security cooperation. In order to promote ASEAN-China cooperation on non-traditional security, the Chinese Premier highly also appreciated the signing of an MoU on disaster management, and declared that China was willing to provide 50 million yuan in emergency disaster aid and that he looked forward to the early identification of projects and their good implementation (Ministry of Foreign Affairs of the People's Republic of China 2014a).

Along with these activities, the Chinese government has invited most Southeast Asian leaders to visit China. In 2013, for instance, President Xi welcomed the state visit of the leaders of eight ASEAN countries – Thailand and the Philippines being exceptions (Ho and Pitakdumrongkit 2013). After the political situation in Thailand returned to stability, Thailand's new prime minister, Prayud O Chan visited China in late December 2014. These activities by China provide an opportunity for ASEAN leaders to become familiar with the new leadership in Beijing, to further develop personal relationships and thereby promote good relations between the Southeast Asian countries and China.

A New Approach to the Problem of Vietnam's East Sea

In order to gain political credibility from the ASEAN countries, only statements of friendship and wishes for cooperation that the Chinese leaders always deliver at every opportunity they meet with ASEAN leaders are not enough. Beijing knows this very well, and cannot ignore the talk about the East Sea of Vietnam issue, the biggest hindrance to ASEAN-China relations.

The new leaders in Beijing have proved to be cleverer than their predecessors when it comes to this issue. To solve the problem of the East Sea of Vietnam, in early 2014, China proposed a dual-track approach, through which China suggested 'specific disputes are to be addressed by countries directly concerned peacefully through negotiation and consultation based on historical facts, international law and the DOC [Declaration of the Code of Conduct] and that peace and security of the South China Sea be jointly upheld by China and ASEAN countries working together'. The approach contains two noteworthy points. First, it repeats China's long-existing viewpoint which states that 'The core of the South China Sea question is the disputes over the sovereignty of some islands and reefs of the Nansha islands and the delimitation disputes over some waters in the South China Sea. It is, in essence, bilateral disputes between China and some ASEAN countries, rather than an issue between China and ASEAN' (Mission of the People's Republic of China to ASEAN 2013). Therefore, resolving such disputes is the work of China and the individual Southeast Asian countries in question. The other point in China's 'dual-track approach' to the problems of East Sea of Vietnam is Beijing's assertion that those responsible for maintaining peace and stability in the East Sea of Vietnam were China and the ASEAN countries, rather than ASEAN as a regional cooperation organisation, or any outsider(s). Therefore, the two sides should 'work together' (Ministry of Foreign Affairs of People's Republic of China 2014).

On the Code Of Conduct (COC), China 'agreed to engage actively in consultations and, on the basis of consensus-building, conclude a code of conduct (COC) at an early date' (Ministry of Foreign Affairs of the People's Republic of China 2014a). To implement such a commitment, China has organised and participated in, for instance, the 6th Senior Officials Meeting (SOM) and the 9th Joint Working Group Meeting held in Suzhou in September 2014 as well as meetings subsequently. The two sides agreed to a list of shared points for reference on the COC. In addition, China also proposed holding a special ASEAN-China SOM meeting in China in September 2015, and the 8th ASEAN-China SOM as well as the 12th Joint Working Group Meeting on the implementation of the DOC meeting in Thailand in October 2015 in order to reach an agreement on classification of the past documents, and to determine the terms for an early conclusion on the COC.

Promoting ASEAN-China Maritime Cooperation

Beijing has called maritime cooperation with ASEAN a new bright spot of ASEAN-China cooperation. The Chinese government attaches great importance to promoting cooperation with ASEAN in this area because if cooperation in the East Vietnam Sea is achieved, China can create the image of peace and cooperation in Vietnam's East Sea. Therefore, ASEAN and international opinion would reduce their attention to China's invasive operations, expansion and renovation in the islands belonging to Southeast Asian countries, particularly Vietnam, that it has invaded.

In order to promote maritime cooperation with ASEAN, China proposed building the 21st Century Maritime Silk Road. The initiative had first been launched by China's President Xi when he delivered the October 2013 at the speech at the Indonesian parliament, and has been called by Chinese Premier Li as one of two biggest initiatives that China has proposed to be jointly conducted with the ASEAN in order to turn the relationship into a 'diamond decade' over the next 10 years. To implement the initiative, China suggested taking up 2015 as the year of China-ASEAN Maritime Cooperation, 'to strengthen cooperation in marine economy, marine science and technology, protection of marine ecology and maritime connectivity, in order to realize shared economic prosperity, expand converging interests and build stronger bonds between the peoples' (Li Keqiang 2014).

The activities were to cover discussions, organising events such as maritime cooperation forum with the expected participation of the maritime ministers from appropriate maritime countries, as well as more dialogue and cooperation among maritime law enforcement agencies and setting up a maritime cooperation centre. In order to facilitate the implementation of these maritime cooperation activities, China also decided to establish the Silk Road Fund to support connectivity development on a priority basis (Ministry of Foreign Affairs of People's Republic of China 2014). The 21st Century Maritime Silk Road initiative by China did not initially get positive responses from the ASEAN.

However, despite the lack of enthusiasm from the ASEAN countries, on the sidelines of the annual Boao Forum on 1 April 2014, China officially announced 2015 as the Year of ASEAN-China Maritime Cooperation. In order to reduce the suspicion of ASEAN towards the 21st Century Maritime Silk Road, China's State Councilor Yang Jiechi in a speech delivered for announcing the event, said that 'China also needs to come up with 'early harvest' projects to demonstrate to ASEAN states that the Maritime Silk Road is in their interest' (Parameswaran 2014). The early harvest projects by the Maritime Silk Road may include an ASEAN-China maritime cooperation centre, setting up an ASEAN-China maritime emergency helpline, and launching the ASEAN-China Ocean College.

Stepping up Relations with Important ASEAN Member States

A notable point in China's ASEAN policy is that it has openly implemented a discriminatory policy towards the ASEAN member countries. In this aspect, Beijing has devoted special attention to three kinds of countries: (i) those that have a strategic location, rich natural resources and play an important role in ASEAN (as Indonesia, Malaysia and Thailand); (ii) oil and gas-rich countries (as Brunei) and (iii) large countries in terms of area and population, and sharing land and maritime borders with China (as Vietnam). The remaining countries are not in China's high priority because they are pro-US (as Philippines and Singapore) or are countries with ongoing political reforms that are not in line with China's interests (as Myanmar), or just small countries where China's influence is already predominant (as Cambodia and Laos). Although the new leaders in China did not publicly announce these priorities, the approach can be clearly seen through China's actions vis-à-vis the countries of Southeast Asia.

President Xi Jinping's first visit to Southeast Asia after taking office was to Indonesia. This choice was not only because Indonesia was the Chair of the 2015 APEC Summit meeting, but also because of the country's political and economic status as well as its strategic position in the region. Moreover, Indonesia is not a claimant in the East Sea. The economic benefits that a country gains from its relationship with China could make Indonesia find it hard to refuse Beijing's invitation for cooperation. The role of Indonesia in ASEAN has also been taken into account by Beijing when implementing the new ASEAN policy. Beijing's new cooperation initiatives with ASEAN would more easily be accepted, if they are also supported by Indonesia. Thus, in his speech to Indonesia's Parliament, Xi affirmed, 'China places great importance on

Indonesia's status and influence in ASEAN. China wishes to work with Indonesia and other ASEAN countries to ensure that China and ASEAN are good neighbors, good friends and good partners who would share prosperity and security and stick together through thick and thin.' (cited in ASEAN-China Center 2013)

During the Xi visit, China and Indonesia agreed to upgrade relations between the two sides to a 'comprehensive strategic partnership', a higher level of relationship compared to the relations China has with the ASEAN as a whole today. Malaysia has also been visited by China's top leader, a choice motivated and prompted by the fact that it is China's largest trading partner in the ASEAN. Despite being a contending party with China in the East Sea, Malaysia's claims do not amount to much. Its approach to the East Sea issue has not been too assertive compared to other Southeast Asian countries. Malaysia is also a country that has an important voice in the ASEAN. Malaysian companies are doing well in China and Xi's visit demonstrated China's respect for Malaysia. Here too, the two sides decided to upgrade their bilateral relations to the level of 'comprehensive strategic partnership' (Ministry of Foreign Affairs of People's Republic of China 2013b).

Vietnam and Thailand are two countries with the most important roles in the Indochina peninsula. China's New Southeast Asian policy would not be a success without the support of these two countries. Besides the above-mentioned shared reasons, the role of each country in China's foreign policy is different. Thailand is a long-standing ally of the US in Southeast Asia. But in the opening years of the 21st century, due to the US' 'indifference' to the region, the Thai government headed by Thaksin Shinawatra pushed Thailand closer to China. After Thaksin was overthrown by a military coup in September 2006, the Thai government led by Abhisit Vejjajiva adjusted the country's China policy in order to balance it with the US. During his five years in office, Thailand's political situation was always volatile because of the fight between Thaksin's supporters, and the supporters of the government. During this time, the Thai economy slowed down and Thailand's position in the ASEAN was also impaired. The above-mentioned situation created favourable conditions for Yingluck Shinawatra, Thaksin's sister, to win in the Thailand's general elections in 2011. After becoming the country's new prime minister, she returned her country closer to China; Yingluck's China policy helped Beijing to regain its lost influence in Thailand, but created disadvantages for the US as well as pro-US strategic forces in the country. In such a context, China placed Thailand at a high priority in order to support Yingluck in implementing her government's new foreign policy. Chinese leaders visiting Thailand promised to buy more rice and rubber in order to ease the economic pressures on Yingluck's government, as well as to help the Thais see the value of the ASEAN-China FTA for the Thai agriculture in particular, and for their country's economy in general.

China's interest in Brunei is mainly due to the country's oil resources. By developing relations with Brunei, China has hoped to obtain long-lasting and stable oil supplies with low transportation costs. In China's Southeast Asia policy, at any time, the position of Vietnam is very important. The security of the southern provinces of China is affected directly by Vietnam and it is also China's most useful gateway to inland Southeast Asia. The role and position of Vietnam in ASEAN have also been increasing. With the US actively promoting activities to pull Vietnam to its side and in order to block the momentum of US-Vietnam relations, Chinese Premier Li Keqiang chose Vietnam as the final destination in his first state trip to Southeast Asia.

While reserving high priority to the relations with the above-mentioned five countries, China has shown its direct hostility to the Philippines. The then Philippines President Benigno Aquino III was not invited to attend the opening ceremony of the 2014 China-ASEAN Expo held in Nanning, for example. However, the relationship between the two countries has changed since the Philippines' new President Rodrigo Duterte came to power in June 2016, who has taken a pro-China slant in the Philippines' foreign policy. As for Myanmar, no high-ranking Chinese leader has visited the country since 2011.

Impact of China's Policy Adjustments on Security and Stability in the ASEAN

China's new policy towards Southeast Asia beginning late 2013 is still a work in progress. Such a policy has been cautiously agreed to by ASEAN, especially for the two major initiatives namely (i) building a community of shared destiny; and (ii) the 21st Century China-ASEAN Maritime Silk Road. This explains why, in the statement by the Chairman of the 17th ASEAN-China Summit, the ASEAN leaders only 'noted with appreciation' (Ministry of Foreign Affairs of the People's Republic of China 2014b) the above-mentioned initiatives by China. Regarding other initiatives, the ASEAN leaders declared: 'We reaffirmed our strong commitment to further strengthen the ASEAN-China Strategic Partnership particularly in the eleven priority areas, namely agriculture, information and communication technology, human resource development, investment, Mekong Basin Development, transportation, energy, culture, tourism, public health and environment' (Ministry of Foreign Affairs of the People's Republic of China 2014b). Seven of the above-mentioned priority areas belong to the economic, cultural and social spheres, which suggests that the ASEAN was not ready to upgrade cooperation with China in the fields of politics, security and defence.

Some visible impacts of China's new policy on politics, security and defence in Southeast Asia can be highlighted.

Positive and Negative Impact

Among the positives has been China's provision of more resources to ASEAN for building the ASEAN Community (AC). Even before the Community was officially formulated on 31 December 2015, China's new Southeast Asia policy played an important role in providing more resources for building the AC. As one of the three pillars of the AC, as planned, the establishment of the ASEAN Political and Security Community (APSC) has also been completed. In the annual report reported at the 25th ASEAN Summit of 11 November 2014 in Nay Pyi Taw, Myanmar, ASEAN Secretary General Le Luong Minh said that until that time, about 85 per cent or 125 out of the 147 action-lines of the APSC Master Plan had been implemented. The successful implementation of the 125 items has had a positive impact on Southeast Asia. Although the regional security environment remains precarious, basically, peace and stability in the region have been maintained.

However, in continuing to realise the APSC, the ASEAN has faced significant challenges. One of the difficulties pointed out by the ASEAN Secretary-General was the shortage of financial resources. So far, the implementation of programmes, projects and activities in the process of ASEAN community building was mainly financed by member countries through in-cash sponsorship and other contributions. In addition to directly providing funding for the operations of the ASEAN Secretariat, centres, special fund and joint funds, member states also had to bear the cost of and contribute manpower, facilities and needed resources for conferences, programmes and projects carried out across the region as well as in their own countries. Although it does not want to rely too heavily on external resources because of concerns over losing its central role in the emerging regional architectures, the ASEAN still has to engage with the dialogue partners and other external partners for financial support and technical aid.

In 2015, the ASEAN carried out several activities to implement the remaining measures of the three Master Plans, to draft documents for the three communities after 2015, and 15 inter-sphere work plans, among other things. To resolve the problem of money for these activities, the Secretary General mooted a comprehensive financial plan, which includes resource mobilisation strategies and a sustainable financial provision mechanism. China is aware of the ASEAN's financial difficulties and in a speech at the 17th ASEAN-China Summit in November 2014, China's Premier Li Keqiang declared,

> 'China is willing to offer ASEAN countries US$10 billion of concessional loans to boost practical cooperation in various fields between the two sides. On top of our commitment last year, we will provide ASEAN with another RMB 50 millions of assistance gratis to support ASEAN community building. Stronger bilateral cooperation between China and ASEAN countries will also be conducive to ASEAN community building' (Ministry of Foreign Affairs of the People's Republic of China 2014a)

In addition to the grants for the activities of the ASEAN Community building, China has also given the Association other aid in carrying out specific goals including confronting non-traditional security challenges. For the ASEAN Economic Community, China pledged to provide the least-developed ASEAN countries RMB 3 billion of non-refundable aid in 2015 to support the efforts of narrowing the development gap within the ASEAN. Within three years (from 2015), the ASEAN would receive US$30 million to support economic and technical cooperation. China also decided to contribute another US$3 billion to raise funds for Phase 2 of the China-ASEAN Investment Cooperation Fund. The China Development Bank has made a special loan of US$10 billion for the development of the ASEAN-China infrastructure.

Other forms of aid have also been pledged by China to assist the ASEAN to carry out the remaining activities in building the ASEAN Social and Cultural Community (ASCC). For the ASCC's objective of human resources development, China has committed to providing training to 100 public health professionals and supporting 100 young scientists from the ASEAN countries to conduct short-term research in China over the next three years. Over the next three to five years starting from 2014, China will provide 15,000 government scholarships to young students from ASEAN countries, and build more educational centres in the ASEAN member states. In addition, China also contributed US$200 million to the Regional Cooperation and Poverty Reduction Fund to provide funding for people-to-people exchanges and capacity building (ASEAN 2013).

No doubt, China has its own intentions and motivation for such generous assistance for the AC's activities and its pillars. But this aid from China has contributed to providing more resources to the ASEAN in implementing the remaining activities in the AC-building process. Therefore, in the statement of the 17th ASEAN-China Summit, the ASEAN leaders have 'welcomed China's support for the implementation of the Roadmap for an ASEAN Community (2009-2015) and the Bali Declaration on ASEAN Community in a Global Community of Nations (Bali Concord III)' (ASEAN 2014)

A second positive impact of the Chinese policies has been the maintenance of the centrality of ASEAN emerging regional architectures. With its wisdom and dynamism, since the end of the Cold War, ASEAN has built up its own regional structures. In many regional organisations, the leadership role belongs to the ASEAN. Powerful states like the US or emerging powers such as China once involved in any regional architecture have to accept the driving role of ASEAN with its membership of small and medium-sized developing countries. This is unprecedented in the history of international relations.

As a driving force, the ASEAN has the power to set the agenda and to take the chairmanship at every annual meeting of such processes. The ASEAN also has the right to direct the activities of all elements in such architectures in addressing emerging problems that would affect the peace, security and development of Southeast Asia.

Another important gain for ASEAN is that the central role of ASEAN has helped create and maintain favourable conditions for the Association to implement a policy of balancing the influence and interests of powerful countries in Southeast Asia. A successful implementation of such policies over the years has contributed significantly to the maintenance of peace and stability in the region. It is perhaps because of the tremendous and important benefits gained from being in a central role that powerful countries including China have been keen to take over the role from ASEAN. In order to have this role, it must firstly be supported by the ASEAN. This is the reason why in recent years, major countries have courted the Association.

For China, even though the country was also desperate to be recognised as a leader in the East Asian integration process, Beijing was well aware that ASEAN and other major countries, especially the US, would never accept its ambitions. Thus, its strong support for ASEAN's central role, would allow China to win goodwill from the Association's leaders, and simultaneously prevent other countries from taking over the role. This Chinese support has over the past few years helped the ASEAN to sustain its central role in the emerging regional architecture in East Asia. An assessment of the significance and importance of China's support for the ASEAN's central role is evident in the statement by the Chairman of the November 2014 ASEAN-China Summit in Nay Pyi Taw where it was declared that the ASEAN Leaders appreciated China's support for ASEAN Centrality in the evolving regional architecture, including through ASEAN-led processes such as the ASEAN Plus Three (APT), the East Asia Summit (EAS), the ASEAN Defence Ministers' Meeting-Plus (ADMM-Plus) and the ASEAN Regional Forum (ARF), in the ASEAN Community building process (ASEAN 2014).

The major negative impact of China's policies including its continuing claims to Vietnam's East Sea has been the threat to ASEAN's own security and stability as a grouping. As discussed above, China's standpoint on the East Sea of Vietnam has basically not changed. The so-called 'dual-track approach', in essence, attempts to push aside the ASEAN, the US and other big countries with interests in the East Sea of Vietnam in the process of seeking solutions to the problem. China's approach is not acceptable to the ASEAN and the Chairman's statement in Nay Pyi Taw also did not have reference to such an approach.

While actively advocating for its new approach in the East Sea of Vietnam, China simultaneously sought to expand and build on some of the islands and reefs it has captured from Vietnam and other ASEAN countries in the past. This shows that China has once again severely violated the DOC and gone against its own leaders' statements of compliance (Neo Chai Chin 2013) .The contradiction between what China says and does in the East Sea of Vietnam has always been evident. The strategic trust that China wants to build with the ASEAN will not be possible, as Beijing does not take seriously commitments that its top leaders have repeatedly and solemnly declared to the leaders of ASEAN.

What to Expect

Lack of Resolution to Vietnam's East Sea Problem in the Short and Medium Term

In the coming years, China's standpoint on the East Sea of Vietnam will not change, because what China wants most in the Sea is turning it into its pond. The reasons behind this ambition are several. First, the East Sea of Vietnam plays an extremely important role in China's economic development. Second, in its global strategy, the role of the East Sea of Vietnam is equally important. If China captures the Spratlys, it would have the ideal location to control the international shipping lanes crossing the Sea, forcing the US and other countries 'to ask for permission' if they wanted to cross. China will also dominate the Southeast Asian nations, cutting off the US' supply routes to Japan, South Korea, Taiwan–American allies in Northeast Asia, in case of a war breaking out between China and one of the above-mentioned countries or territories. Third, at present, China is aspiring to become an ocean power in order to be capable of matching the US, Russia, Britain and other ocean powers. To fulfill this ambition and to support its territorial ambitions both on land and in the East Sea of Vietnam, China is working hard to develop its naval power. But if there is no way out, China's navy could only be a presence in the waters around its territory. Even if China possessed the East China Sea, it could only enter the Pacific Ocean. But even this possibility is very difficult because of Japan's huge naval forces supported by the US. If China captures Vietnam's East Sea on the other hand, Chinese naval forces would have a convenient exit to all the world's largest oceans.

For these reasons, China is increasingly uncompromising in its claims of sovereignty over the East Sea of Vietnam. Relations with the ASEAN are important, but occupying the territory of the East Sea of Vietnam is even more important. This explains why China can compromise with the ASEAN on many issues, but never change its standpoint of resolving the maritime dispute bilaterally with relevant countries. The essence of this viewpoint is that China will prolong the sovereignty dispute in the East Sea of Vietnam until it is capable of fully controlling the Sea. At present, China is trying to foster the 'dual-track approach' in the East Sea of Vietnam. If this approach is not accepted by the ASEAN, it may propose another initiative but China's standpoint on the Sea will never change. China says it expects the COC to be signed soon, but always refuses to continue negotiations on the COC for various reasons. This is in essence because China does not want to be bound by the COC, and prefers the DOC, a legally non-binding declaration.

Due to this Chinese attitude, the problem of sovereignty disputes in Vietnam's East Sea will not be resolved in the short- or medium-term. The situation in the Sea will be a case of both peace and disturbance. Peace and stability in the East Sea of Vietnam, therefore, will be very fragile. The most disturbed area in the East Sea of Vietnam in the coming years will be the that surrounding Vietnam's Paracel Islands, because the Paracels are not considered by the ASEAN as a disputed territory between China and ASEAN but only as a bilateral-level dispute between Vietnam and China. If Beijing conducts aggressive activities in the islands, Vietnam can not stand alone in confronting China and nor can it rely on any big country, whether under a strategic partnership or a comprehensive strategic partnership. China knows this very well, and thus, its recent aggressive activities have only taken place mainly in the waters around the Paracels. To protect its sovereignty, Vietnam will have to respond, creating a difficult situation in the Paracels.

China may also conduct aggressive activities in the Spratlys. But the area in which China will carry out such activities in the coming years will also be in the disputed areas between Vietnam and China. For the Philippines, China will have to be more cautious because of concerns about possible reactions from the US. Malaysia and Brunei will not suffer much from the Chinese aggression as their dispute with China in the East Sea of Vietnam is not serious. Beijing also needs Malaysia's cooperation to implement its new Southeast Asia policies while the oil supply from Brunei would make Beijing unwilling to attack it.

Aggravation of Divisions within the ASEAN

China's discriminatory policies towards the ASEAN member countries have made intra-ASEAN divisions more serious. The divisions within ASEAN due to China's influence have been latent for a long time. The situation was publicly disclosed in late 2012, when Cambodia was the chairman of ASEAN. For the first time in the Association's over-40-year history, the 45th ASEAN Ministerial Meeting did not issue a joint statement due to disagreements between the Philippines and Cambodia regarding the East Sea issue.

China has given high priority to some ASEAN countries, while showing its hostility to the Philippines, and having cool ties with Singapore and Myanmar. This has led the ASEAN countries to suspect each other and has led to a division in their China policy. Countries prioritised by Beijing receive more gains from their relations with China and are more than happy to support the Chinese-led cooperation projects. By contrast, countries cold-shouldered by Beijing, will have to find ways to appeal to China, or seek closer links with the US. In such a context, the collective strength of the ASEAN deteriorates.

Risk of an Arms Race

Arms procurement and military modernisation in the ASEAN countries have taken place at a rapid pace in the 21st century. There are many reasons for this situation. One of the main reasons is that the ASEAN countries are concerned that China would be able to direct its military might against them. Countries that are disputing Chinese sovereignty in the East Sea of Vietnam naturally have more reasons to fear.

Following the September 2006 coup, the Thai Military Council decided to increase the defence budget by 34 per cent in 2007 and 28 per cent in 2008. In November 2007, the Thai Military introduced a 10-year national defence modernisation programme with a total budget increase of 9.8 per cent. This programme implemented since 2009 is expected to push defence expenditures from 1.58 per cent to 2 per cent of GDP by 2014. Meanwhile, according to the Stockholm Peace Research Institute, Malaysia's defence spending increased 75 per cent for the period from 2000 to 2006, from US$1.7 billion to US$3 billion (according to the 2005 dollar exchange rate). Indonesia's defence spending increased 68 per cent from US$2.2 billion to US$3.7 billion in the same period, excluding weapons purchased under export credit. Singapore's budget for defence increased 24 per cent from US$4.6 billion in 2000 to US$5.7 billion in 2006

The tendency towards arms procurement and defence modernisation in the ASEAN countries is also in line with the increase in China's defence budget. The situation makes the environment of peace and security in Southeast Asia already precarious, and even more fragile in the years to come.

Balance of Power in Southeast Asia shifts towards China

In the last decade of the 20th century, with a declining interest in Southeast Asia, it was the US that gave China the opportunity to increase its influence in Southeast Asia. China's influence predominated in most Southeast Asian countries, including in Thailand and the Philippines—the two traditional allies of the US in the region.

However, the situation has changed in the 21st century, especially since Barack Obama became the 44th President of the US in January 2008. Concerned about China's growing rise, the US aggressively deployed a rebalancing strategy in the Asia-Pacific whose real purpose is to contain China's rise.

In the rebalancing strategy of the US, the position of Southeast Asia is very important. The then US Secretary of State Hillary Clinton viewed the ASEAN as 'the fulcrum for the region's emerging regional architecture' (United States Mission to ASEAN 2010) and as a result, Southeast Asia became a cornerstone of the US rebalancing policy since 2009.

The US has part of the rebalance strengthened security relations with Thailand and the Philippines. It is noteworthy that when the US launched the pivot Asia-Pacific policy, the relations between China and these two countries were developing very well. The strong developments in China's relations with Thailand and the Philippines posed great challenges to the US; if the momentum of these relations could not be inhibited, it would lose its influence in its own allies in Southeast Asia. In order to prevent this, the US quietly backed pro-US military forces in Thailand to overthrow the Thai Premier Thaksin Shinawatra's government in September 2006. Washington also actively supported opposition forces in the Philippines to bring down the pro-China Gloria Arroyo as president during the May 2010 elections. After taking the office 30 June 2010, the then Philippine President Benigno Aquino III adjusted relations with China. Manila's standpoint on the East Sea issue has also become more assertive and relations between the Philippines and China have been deteriorated since then. As part of its efforts, the US also promoted and strengthened relations with countries that were considered close to China such as Laos, Cambodia, Myanmar and Vietnam.

The process of implementing the rebalancing policy in Southeast Asia has created a momentum for ASEAN-US relations. In 2005, the US State Department launched the ASEAN Development Vision to Advance National Cooperation and Economic Integration (the ADVANCE program) in order to promote the ASEAN economic integration and cooperation. The US also pledged to provide US$150 million aid to ASEAN to implement the objectives in the cooperation agreements and plans between the US and ASEAN in eight years. Some projects have achieved good results.

Regarding the Vietnam East Sea issue, there were also some important adjustments in the US policy. Instead of holding a neutral standpoint on the sovereignty dispute, Hillary Clinton declared at the ARF meeting in Hanoi in July 2010 that freedom of navigation in the East Vietnam Sea was an American national interest and that it was the US standpoint on the East Vietnam Sea to respect freedom of navigation, peaceful resolution of disputes, freedom of commerce, and support negotiation of a CoC for dispute resolution and—the most relevant here—the view that claims to water could only be based on legitimate land-based claims (Bader 2014). ASEAN-US relations made a breakthrough when the US officially signed the Treaty of Amity and Cooperation (TAC) for joining the East Asian Summit (EAS) in July 2009.

The highlights of ASEAN-US relations were the ASEAN-US Leaders Meeting held in Singapore on 15 November 2009. This was the first summit between the top leaders from the two sides.[2] In the Joint Declaration with ASEAN leaders, President Obama said that his country welcomed the ASEAN's plans to achieve an ASEAN Community by 2015 based on the ASEAN Charter, and reaffirmed American commitment to support those plans (ASEAN 2009). The two sides agreed to step up cooperation and to set up a group of outstanding individuals to support strengthening ASEAN-US relations in addressing regional and global issues. In the above statement, the ASEAN and the US also pledged to promote cooperation in the fields of education, science and technology, labour, cooperation against international terrorism, commitment to nuclear non-proliferation and disarmament, and long-term cooperative actions to address climate change, and so on.

The increasingly active involvement of the US in Southeast Asia, particularly in the East Sea issue, have been warmly applauded by the ASEAN and its member countries, because this is in line with the ASEAN's standpoint. The ASEAN countries having sovereignty disputes with China in the East Vietnam Sea would feel more reassured when the US shares with them basic common interests in the East Vietnam Sea. American influence has grown rapidly in the region, including in Myanmar, where China's influence has predominated since 1988.

However, since the end of 2013, due to domestic problems, the emergence of the Ukrainian crisis and the rise of radical Islamic forces under the leadership of the Islamic State, the US has been unable to sustain the momentum of its rebalancing strategy in Asia, in general, and in Southeast Asia, in particular. The US President was unable to attend the APEC Summit held in Indonesia in October 2013 and the East Asia Summit in Brunei in November 2013. The absence of the American President provided an opportunity for the Chinese leaders to exert their influence in these two forums and to propose the new cooperation initiatives with the ASEAN as mentioned above. Except for the ASEAN Summit in Phnom Penh in November 2012, Obama only met with the Thai Prime Minister and the Myanmarese Prime Minister and welcomed the leaders of Singapore and Brunei since being re-elected for a second term as President.

For the past several years and perhaps, it has become increasingly less likely for the US to focus its attention back on Southeast Asia. The possibility of China alone as the leader of the region as once warned by Singaporean Prime Minister Lee Kuan Yew, looks increasingly likely. Since end-2013, China seems to have had the upper hand and under Xi Jinping, 'it would seem that Beijing's focus on Southeast Asia has gained further momentum' (Ho and Pitakdumrongkit 2013).

Conclusion

The strategic adjustments and reforms of China's development methods set by the 18th National Congress of the Communist Party of China in November 2012 led to changes in its foreign policy in general, and those for Southeast Asia, in particular. This was especially reflected in the proposal to build the 'community of shared destiny' launched by Xi and was elaborated by Li Keqiang in the ASEAN-China Framework 2+7.

In order to implement this policy, China has for the past few years, developed and implemented a number of specific cooperation initiatives. Four prominent initiatives include (i) the proposal of a 'dual-track' approach to tackling the East Sea of Vietnam issue; (ii) establishment of the Asian Infrastructure Investment Bank (AIIB); (iii) making 2014 the year of ASEAN-China cultural exchanges; and (iv) declaring 2015 as the year of ASEAN-China Maritime Cooperation.

Due to ASEAN's prudence, however, some of the Chinese policies could not be implemented strongly. So far, the ASEAN has maintained its central role in the emerging regional architectures. The most obvious negative impact is that the situation in the East Sea continues to be difficult.

In the coming years, the implementation of China's new Southeast Asia policy will have more negative impacts than positive ones. The crisis in Vietnam's East Sea will not be resolved in the short- or medium-term. Intra-ASEAN divisions will likely be exacerbated by the impact of China's discriminatory policies towards the ASEAN states. The risk of an arms race in the region will increase and if the US cannot regain momentum in the implementation of its rebalancing policy in Southeast Asia, China's influence is likely to dominate in the region.

NOTES

1. Internationally, it is called the South China Sea. For the sake of Vietnamese sovereignty, in this paper we call it the East Sea of Vietnam as it is officially and popularly used in Vietnam.
2 During his term (2000-2008), the President George W. Bush had met many times with the seven ASEAN leaders: in October 2002 in Los Cabos, Mexico; in December 2005 in Busan, South Korea; and in September 2007 in Sydney, Australia. However, these meetings took place when they gathered for an APEC meeting. Cambodia, Laos, and Myanmar had not been invited to participate because they were not the members of the APEC.

REFERENCES

ASEAN. 2009. 'Joint statement- 1st ASEAN-US Leaders Meeting Singapore', 15 November, http://asean.org/?static_post=joint-statement-1st-asean-us-leaders-meeting-singapore-15-november-2009 (accessed on 23 July 2015)

ASEAN. 2013. 'Chairman's Statement of the 16th ASEAN-China Summit', 9 October, http://asean.org/wp-content/uploads/images/archive/23rdASEANSummit/chairmans%20statement for%20the%2016th%20asean-china%20summit%20-%20final%203.pdf (accessed on 21 July 2015)

ASEAN. 2014. 'Chairman's Statement of the 17th ASEAN-China Summit', 13 November, http://www.asean.org/storage/images/Chairmans_statement_of_17th_ASEAN-China_Summit.pdf (accessed on 21 July 2015)

ASEAN-China Centre. 2013. 'Speech by Chinese President Xi Jinping to Indonesian Parliament' ASEAN China Centre. 3 October, http://www.asean-china-center.org/english/2013-10/03/c_133062675.htm (accessed on 15 June 2015)

Bilahari Kausikan. 2014. 'ASEAN-China Relations: Building a Common Destiny?', *The American Interest*. 23 September, www.the-american-interest.com/2014/09/23/asean-china-relations-building-a-common-destiny (accessed on 8 March 2017)

China Daily Europe. 2014. 'China-ASEAN strategic partnership enter new stage'. 10 August, http://europe.chinadaily.com.cn/china/2014-08/10/content_18280239.htm (accessed on 15 June 2015)

Ho, Benjamin and Kaewkamol Pitakdumrongkit. 2013. 'Beijing's ASEAN Embrace: Making Hay

While the Sun Shines', *Multilateral Matters,* October, Issue 9, Singapore, 1-6 http://www.rsis.edu.sg/wp-content/uploads/2014/08/CMS_Bulletin009.pdf (accessed on 15 July 2015)

Bader, Jeffery A.. 2014. 'The US-China Dash line: Ending the Ambiguity' 6 February, https://www.brookings.edu/opinions/the-u-s-and-chinas-nine-dash-line-ending-the-ambiguity/ (accessed on 26 August 2015)

Li Kaisheng. 2013. 'Economic ties not enough to build lasting ASEAN relations', *Global Times.* 15 October, http://www.globaltimes.cn/content/817779.shtml (accessed on 8 March 2017)

Li Keqiang. 2014. 'Jointly open up a brighter future for China-ASEAN relations' *Philstar Global.* 11 November, http://www.philstar.com/letters-editor/2014/11/11/1390363/jointly-open-brighter-future-china-asean-relations (accessed on 22 July 2015)

Ministry of Foreign Affairs of the People's Republic of China. 2013a. 'Remarks by H.E. Li Keqiang — Premier of the State Council of the People's Republic of China At the 16th ASEAN-China Summit', 10 October, http://www.fmprc.gov.cn/mfa_eng/topics_665678/lkqzlcxdyldrxlhy_665684/t1089853.shtml (accessed on 8 March 2017)

Ministry of Foreign Affairs the People's Republic of China. 2013b. 'President Xi Jinping Holds Talks with Prime Minister Najib Razak of Malaysia, Deciding to Establish China-Malaysia Comprehensive Strategic Partnership', 10 April http://www.fmprc.gov.cn/mfa_eng/topics_665678/xjpfwynmlxycx21apec_665682/t1085197.shtml (accessed on 8 March 2017)

Ministry of Foreign Affairs of the People's Republic of China. 2014a. 'Remarks by H.E. Li Keqiang Premier of the State Council of the People's Republic of China At the 17th ASEAN-China Summit', 13 November, http://www.fmprc.gov.cn/mfa_eng/zxxx_662805/t1212266.shtml (accessed on 8 March 2017)

Ministry of Foreign Affairs of the People's Republic of China. 2014b. 'Chairman's Statement of the 17th ASEAN-China Summit', 1 December, http://www.fmprc.gov.cn/mfa_eng/topics_665678/lkqzlcxdyhzldrxlhybdmdjxzsfw/t1215668.shtml (accessed on 15 July 2015)

Mission of the People's Republic of China to ASEAN. 2013. 'Chinese Ambassador to ASEAN, H.E. Mme. Yang Xiuping answers journalists' questions on the occasion of the Reception in Celebration of the 10th Anniversary of ASEAN-China Strategic Partnership'. 26 November, http://asean.chinamission.org.cn/eng/stxw/t1102542.htm (accessed on 23 July 2015)

Neo Chai Chin. 2013. 'China, ASEAN should work together for peace in South China Sea: Premier Li', *Today,* 10 October, http://www.todayonline.com/world/asia/china-asean-should-work-together-peace-south-china-sea-premier-li (accessed on 21 July 2015)

Parameswaran, Prashanth. 2015. 'China Plan for ASEAN-China Maritime Cooperation' *The Diplomat,* 1 April, http://thediplomat.com/2015/04/chinas-plan-for-asean-china-maritime-cooperation (accessed on 22 July 2015)

Parameswaran, Prashanth. 2013. 'Beijing Unveils New Strategy for ASEAN-China Relations', *China Brief,* Volume: 13 Issue: 21, 24 October, www.jamestown.org/programs/chinabrief/sin/?cHash=402b2503bf1b47209b28edc1bcc34$tx_ttnews%65btt_news%5D=4126#VR9bJvzF9gcgle (accessed on 8 March 2017)

The State Council of the People's Republic of China.2014. 'China, ASEAN embarking on cooperation of 'diamond decade'', *Xinhua.* 12 November, http://english.gov.cn/premier/news/2014/11/12/content_281475008995238.htm (accessed on 8 March 2017)

United States Mission to ASEAN. 2010. 'Secretary Clinton's Speech on Regional Engagement in Asia', 28 October, https://asean.usmission.gov/secretary-clintons-speech-on-regional-engagement-in-asia/ (accessed on 21 July 2015)

Wang Yuzhu. 2014. 'Premier Li improves prospects of China-ASEAN relationship', *CCTV.* 18

November, http://english.cntv.cn/2014/11/18/ARTI1416299817197110.shtml (accessed on 8 March 2017)

Zhai Kun. 2015. ' Chinese Diplomacy Towards Southeast Asia in 2014', *China US Focus*. 16 January, http://www.chinausfocus.com/foreign-policy/chinese-diplomacy-towards-Southeast-asia-in-2014/ (accessed on 8 March 2017)

Zhang Yuanan. 2013. 'What China Sees When It Looks at Southeast Asia', *Real Clear World*. 17 October, http://www.realclearworld.com/articles/2013/10/17/what_china_sees_ when_ it_ looks_at_southeast_asia_105526.html (accessed on 8 March 2017)

4

The East Sea Issue in Vietnam-China Relations after Normalisation

Bui Thi Thu Hien

Vietnam and China are two neighbouring countries with many similarities in political institutions and also share common land and sea borders. After 25 years of normalisation, the bilateral relationship has achieved rapid development in terms of politics, economics and culture. However, in recent years, there have also been difficult periods in bilateral relations as well as the decline of political trust between the two parties, the two countries and peoples. The reason for this situation is that there still remains much disagreement between the two sides over the settlement of border and territory issues in the East Sea of Vietnam.

Vietnam-China relations in the Post-Normalisation Period

After 25 years of normalisation of relations between Vietnam and China, the bilateral relationship has experienced rapid development. Scholars from Vietnam and China have different ways of dividing the stages of development of the relationship but regardless of the methods, one can easily see that ties since normalisation have had their ups and downs. According to Vietnamese scholars, Vietnam-China relations are divided into four main stages.

1991 to 2000

In this period, the relationship was gradually restored but economic and trade exchanges between the two countries remained low. However, this was an important stage for the rapid development of bilateral relations in the later stages. Realising the factors hindering a healthy development of bilateral ties were the border disputes on land and at sea, the leaders of the two countries began boundary delimitation negotiations on land and at sea as a key task. In this period, the two countries signed agreements on the delimitation of the border (1999), on delimitation of the Tonkin Gulf (2000) and on fisheries cooperation (2000). These agreements contributed to political and economic relations between Vietnam and China entering a phase of strong and rapid development.

2000 to 2014

In this period, bilateral relations flourished on many fronts, particularly in the fields of politics and economics. On the political aspect, in 2008, the two countries established a 'comprehensive strategic cooperation partnership'. High-level meetings are maintained under many forms, to enhance political trust, promote cooperation and create conditions for the two sides to gradually resolve disputes and disagreements (Ministry of Foreign Affairs of the People's Republic of China 2008). Cooperation between the two sides is constantly promoted through delegation exchanges, forming various cooperation and exchange mechanisms between the respective Communist Party Committees, and organising seminars. The two sides also set up a bilateral cooperation Steering Committee (2006) while relations at local levels between the two countries have strengthened. Exchange activities between the two peoples such as youth and scholar exchange programmes are also promoted.

On the economic side, since normalisation, the trade turnover between Vietnam and China has increased more than 1,800 times, from US$32 million (1991) to US$100 billion dollars (2016) (Dao 2016). In terms of investments, China now has more than 4,000 investment projects in Vietnam, with a total of US$56.7 billion, ranked 9th out of 101 countries and territories (Vietnam's Association of Foreign Invested Enterprises 2016).

In recent years, the issues of borders on land and demarcation of the Gulf of Tonkin have basically been resolved. For the East Sea issue, Vietnam and China signed an agreement to guide the settlement of maritime issues (2011) as the basis for the East Sea issue settlement. The two sides agreed to seek a peaceful resolution based on international laws, the 1982 UN Convention of Law of the Sea (UNCLOS) and the 2002 ASEAN Declaration on the Code of Conduct of Parties in the East Sea/South China Sea (DOC). ASEAN and China are now negotiating the Code of Conduct itself (COC) to ensure peace, security and stability in the region.

2014 to the Present

In early May 2014, China blatantly contravened UNCLOS by moving its drilling rig Haiyang Shiyou 981 to a location which was just 17 nautical miles south from Tri Ton Island (the Paracel Islands, Vietnam), about 120 nautical miles to the east of Ly Son Island (Quang Ngai, Vietnam) and staying deep in the 200 nautical miles exclusive economic zone of Vietnam. This incident caused a wave of indignation in the Vietnamese people at home and abroad. Bilateral relations fell to their worst stage since the two countries' official normalisation of relations in 1991. In late 2014, after several visits by high-level leaders of the two countries, relations gradually recovered and in November 2015, President Xi Jinping of China paid a high-level visit to Vietnam. While bilateral relations have gradually gotten back to normal, the East Sea issues between the two countries remain affecting Vietnam-China relations.

Especially, over the last few years, China has defied international condemnation by constantly conducting construction and renovation activities on artificial islands in Vietnam's Spratly archipelago area that it had illegally occupied. In mid-2016, after the Court of Arbitration's ruling on the lawsuit between the Philippines and China concerning their East Sea disputes, the newly-elected president of the Philippines has actively changed his country's foreign policy with China and is also taking the initiative to alleviate the situation by not continuing its tough military actions in the region. It seems that although the situation in the East Sea area in late 2016 and in 2017 is relatively in détente as predicted by many experts and scholars (Wu 2017), related issues will remain complicated and unpredictable in the future due to the existence of large-scale artificial islands located at key geographical positions and militarised by China.

The East Sea Issue in Vietnam-China Relations

The East Sea (as the Vietnamese call it) or Nan Hai (南海 in Chinese) is among the most important and busiest shipping routes of the world. For

Vietnam, a coastal state with a coastline of about 3,260 km, the East Sea has a very important role in terms of economics, socio-politics and national security. In addition to the two offshore islands namely the Paracel Islands and the Spratly Islands in the East Sea, Vietnam's islands and archipelagos total number nearly 2,800 islands (Le Thi Kim Thoa 2015: 17). From the feudal era, Vietnam fishermen have known and exploited natural resources in the East Sea region due to its very important geopolitical position and abundant valuable resources. Along with historical changes, the East Sea has become the object of sovereignty disputes for many countries in the region. These disputes have existed for more than a hundred years over the Paracel islands and for eighty years over the Spratly islands (Nguyen Hong Thao 2016). Sovereignty disputes over only the Paracel Islands exist between Vietnam and China and were marked by China's use of military forces twice in 1956 and in 1974 to invade the Paracel Islands under Vietnam's territorial sovereignty (then under the management of the Democratic Republic of Vietnam).

Sovereignty disputes over the Spratly Islands started and developed after the end of World War II, together with the new world order, the development of science and technology, the oil crisis and the new maritime legal order established in the 1970s and 1980s. Since 1965 and particularly in the late 1970s, new disputants have appeared such as the Philippines, Malaysia and Brunei. After two naval attacks in 1974 and in 1988, China occupied all of the Paracel Islands and several rocky outcrops in the Spratly Islands (Nguyen Hong Thao 2016). After the Mischief Reef incident in 1995 between China and the Philippines, and after a period of negotiations between China and ASEAN, the two sides signed the DOC in 2002. In 2009, however, China officially submitted the U-shape map (the 9-dash line) to the UN Commission on the Limits of the Continental Shelf (CLCS) to represent its official views on its claims.

In parallel with the proposal, China has made several statements on what it calls its 'core interests' in the East Sea (Nguyen Hong Thao 2016). This increased tensions in the region, slowing down the negotiation process between China and ASEAN in formulating the COC. Chinese scholar Wu Shicun, Director, National Institute for South China Sea Studies, predicted that in the first six months of 2017, China and ASEAN would 'complete the outline discussions on the Code of conduct' (Wu 2017) to accelerate the negotiation and conclusion process of this important document, creating a maritime cooperation framework between China and the ASEAN countries for the future. However, this collaboration possibility remains unlikely.

China is a big country, with a long coastline and four territorial seas namely Bohai, Huanghai, Donghai, and Nanhai/East Sea. In history, a lot of Chinese documents and maps showed the Hainan Island as the southern end of China. After nearly 40 years of reform and open-door policy, China has made great economic progress, becoming the second-largest economy in the world since 2010. Given its demand for energy needed for growth, China needs to have a long-term strategy to approach and control the sea waters with a rich potential of natural resources and turn them into stepping stones to move on to the other oceans. The 18th Congress of Chinese Communist Party in 2012 outlined a strategy of building China up as 'a maritime power' in its Party documents (Zhang et al. 2014). Xi stressed 'building a maritime power has an important significance in promoting healthy and sustainable economic development, national security and sovereignty protection, benefits' (Zhejiang Province Development and Reform Commission 2013). China's 13th Five-Year Plan has included the 'expansion of blue economy space' for the purpose of 'marine economic development, science and technology applications to exploit marine resources for the benefits of maritime protection and the build-up of a maritime power' (Chapter 41 in *iNews* 2016). In the near future, therefore, China will continue to 'expand the marine economy' through 'improving and optimizing marine industries structure, developing offshore fishing industry, promoting large-scale applications of seawater filtration, manufacturing drugs from marine organisms...' The 13th FYP has, for the first time, officially defined the objective of 'supporting Hainan to develop special maritime economics by taking advantage of the South China Sea resources' (Chapter 41 in *iNews* 2016).

China has long wanted to possess and claim the sovereignty of the East Sea's vast and resource-rich waters. However, since China's economic strengths in the previous period were limited, insufficient and unable to dominate and control the area, China has only now advocated specific policies in the East Sea issues and used the historically vague '9-dash line' to support its claims. In recent years, China's policies on the East Sea have changed markedly owing to its economic development and especially since its new status in 2010 as the second-largest economic power in the world.

Causes for Disagreements

With the sovereignty claims over the East Sea between Vietnam and China, disagreements between the two countries can be identified in the following aspects. First, in the Tonkin Gulf, as a coastal state, Vietnam has the right to draw straight baselines, thereby determining the economic exclusive zone and the continental shelf over which Vietnam has full sovereignty, sovereign rights and jurisdiction rights under the UNCLOS. However, China makes its claims based on the U-shape line including the waters of the Tonkin Gulf saying this is a historical claim.

Second, however, according to the UNCLOS, China's historical evidence is not convincing enough because 'the claims of historical rights provided by the coastal states were based on a long history of maritime use, legally recognized by tribunals with valid recognition of the stakeholders' (Nguyen Thi Lan Anh 2015: 325). Meanwhile, in addition to historical evidence related to the Paracel and Spratly Islands and on the basis of the UNCLOS, Vietnam has sufficient legal grounds to claim sovereignty over the two islands chains. The fact that China used military forces to illegally invade the Paracel Islands in 1956 and in 1974 as well as a number of islands in the Spratly Islands in 1988, is contrary to the international law and thus, not recognised by other countries. This is also an important reason that China has always stubbornly refused to resolve the East Sea disputes through legal procedures.

Third, the issue of sovereignty of the Spratly Islands involves five countries and six parties claiming sovereignty over a number of rocky islands either in whole or in part. Before the Permanent Court of Arbitration's (PCA) ruling on a dispute between the Philippines and China in the East Sea, China had used the U-shape line to claim a vast area of waters including 80 per cent of the East Sea area and created large overlapping zones with other countries in the region. The PCA's ruling has formally rejected the legality of the U-shape line, which China created in the East Sea, while at the same time, also narrowing the disputed waters after reviewing legal regulations of the entities in this area.

Impact on Bilateral Ties

The impacts of the East Sea issue on Vietnam-China ties can be seen in several respects. First, in political terms, the issue of territorial sovereignty disputes in the East Sea has caused the decline of political trust between Vietnam and China (Nguyen Dinh Liem 2013: 139) and thus caused ups and downs in cooperation relations between the two countries – 'the East Sea is like a rope that will pull back to the starting point whenever there is a step forward in the Vietnam-China relationship', as one Chinese source put it (*Huanqiu Shibao* 2017). After the normalization of relations, in order to deal with the issue of strategic trust, the leaders of the two countries have continuously put in their efforts into border demarcation negotiations, especially maritime borders. The agreement on the demarcation of the Gulf of Tonkin (*Vnexpress* 2015) was concluded after a long period of negotiations. With regard to the Paracel and Spratly Islands, there was no progress in negotiations and dispute resolution due to two critical reasons. One, China has always denied the existence of any dispute over the Paracel Islands (after in reality, using military forces to illegally occupy and control the islands until the present day). Two, as regards the Spratly Islands, China always wanted to resolve the dispute through one-on-one negotiations with economically and militarily weaker countries to gain better advantages in negotiations.

In the context where the existing disputes and negotiations have always reached an impasse, from 2009 to now, China has actively increased its provocative activities in the field, in order to illegally claim sovereignty in the U-shape line area, for example cutting the *Viking* and *Binh Minh 02* cables while these ships were performing oil and gas exploration activities in the continental shelf and exclusive economic zone of Vietnam, or by its poor treatment of Vietnamese fishermen after unilaterally and blatantly imposed a fishing ban in the East Sea (*Vnexpress* 2016). In addition, as mentioned above, there was the 2014 Haiyang Shiyou 981 oil rig incident that led to protest demonstrations in several big Vietnamese cities like Hanoi, Ho Chi Minh City, and Da Nang (*Vnexpress* 2014). Thus, it is clear that the disputes over maritime territorial sovereignty have deeply affected the political trust as well as bilateral relations in recent years. If there are no substantive and progressive talks in the future, the East Sea issues will remain destabilising factors in the Vietnam-China relationship.

Second, in terms of economic aspects, after the incident of illegally moving the Haiyang Shiyou 981 oil rig into the continental shelf and exclusive economic zone of Vietnam, there were some sceptical opinions in Vietnam about trade and economic cooperation activities with China (*Vietnamnet* 2014). The incident has caused tremendous impact on Vietnam's economy in certain areas such as tourism and seafood exports. Besides, this incident has also had a direct influence on some businesses from China and on those from Hong Kong and Taiwan (*Dantri* 2014), with bilateral trade activities during the period also showing signs of decline. However, after China withdrew the Haiyang Shiyou 981 oil rig, bilateral trade between the two sides has speedily recovered and by the end of 2014, trade turnover between the two countries continued to increase in both exports and imports *(Vinacorp* 2015). This meant that the demands for trade and economic cooperation between the two countries were very high in the context of globalisation and regionalisation, especially when both countries could take advantage of close geographical positions. 2015 recorded a large stream of Chinese investment into Vietnam, especially in low-tax industries for member states under the proposed Trans-Pacific Partnership (TPP) (Pho Noi Textile & Garment Industrial Park 2013).

Third, in terms of the people's awareness, after the incident of Haiyang Shiyou 981 oil rig incident, the Vietnamese and Chinese naturally reported matters differently. This has led to different perceptions from the two peoples on the maritime disputes between their countries. The Chinese media distorted the truth and stated that Vietnamese military forces had actively collided with the oil rig to obstruct China's 'legal' oil and gas exploration activities (*360 doc* 2014). In fact, it is clear that China has blatantly violated the waters under Vietnam's sovereignty in the contravention of the UNCLOS to which both countries are signatories, and Vietnam has properly reacted to peacefully safeguard its legitimate maritime sovereignty (Huongvebien Dong 2014). Vietnam is a coastal state with a long coastline from the north to the south, and historically, Vietnamese fishermen have long been active and fished in these traditional fishing grounds. The Vietnamese people have always attached great importance to maritime territorial sovereignty that many Vietnamese generations sacrificed their lives for. Therefore, it is entirely rightful and natural (Truong Luu 2014) for the Vietnamese people and military forces to respond to China's violation of sovereignty.

Fourth, China has undermined peace and stability in the region. After the Haiyang Shiyou 981 incident, the United States published a series of satellite photographs revealing China's accretion and renovation of rocky islands illegally occupied by Chinese military forces. The situation in the region has continued to heat up, with China this time blatantly declaring that 'this is a legitimate activity in China's sovereign territory' as it could not hide its illegal renovation activities on the rocky islands. To challenge the claims that go against the spirit of the UNCLOS and to affirm the right of freedom of navigation and aviation as stipulated by international law, the US and its allies have conducted many patrol operations in the area around China's artificial islands. These activities have caused tensions in recent years in the area. As a result, it can be seen that the East Sea situation has been continuously in turmoil in recent years due to China's behaviour towards other countries in the region in defiance of international law.

Recommendations for Going Forward

Although in many exchange forums between the two countries, where the state and party leaders or scholars have always affirmed that 'Vietnam-China relations include not only the East Sea issues', we can see that the disagreements on maritime territorial sovereignty are also always considered as the contributing factor for the decline of strategic trust, affecting economic cooperation, the two peoples' feelings and causing extreme instability in the reign. The East Sea issues play an important role in Vietnam-China relations, and it will take a long time and will need great efforts from the leaders and peoples of both countries to resolve for a number of reasons.

The nature of the East Sea disputes and the importance that China and Vietnam attach to the issues of sovereignty, sovereign rights and jurisdiction over the sea, are major factors. For any country, especially Vietnam—a country that has suffered from many years of wars and sacrifices—territorial sovereignty is always a most sacred issue. In the context where the world is witnessing a strong growth of populist movements leading to the United Kingdom's exit from the European Union, the election of Donald Trump as American President with his protectionist agenda, and continuing national sovereignty issues in Asian countries, mutual concessions on sovereignty issues among the disputing countries in the East Sea region will now be more difficult than ever.

Also, the East Sea disputes are links in a network; thus, if there is any change in a link, it also leads to changes in that network. It can be seen that in late 2016, the East Sea situation changed markedly owing to strategic choices of the concerned countries, for example, the Philippines. Although the Philippines won the legal battle with China in the maritime dispute, the newly-elected president chose a policy of détente and strengthened economic cooperation with the Chinese and sped up bilateral cooperation negotiations on resource exploitation and fishing in the region. In response to this strategic shift of the

Philippines, China also shows more peaceful reactions, lowering tensions in the East Sea region.

Furthermore, along with the change of governments in some other countries in the world such as in the US, in Taiwan and in the context of the new populism in Europe and Asia, there will be more unpredictable impacts on the East Sea issues in the coming times. Any development in the East Sea will also have an enormous influence on Vietnam as a coastal state. Therefore, stability and peace in the East Sea for Vietnam is a consistent policy guideline for Vietnamese leaders – instability in the East Sea has a bad impact on both countries. Cooperation and negotiations to settle disputes are the only solutions to deal with all the remaining issues.

Therefore, a cooperative perspective between the two countries for going forward will include the following steps. First, fostering peace and friendship relations between Vietnam and China is an important base for peace and stability in the East Sea region and vice versa. China and Vietnam should strengthen political confidence and cooperation between their governments and ministries in implementing commitments of their leaders to achieve good relations in all aspects.

Second, Vietnam and China should increase their maritime cooperation in less sensitive areas such as fisheries, anti-piracy and rescue efforts. Sovereignty-related problems have always been the most sensitive, thorny and difficult issues to resolve, therefore, much time on talks and negotiations will be needed. As a result, currently, China and Vietnam should focus on handling maritime conflicts, developing cooperation in less sensitive areas in order to increase mutual understanding between the two peoples and authorities. Third, in order to establish a strong foundation for cooperation, China and the ASEAN member states must achieve the early conclusion of the COC, which creates an important framework for long-term cooperation between China and related countries in the East Sea region.

Fourth, the two parties and governments have to manage well their propaganda to prevent their people being aroused by hostile forces. In recent years, hostile forces from other countries and governments have been taking advantage of some people's legitimate patriotism and transferring their reactions into damaging activities towards foreign businesses. Media agencies should honestly report the nature of the disputes to give the people a better understanding about the issues, and the leaders of the two countries too, should promote dispute resolution guidelines and policies. Vietnam and China should settle their disputes in accordance with international law so that mainstream media agencies can positively impact radical public opinion at home and abroad.

Fifth, apart from economic cooperation, Vietnam and China should continuously strengthen maritime patrol cooperation and condemn inhuman treatment towards fishermen carrying out activities in their traditional fishing grounds. Authorities of both countries are to enhance their fishermen's understanding of the major principles of natural resource protection, environmental protection and fishermen rescue. Humane treatment of each other's fishermen would help reduce tensions in the conflicts between the two countries even if disputes on territorial sovereignty remain unresolved. These will also be beneficial to confidence-building between the two peoples and promote bilateral maritime cooperation.

Vietnam and China are two neighbouring countries, still having many disagreements over maritime territorial borders. The two countries therefore, need to quickly settle their maritime disputes, strengthen maritime cooperation and continuously promote a common code of conduct for the East Sea area, and thus contribute to the preservation of peace and stability in the region.

REFERENCES

360 doc. 2014. 'Nanhai 981 fasheng dashi: Zhong-Yue jilie jiaofeng' (南海 981 发生大事：中越激烈交锋) [South China Sea 981 Major Incident: China and Vietnam engage in sharp clash], 26 June, http://www.360doc.com/content/14/0626/20/11548039_390076325.shtml (accessed on 15 February 2017).

Dantri. 2014. 'TS Nguyen Duc Thanh: Gian khoan Hai Duong 981 lam mat 0,7% GDP' [Haiyang Shiyou 981 oil rig caused 0.7% loss of GDP], 28 July, http://dantri.com.vn/kinh-doanh/ts-nguyen-duc-thanh-gian-khoan-hai-duong-981-lam-mat-07-gdp-1407084629.htm (accessed on 15 February 2017).

Dao Tung. 2016. 'Kim ngach Viet-Trunghuongtoi 100 ti USD nam nay' (Vietnam-China trade turnover will reach US$100 billion in this year), *Tin téc*. 8 March, http://baotintuc.vn/kinh-te/kim-ngach-viettrung-huong-toi-100-ti-usd-nam-nay-20160308193118005.htm (accessed on 15 February 2017).

Huanqiu Shibao (环球时报). 2017. 'Ruan Fuzhong Nguyen Phu Trong fang-Hua shi Zhong-Yue youhao gonggu dexinhao' (阮富仲访华是中越友好巩固的信号) [Visit by Nguyen Phu Trong to China signals strengthening of China-Vietnam friendship], 9 January, http://opinion.huanqiu.com/editorial/2017-01/9921028.html (accessed on 15 February 2017).

Huongvebien Dong. n.d. 'Tai sao tau Viet Nam phai tim cach ap sat gian khoan HD-981 cua Trung Quoc?' [Why has Vietnam not used naval forces to resolve the issue of Haiyang Shiyou 981 oil rig?], https://biengioihaidao.wordpress.com/2014/06/26/tai-sao-tau-viet-nam-phai-tim-cach-ap-sat-gian-khoan-hd-981-cua-trung-quoc/ (accessed on 15 February 2017).

iNews (凤凰财经). 2016. 'Shisan Wu guihua gang yao fabu (quanwen)' (十三五规划纲要发布(全文))

[Outline of the 13th Five-Year Plan (Full Text), http://finance.ifeng.com/a/20160317/14275496_0.shtml (accessed on 15 February 2017).

Le Thi Kim Thoa. 2015. 'Tam quan trong cua dao va quan dao Viet Nam va van de tranh chap chu quyen bien dao tren Bien Dong' [The importance of Vietnam's Islands and the Problem of Sovereignty over the Sea and Islands in the East Sea], in Do Tien Sam (ed.). 2015. *Bien Dong: Lich su, phap ly va quan he quoc te* [East Sea/South China Sea: History, Legal and International Relations]. Hanoi: The Social Sciences Publishing House, 17-45.

Ministry of Foreign Affairs of the People's Republic of China. 2008. 'China-Viet Nam Joint Statement', 25 October, http://www.fmprc.gov.cn/mfa_eng/wjb_663304/zzjg_663340/yzs_663350/gjlb_663354/2792_663578/2793_663580/t520438.shtml (accessed on 15 February 2017).

Nguyen Dinh Liem. 2013. *Quan he Viet-Trung truoc su troi day cua Trung Quoc* [Vietnam-China relations Before the Rise of China]. Hanoi: Encyclopedia Publishing House.

Nguyen Hong Thao. 2016. 'The East Sea—Three stages, four challenges, two regional approaches and a belief', in Tran Truing Thuy (ed.), *The South China Sea: Towards a Region of Peace, Security and Cooperation*. The Diplomatic Academy of Vietnam (Hanoi: The Gioi Publishers), 269-289, http://nghiencuubiendong.vn/trung-tam-du-lieu-bien-dong/doc_view/997-the-south-china-sea-towards-a-region-of-peace-security-and-cooperation-full-version?tmpl=component&format=raw (accessed on 15 February 2017).

Nguyen Thi Lan Anh. 2015. 'Tai sao Quyen lich su bi Cong uoc luat bien 1982 dua vao lich suCac van de phap ly trong tranh chap Bien Dong' [Why Historical Rights were inserted into the 1982 United Nations Convention on the Law of the Sea in the East Sea/South China Sea], in Dang Dinh Quy (ed.). 2015. *Tim kiem giai phap vi hoa binh va cong ly o Bien Dong* [Seeking Solutions for Peace and Justice in the East Sea]. Hanoi: The World Publishing House, 325-343

Nhu Tam. 2014. 'Bieu tinh phan doi Trung Quoc gay tieng vang tren bao quoc te' [Chinese protests in international newspapers], *VnExpress*. 11 May, http://vnexpress.net/tin-tuc/the-gioi/bieu-tinh-phan-doi-trung-quoc-gay-tieng-vang-tren-bao-quoc-te-2989137.html (accessed on 15 February 2017).

Pho Noi Textile & Garment Industrial Park. 2013. 'Doanh nghiep Trung Quoc don song TPP o Viet Nam' [Chinese businesses and the TPP wave in Vietnam], 9 September, http://vinatexid.com.vn/chi-tiet/23/doanh-nghiep-trung-quoc-don-song-tpp-o-viet-nam (accessed on 15 February 2017).

Truong Luu. 2014. 'Nhin lai su kien Trung Quoc ha dat gian khoan Hai Duong – 981 xam pham chu quyen bien dao cua Viet Nam' [A review of the of Haiyang Shiyou 981 oil rig incident that violated Vietnam's maritime sovereignty], Vietnam Institute of Chinese Studies. 27 August, http://vnics.org.vn/Default.aspx?ctl=Article&aID=508 (accessed on 15 February 2017).

Vietnam's Association of Foreign Invested Enterprises (Hiep Hoi Doanh Nghiep Dau Tu Nuoc Ngoai). 2016. 'Trung Quoc dau tu 4.759 du an tai Viet Nam' (China's investment in 4,759 projects in Vietnam), 5 May, http://www.vafie.org.vn/detail/trung-quoc-dau-tu-4759-du-an-tai-viet-nam.html#top (accessed on 15 February 2017).

Vietnamnet. 2014. 'Gian khoan Hai Duong 981 va kich ban kinh te Viet - Trung' [Haiyang Shiyou 981 oil rig and Vietnam-China economic scenarios], 16 August, http://vietnamnet.vn/vn/kinh-doanh/gian-khoan-hai-duong-981-va-kich-ban-kinh-te-viet-trung-186221.html (accessed on 15 February 2017).

Vinacorp. 2015. 'Quan he thuong mai Viet - Trung qua nhung con so' [Vietnam-China trade relations in figures], 21 January, http://vinacorp.vn/news/quan-he-thuong-mai-viet-trung-qua-nhung-con-so/ct-570210 (accessed on 15 February 2017).

Vnexpress. 2014. 'Bieu tinh phan doi Trung Quoc gay tieng vang tren bao quoc te' [Chinese protests in international newspaper], 11 May, http://vnexpress.net/tin-tuc/the-gioi/bieu-tinh-phan-doi-trung-quoc-gay-tieng-vang-tren-bao-quoc-te-2989137.html (accessed on 15 February 2017).

Vnexpress. 2015. 'Viet - Trung phan chia trong Vinh Bac Bo nhu the nao' [How Vietnam and China divided the Gulf of Tonkin], 14 May, http://vnexpress.net/tin-tuc/the-gioi/tu-lieu/viet-trung-phan-chia-trong-vinh-bac-bo-nhu-the-nao-3133678.html (accessed on 15 February 2017).

Vnexpress. 2016. 'Trung Quoc doa siet lenh cam danh bat ca o Bien Dong' [China threatens to ban fishing in the East Sea], 7 May, http://vnexpress.net/tin-tuc/the-gioi/trung-quoc-doa-siet-lenh-cam-danh-bat-ca-o-bien-dong-3398996.html (accessed on 15 February 2017).

Wu Shicun (吴士存). 2017. 'Nanhai jushi qu huan haishi qujin' (南海局势趋缓还是趋紧?) [Is the South China Sea situation easing up or becoming increasingly tense?], *Cankao Xiaoxi* (参考消息), 3 January, http://www.nanhai.org.cn/index.php/Index/Research/review_c/id/190.html (accessed on 15 February 2017).

Zhang Ye, Deng Chuxiong, Xie Binggeng, Liu Like, Lei Guoqiang (张晔, 邓楚雄, 谢炳庚, 刘利科, 雷国强). 2014. 'Jiyu BP rengong shenjing wangluo de "meili Hunan" jianshe shuiping dingliang zonghe pingjia' (基于 BP 人工神经网络的'美丽湖南'建设水平定量综合评价) [Quantitative and Comprehensive Evaluation of Beautiful Hunan Construction Level Based on BP Artificial Neural Network], *Tropical Geography*. 34 (4): 553-560, July, http://www.rddl.com.cn/CN/article/downloadArticleFile.do?attachType=PDF&id=2508 (accessed on 15 February 2017).

Zhejiang Province Development and Reform Commission (浙江省发展和改革委员会). 2013. 'Zhonggong zhongyang zhengzhiju jiu jianshe haiyang qiangguo yanjiu jinxing di-ba ci jiti xuexi' (中共中央政治局就建设海洋强国研究进行第八次集体学习) [The CPC Central Committee Political Bureau conducted the eighth collective study on the construction of maritime power], 6 August, http://www.zjdpc.gov.cn/art/2013/8/6/art_1285_565778.html (accessed on 15 February 2017).

5

Sino-Indian Maritime Interface: Assessing the Vietnam Factor

Kush Kumar Gayasen

China's rise as an assertive maritime power and India's growing maritime ambition with a rapidly transforming navy have resulted in a geopolitical shift in Asia. Moreover, the seas surrounding India and China have become a consequential theatre of interplay between them. China has the second-largest navy in the world which is undergoing a rapid modernisation programme. The PLA Navy is now aspiring to establish its presence in the far-flung areas of the Indian Ocean. The urge to expand Chinese naval power in the Indian Ocean is also seen as part of China's 'Go West' strategy, to link western China with the Indian Ocean (Mohan 2013). It is argued that the ever-increasing Chinese footholds and diplomatic ties in the region have limited India's ability to project its maritime power (Pant 2010).

India has long been conscious of Chinese naval expansion in the vicinity of the Indian Ocean and South Asia. Emergence of conflicting maritime issues has further pushed India to restructure its relations with Southeast Asian countries. Among the Southeast Asian countries, Vietnam serves India's ambition of playing a significant role in the Western Pacific Ocean. It is generally argued that the potential role of Vietnam to counterbalance China's growing maritime power has triggered India's strengthening of its economic, political and strategic engagements with Vietnam (Jha 2011: 58; Sokinda 2015: 4). As a matter of fact, India's overall economic, political and strategic interests in Southeast Asia, which include a huge amount of Indian trade that passes through the South China Sea and exploring oil deposits off the coast of Vietnam, compel India to assert its presence in the region and play a constructive role in the developments taking place in the area. With regard to the South China Sea maritime disputes, the Indian government's position is to support 'freedom of navigation and over flight, and unimpeded commerce, based on the principles of international law, as reflected notably in the UNCLOS' (MEA 2016a). In order to maintain its economic, political and strategic engagements with the Southeast Asian countries, India looks at the region as a platform to establish its growing maritime influence. This in turn has made it an important player in the South China Sea.

Sino-Indian Maritime Interface and Vietnam

Over the last few decades, the growing maritime prowess of both India and China has allowed them proactive maritime operational capabilities. The enunciation of India's maritime doctrines in 2004 and thereafter, reflects a transformation in India's maritime strategy for the first time in its long maritime traditions (Integrated Headquarters Ministry of Defence, Navy, 2004, 2007, 2009 and 2015). These formal expositions underline China's rise as a threat to India's maritime interests. The Indian Navy, by endorsing the Indian Ocean Naval Symposium, participating in multilateral-regional institutions, frequent joint naval exercises and strategic-diplomatic collaborations with littoral states has gradually strengthened its presence in the Indo-Pacific region to face growing traditional and non-traditional challenges and to maximise India's maritime interests. India's maritime trade is at its all-time high, expanding across countries of both the Indian and Western Pacific Ocean.

The 2009 Maritime Doctrine of India clearly expands its maritime domain by 'including for the first time SCS, other areas of west Pacific Ocean and friendly littoral countries located in the region' (Integrated Headquarters Ministry of Defence, Navy 2009: 65-68). The Maritime Strategy Document 2007 underlines how events in the South China Sea can affect India's position in the Indian Ocean region. On the other hand, according to one Chinese scholar Hou Songlin, 'India's 'Look East Policy' toward the Association of South East Asian Nations (ASEAN) carries maritime implications' (Holmes and Yoshihara 2008: 368). He prophesies that Indo-ASEAN cooperation on counter-terrorism, maritime security and transnational crime-fighting represents part of an Indian 'grand strategy to control the Indian Ocean, particularly the Malacca Strait' (cited in Holmes et al. 2009: 133). Another commentator perceives the Indian naval presence in the Andamans as evidence that New Delhi is seeking to monitor Chinese naval activities near the Strait, a strategic point linking the Indian Ocean and the Pacific (cited in Holmes et al. 2009: 134). As a result, the struggle for maximising maritime influence has brought India and China to the shores of the South China Sea.

Any problem surfacing either in the Indian Ocean or the South China Sea has a spillover effect on other countries. As one scholar puts it, 'whereas the Indian Ocean is India's strategic backyard in which China is coming, the situation is reversed in the South China Sea which is China's strategic backyard into which India is coming' (Scott 2016). Their competition for resources and growing maritime capabilities has brought them to a junction where their interests are intersecting each other. The significance of Vietnam for both India and China increases as the relations become sour between India and China over the issue of the South China Sea. With regard to India's oil exploration in the waters, the Chinese media has termed India's deal with Vietnam for oil exploration as a 'serious political provocation', and advocates every means possible' to stop this (cited in Muni 2011: 2). On the contrary, Vietnam has supported India in its bid to explore oil resources. Vietnam 'reaffirmed that it is within its rights to invite India to explore for oil in this area, but China claims that this basin is within the 'nine dotted line' or its zone of influence' (cited in Panda 2013). In 2006, the Indian oil firm ONGC Videsh first signed a contract to explore a Vietnamese oil block known as Block-128. In July 2017, Vietnam granted a two-year extension of the contract in the area that was by now a prominent part of the South China Sea dispute between China and Vietnam (*The Times of India* 2017). China sees India's efforts at naval diplomacy to garner support from Australia, Japan and Vietnam as part of India's counterbalancing strategy against China's maritime expansion in the Indian Ocean region (*The Economic Times* 2015).

India-Vietnam Interactions

Though, India and Vietnam are not immediate neighbours in Asia, the geographical distance has never been a factor in determining the depth of relationship between the two countries. Historically, India and Vietnam share cultural and economic links and in the Cold War era, Indian leaders had proactively strengthened ties with Vietnam. This was reflected in India's support to Vietnam during the US-Vietnam and the Cambodia-Vietnam wars. Thus, the bilateral relationship between India and Vietnam has evolved over the years in all three dimensions: economic, political and military-strategic. Initially, the economic relationship got momentum with the implementation of India's 'Look East' policy in early 1990s. Vietnam's geostrategic location was seen as vital. A rising demand for energy led both countries to engage in exploring oil resources in the South China Sea and the Look East Policy also became a platform for India's defence diplomacy after 1992 to safeguard its eastern seaboard and secure its strategic interests in Southeast Asia (Jha 2011: 47).

The strategic engagement between India and Vietnam began during the 1980s and got strengthened in the form of structured and institutional arrangements during the 1990s (Muni 2011: 6). In later years, emphasis on a renewed political relationship with Vietnam received greater momentum. The then Defence Minister, George Fernandes, portrayed Vietnam as India's most trusted friend and ally and suggested that India develop a naval presence in the South China Sea through access to the Cam Ranh Bay naval and air base and also that India should provide training and advanced weapons to Vietnam (Brewster 2012).

A landmark strategic partnership agreement was signed between India and Vietnam in 2007 that set the ground for cooperation in the following areas – political, defence and security cooperation, economic cooperation and commercial engagement, closer trade and investment, science and technology, cultural and technical cooperation, and cooperation at multilateral and regional forums (Panda 2013). This partnership has flourished to the extent that India has agreed to partner with Vietnam in areas of submarine and fighter aircraft training and transfer of medium-sized warships (*The Hindu* 2013). In 2014, Indian Prime Minister Narendra Modi stated that 'our defence cooperation with Vietnam is among our most important ones. India remains committed to the modernisation of Vietnam's defence and security forces that will include the expansion of our training programme, joint exercises and cooperation in defence equipment' (*The Indian Express* 2014). During an official visit to Vietnam from 2-3 September 2016, Prime Minister Modi termed Vietnam a strong pillar of India's Act East Policy and reiterated India's interest in promoting defence industry cooperation between the two sides and committed to provide a new Line of Credit for Vietnam in this area (MEA 2016b). Both India and

Vietnam signed the contract for Offshore High-speed Patrol Boats between Larsen & Toubro and Vietnam Border Guards utilising the US$100 million Line of Credit for defence procurement extended by India to Vietnam (MEA 2016b).

In order to further fortify the relationship in the defence sector, India has offered to provide the Brahmos medium-range anti-ship cruise missile to Vietnam. Reportedly, the negotiations with Vietnam to supply the BrahMos missiles were at an advanced stage during Indian Defence Minister Manohar Parrikar's visit to Hanoi between 5 and 6 June 2016 (*IHS Jane's Defence Weekly* 2016). It is argued that the conclusion of a BrahMos deal with Vietnam would signify a major success for India's defence industry and for Vietnam; the anti-ship variant would represent a potent deterrent tool (Panda 2016).

The increasing maritime engagement between India and Vietnam has taken a great leap and has contributed in strengthening their ties significantly in the recent years. Indian warships have made forays in the Vietnamese seas for goodwill visits and in 2011, after reports of a radio incident between a Chinese ship and the Indian warship *INS Airavat* in the South China Sea, Vietnam came forward and backed continued visits of Indian ships to its waters (*The Times of India* 2011). In addition, in 2016, in a demonstration of India's Act East Policy and the Indian Navy's increasing footprint and operational reach, two Indian warships as part of the deployment of the Indian Navy's Eastern Fleet to the South China Sea and Western Pacific, arrived at Cam Ranh Bay in Vietnam for a four-day port visit (Indian Navy 2016). Such naval exchanges not only strengthen maritime engagements between the two navies but also 'reinforce the strong bonds of friendship between India and Vietnam and contribute to security and stability in this vital part of the world' (Press Information Bureau 2016).

It is noteworthy that a similar demonstration of naval operational reach had taken place in 2015 as well. According to the Indian Ministry of Defence, the purpose of the visits of Indian warships to Vietnam is to strengthen military-diplomatic ties and even more importantly, to enhance interoperability between the Indian Navy and Vietnam's People's Navy, as well as maritime cooperation (Gady 2016). India has been active in shifting its maritime strength in accordance with China's assertiveness in the Indian Ocean. In addition to the setting up of a special tri-service command in the Andaman and Nicobar group of islands close to the Malacca Strait since 2001, India has also been busy overhauling its Eastern Naval Command and building fresh infrastructure, assets and organisation (Singh 2011).

China-Vietnam Interaction

China and Vietnam relations are presently broadly determined by their past experiences and the South China Sea maritime disputes. Bilateral relations between China and Vietnam have mostly witnessed instability so far. Though both the countries share socialist linkages, the mismatch in the power equation between them and unresolved issues have been impediments to facilitating a stable relationship (Jacob 2015). Both China and Vietnam have been focusing on enhancing trade and promoting a rapid development of the bilateral economic and trade relationship (*Xinhua* 2005). China is Vietnam's largest trading partner. There has been an attempt to set up an 'economic corridor' from China's Yunnan province to Vietnam's northern regions, and similar economic zones linking China's Guangxi province with Vietnam's Lang Son and Quang Ninh provinces and the cities of Hanoi and Haiphong (*Asia Times Online* 2005). As per one official website of Vietnam, 'the economic corridor linking four Vietnamese Northern provinces and Chinese southwestern province of Yunnan has helped to reinforce mutual understanding, trust and cooperation among respective localities' (Ministry of Planning and Investment, Vietnam 2009).

In April 2015, General Secretary of the Communist Party of Vietnam Nguyen Phu Trong visited China and signed MoUs with Chinese counterparts to form two working groups—one for infrastructure cooperation and one for finance and currency cooperation (*Xinhua* 2015). Similarly, in November 2015, Chinese President Xi Jinping during his state visit to Vietnam advocated for the two sides to align their development strategies and work together to push forward both China's 'Belt and Road Initiative' and Vietnam's 'Two Corridors and One Economic Circle' plan (*Xinhua* 2015). China's ambitious 'Belt and Road Initiative' (also known as the 'one belt, one road' (OBOR)) creates opportunities for China as well as regional countries such as Vietnam to work towards the economic integration of the region. However, everything including flourishing trade relationships hinge upon the stability of the region. According to many Chinese scholars, stability in Sino-Vietnamese relations is important for the successful implementation of China's OBOR initiative (Jacob 2015).

There has been a constant effort from both China and Vietnam to normalise the relationship by establishing exchanges of visits between the leaders and friendly exchanges and mutually beneficial cooperation in various fields. According to one Chinese official, bilateral trade between China and Vietnam was expected to reach US$100 billion in 2016 (*China Daily* 2016). However, the economic relationship is basically in China's favour with Vietnamese exports totalling only US$17 billion out of a total trade of US$66 billion (cited in Suri 2016). Besides, the maritime dispute in the South China Sea has further hampered their efforts to work towards strengthening their economic, political and strategic ties. According to the International Monetary Fund (IMF) representative in Vietnam, 'domestic demand remains weak and the economy is running on a single engine of external demand and exports' (cited in Hayton 2015: 4). In 2014, Vietnam's two major export markets were the United States and European Union (Hayton 2015: 4). The statistics in Figure 1 below depict the current trend in Vietnam's trade pattern with major countries. The US is the number one exporting market for Vietnam with the maximum turnover while China with US$9.1 billion occupies the second place. Germany, Netherlands and the United Kingdom are the three EU countries among the top ten main exporting markets for Vietnam.

Figure 1: Top 10 Export Markets of Vietnam in the First Half of 2016

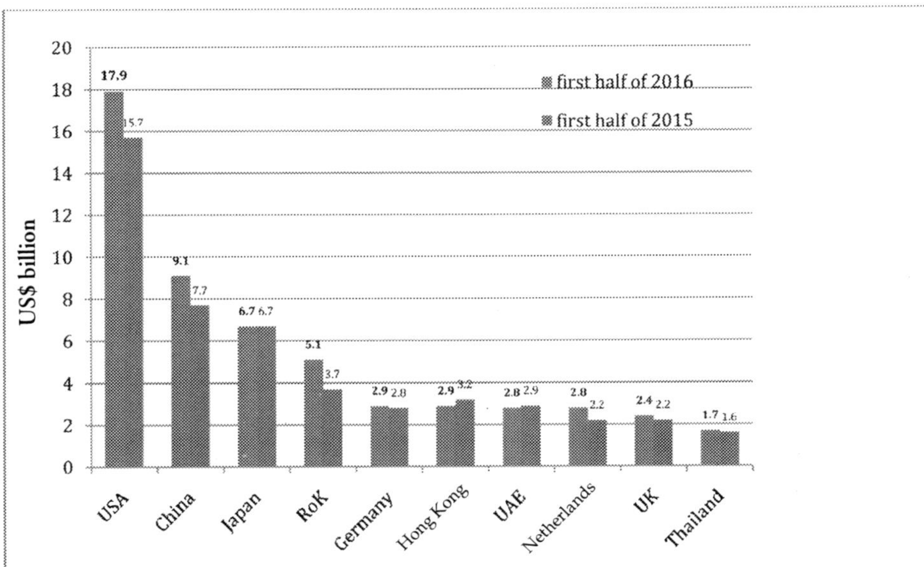

Source: Vietnam Customs 2016.

Figure 2 shows that among the top ten partners exporting goods to Vietnam, China remains the biggest importing market for Vietnam. There has been an increasing Vietnamese trade deficit with China in each of the last ten years (*Radio Free Asia* 2015). According to one source, over the period 2001-14, Vietnam's trade deficit with China rose from US$200 million to at least US$28 billion (cited in Hayton 2015: 11).

Figure 2: Top 10 Import Markets of Vietnam in the First Half of 2016

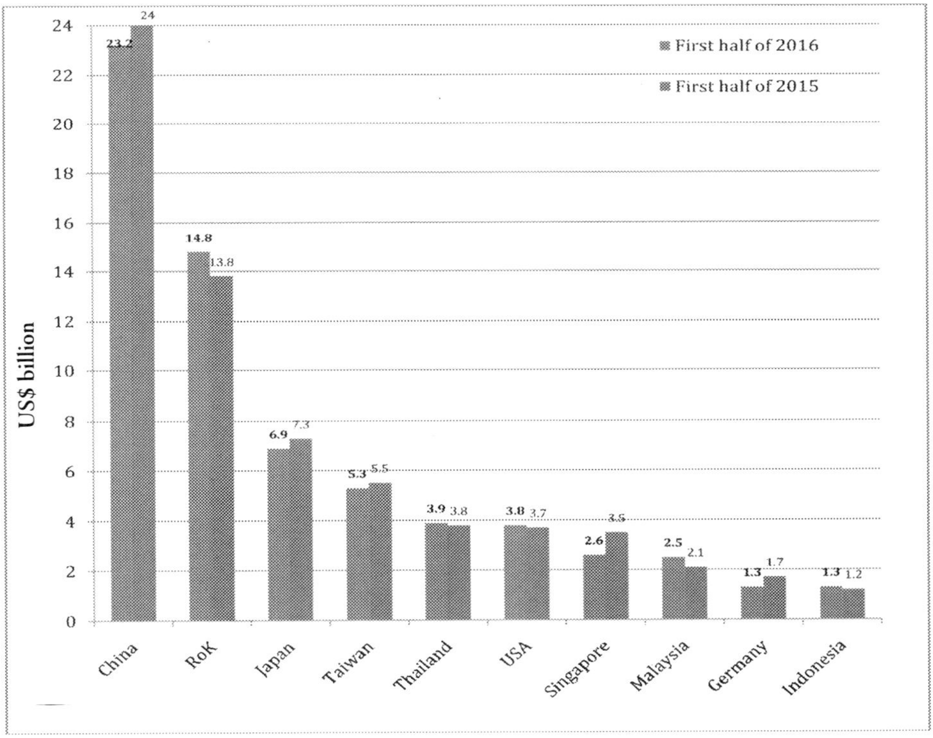

Source: Vietnam Customs 2016

Vietnam's differences with China on the issue of maritime disputes, and its associated fish stocks, hydrocarbon reserves and sea lanes, are the main concerns in the South China Sea (Hayton 2015: 5-6). Over the last few years, Vietnam has increased its defence spending by 60 per cent between 2010 and 2014 and has become one of the largest spenders on defence equipment in the last decade in Southeast Asia (cited in Hayton 2015: 5-6). It is noteworthy that after the collapse of the Soviet Union, Vietnam has publicly advocated a policy of 'three noes': no to foreign bases on its territory, to military alliances and to using a third country to oppose another country (Hayton 2015: 4). To a large extent, this policy has been apparent in Vietnam's relationships with different countries so far. Vietnam has focused on uninterrupted economic growth and looked outward to strengthen its overall position in a region marred by territorial disputes and the domination of a belligerent China.

Assessing the Vietnam Factor

The new maritime dimension of Indian engagement in the Southeast Asian region is being seen as the manifestation of India's recently announced 'Act East Policy'. According to one scholar, due to India's long-standing ties with East and Southeast Asian countries, in 'Acting East', the difference is of degree only, with an increasing maritime component (Cheney-Peters 2015). In order to maximise maritime gain, both India and China have underlined the significance of Vietnam. As far as Vietnam is concerned, it maintains its relationship with India and China differently. On the one hand, owing to a stable past relationship, Vietnam has considered India as a reliable friend and an emerging power in Southeast Asia that can play an important role to complement Vietnam's interests in the region. The relationship with China meanwhile, has been perceived differently by Vietnam at different phases of the past. The previous ups and downs in relations along with the current maritime disputes in the South China Sea have made the Sino-Vietnamese equations complicated.

China opposes any third party involvement in resolving its maritime dispute with Vietnam. China no doubt believes negotiating bilaterally would be more conducive to the implementation of its ambitious new Silk Road initiatives. Therefore, from China's perspective, the maritime divergence with India should not be mixed up with regional actors such as Vietnam. That is the principal reason why China wants India to stay away from the disputed waters of the South China Sea. Obviously, Vietnam remains the most beneficial party as it can maintain its friendly relationship with India and at the same time, check Chinese aggression in the region. As far as India is concerned, its ties with Vietnam are based on long friendly relations that have grown over the years. It has got a new spark in the strategic sphere under the umbrella of India's Act East Policy. These maritime developments would not have been possible without a resurgent maritime consciousness in Indian maritime thinking that is reflected in the repeated enunciation of maritime doctrines and strategy documents (Integrated Headquarters Ministry of Defence (Navy) 2004, 2007, 2009, 2015).

The rapidly growing maritime component in India's engagement with Southeast Asia shows a new awakening in the maritime domain. This ranges from training, repairs and maintenance support, exchanges between thinktanks, study tours and ship visits. Predominantly, the last few years have witnessed increasing forays by the Indian naval ships to Vietnam. In order to demonstrate India's maritime outreach, 'four Indian naval ships which included the indigenously built stealth frigate *INS Satpura* and fleet tanker *INS Shakti* with a complement of around 1,200 officers and sailors visited Da Nang from 6-10 June 2013'. Later in August 2015, a Coast Guard ship *Sarang* visited Ho Chi Minh City (MEA 2016c). In February 2016, for the first time, the Vietnamese HQ-011 frigate named *Dinh Tien Hoang* participated in the International Fleet Review at Vishakhapatnam (*Vietnam Breaking News.com* 2016). Between 30 May and 2 June 2016, the Indian Naval Ships *Satpura* and *Kirch* visited the Cam Ranh Bay as part of the deployment of the Eastern Fleet to the South China Sea and Western Pacific (Embassy of India, Hanoi 2016). Thus, the regular visits of both the navies to each other's ports and cooperation in various domains have taken the engagement between India and Vietnam to a higher level.

India's strengthening security links with Vietnam continue to have a strong maritime flavour as India has provided supplies to the Vietnamese navy and Vietnam has provided berthing facilities for India at the Cam Ranh Bay (Scott 2016). This has led to a growing maritime consciousness which emphasises securing energy routes, the use of naval diplomacy and engagements with East and Southeast Asian states, participating in regional institutions, counter-terrorism, anti-piracy and disaster relief, etc. There has also been a trend of seeing India's engagements in the South China Sea with regional players like Vietnam through the prism of tensions prevailing in the disputed waters (Baruah 2014; Brewster 2009). Sino-Indian maritime competition does have a bearing on India's overall engagements with the region. However, it is also evident that India has had a good relationship with Vietnam for long, along with its maritime extension in the Western Pacific since the advent of the Look East policy. It is also noteworthy that the realisation of Indian maritime ambitions in the South China Sea remains a work in progress for the Indian Navy lacks the capacity to defend its interests in the area. The Indian Maritime Strategy Document 2007 and its revised version in 2015, in fact, underline this region as India's secondary area of interests (Integrated Headquarters Ministry of Defence (Navy) 2007, 2015). It also implies that 'as India's interactions across the world and the effects of globalisation will increase, the areas of interest would correspondingly evolve' (Integrated Headquarters Ministry of Defence (Navy) 2015).

Conclusion

This chapter has argued that the growing India-Vietnam equation in the strategic-military realm can be seen as the extension of India's own growing maritime power and its consistent, proactive maritime engagements towards Southeast Asia and not as merely a reaction to China's increasing maritime influence. Given the complex situation in the South China Sea, its ties with Vietnam are crucial for India in the South China Sea.

India is looking at its east in strategic terms where it considers Vietnam as one of its most important partners. The maritime component of India's Act East policy complements India's maritime aspirations in the South China Sea. For Vietnam, too, in order to check China's dominance, India is seen as one of the most reliable strategic allies even as it maintains its engagements with other powers such as the US, Russia, Australia, Japan and South Korea. India's emerging maritime posture and naval transformations on the one hand and China's aggression in the South China Sea on the other, coincide with India's increased cooperation with Vietnam in particular, and its overall relationship with Southeast Asia in general. Meanwhile, this in turn has further complicated the Sino-Indian maritime tussle. Thus, the significance of Vietnam for both India and China also increases with the increasing tensions in the relations between India and China in the maritime realm.

REFERENCES

Asia Times Online. 2005. 'China, Vietnam Find Love', 21 July, http://www.atimes.com/atimes/Southeast_Asia/GG21Ae01.html (accessed on 1 June 2016).

Baruah, Darshana M. 2014. 'South China Sea: Time for India to Mark its Presence', *RSIS Commentary*, No. 225, 17 November, https://www.rsis.edu.sg/wp-content/uploads/2014/11/CO14225.pdf (accessed on 1 September 2016).

Brewster, David. 2009. 'India's Strategic Partnership with Vietnam: The Search for a Diamond on the South China Sea?' *Asian Security*, Vol. 5, No. 1, https://openresearch-repository.anu.edu.au/bitstream/1885/13058/1/Brewster,%20D.%20India's%20Strategic%20Partnership%20with%20Vietnam%202009.pdf (accessed on 10 May 2016).

Brewster, David. 2012. *India as an Asia Pacific Power*. London and New York: Routledge.

Cheney-Peters, Scott. 2015. 'India's Maritime Acts in the East', Asia Maritime Transparency Initiative, http://amti.csis.org/indias-maritime-acts-in-the-east/ (accessed on 10 May 2016).

China Daily. 2016. 'China, Vietnam to fulfill trade target of $100b in 2016', 9 March, http://

www.chinadaily.com.cn/business/2016-03/09/content_23791827.htm (accessed on 25 June 2016).

Embassy of India, Hanoi. 2016. 'India-Vietnam Relations', June, http://indembassy.com.vn/India_viet_nam_relations.php?id=8 (accessed on 13 May 2016).

Gady, Franz-Stefan. 2016. 'South China Sea Deployment: Indian Stealth Warships Visit Vietnam', *The Diplomat*, http://thediplomat.com/2016/06/south-china-sea-deployment-indian-stealth-warships-visit-vietnam/ (accessed on 25 June 2016).

Hayton, Bill. 2015. 'Vietnam and The United States: An Emerging Security Partnership' United States Studies Centre, http://ussc.edu.au/ussc/assets/media/docs/publications/Emerging-Asia-Reports/MacArthur-Vietnam-ONLINE.pdf (accessed on 25 June 2016).

Holmes, J.R. and T. Yoshihara. 2008. 'China's Naval Ambitions in the Indian Ocean', *The Journal of Strategic Studies*, Vol. 31, No. 3, 367–394.

Holmes, J. R. et al. 2009. *Indian Naval Strategy in the Twenty-First Century*. London: Routledge.

IHS Jane's Defence Weekly. 2016. 'India plans expanded export of BrahMos cruise missiles', 14 June, http://www.janes.com/article/61334/india-plans-expanded-export-of-brahmos-cruise-missiles (accessed on 30 August 2016)

Indian Navy. 2016. 'Visit of Indian Warships to Cam Ranh Bay, Vietnam', *Press Release*, http://www.indiannavy.nic.in/content/visit-indian-warships-cam-ranh-bay-vietnam (accessed on 11 June 2016).

Integrated Headquarters, Ministry of Defence (Navy). 2004. *Indian Maritime Doctrine,* INBR 8.

Integrated Headquarters, Ministry of Defence (Navy). 2007 *Freedom to Use the Seas: India's Maritime Military Strategy*, https://www.scribd.com/doc/31917366/India-s-Maritime-Military-Strategy#scribd (accessed on 13 May 2016).

Integrated Headquarters, Ministry of Defence (Navy). 2009. *Indian Maritime Doctrine 2009*, INBR 8.

Integrated Headquarters, Ministry of Defence (Navy). 2015. *Ensuring Secure Seas: Indian Maritime Security Strategy,* http://indiannavy.nic.in/sites/default/files/Indian_Maritime_Security_Strategy_Document_25Jan16.pdf (accessed on 13 May 2016).

Jacob, Jabin T. 2015. 'China and Vietnam: Neither Thick Friends nor Constant Antagonists', *ICS Analysis*, No. 30, May, http://www.icsin.org/uploads/2015/05/15/e0027ca3a5b3be0710cd5a55a34a891c.pdf (accessed on 10 February 2016).

Jha, Pankaj Kumar. 2011. 'India's Defence Diplomacy in Southeast Asia', *Journal of Defence Studies*, Vol. 5, No. 1, 47-63.

Ministry of External Affairs, Government of India. 2016a. Gen. (Dr) V.K. Singh (retd) (MEA-VKS), Question No. 2014 'India's Interest in South China Sea Region', 4 August, http://www.mea.gov.in/rajya-sabha.htm?dtl/27229/QUESTION+NO2014+INDIAS+INTEREST+IN+SOUTH+CHINA+SEA+REGION (accessed on 3 September 2016).

Ministry of External Affairs, Government of India. 2016b. 'Banquet Speech by Prime Minister during his visit to Vietnam', 3 September, http://www.mea.gov.in/Speeches-Statements.htm?dtl/27364/Banquet+Speech+by+Prime+Minister+during+his+visit+to+Vietnam+September+03+2016 (accessed on 3 September 2016).

Ministry of External Affairs, Government of India. 2016c. 'India-Vietnam Relations', January, https://www.mea.gov.in/Portal/ForeignRelation/Vietnam_13_01_2016.pdf (accessed on 13 May 2016).

Ministry of Planning and Investment of the Socialist Republic of Vietnam. 2009. 'Vietnam, China foster the formation of economic corridor', 21 November, http://www.mpi.gov.vn/en/Pages/tinbai.aspx?idTin=23214&idcm=133 (accessed on 13 August 2016).

Mohan, C. Raja. 2013. *Samundra Manthan: Sino-Indian Rivalry in the Indo-Pacific*. New Delhi: Oxford University.

Muni, S.D. 2011. 'The Turbulent South-China Sea Waters: India, Vietnam and China', *ISAS Insights*, No 140, http://www.isas.nus.edu.sg/ISAS%20Reports/ISAS%20Insights%20140%20-%20Email%20-%20The%20Turbulent%20South-China%20Sea%20Waters-%20India%20Vietnam%20and%20China.pdf (accessed on 10 May 2016).

Panda, Ankit. 2016. 'Vietnam May Purchase India's Deadly Supersonic BrahMos Cruise Missile', *The Diplomat*, 2 June, http://thediplomat.com/2016/06/vietnam-may-purchase-indias-deadly-supersonic-brahmos-cruise-missile/ (accessed on 3 September 2016).

Panda, Rajaram. 2013. 'India & Vietnam: Defence Cooperation, Economic Ties and a Strategic Partnership', *IPCS Special Commentary*, http://www.ipcs.org/article/india/ipcs-special-commentary-india-vietnam-defence-cooperation-economic-ties-and-4080.html (accessed on 10 May 2016).

Pant, Harsh V. 2010. *The China Syndrome: Grappling With An Uneasy Relationship*. New Delhi: HarperCollins Publishers.

Press Information Bureau. 2016. 'Visit of Indian Warships to Cam Ranh Bay, Vietnam, 30 May-03 June 2016', Government of India Ministry of Defence, 30 May, http://pib.nic.in/newsite/PrintRelease.aspx?relid=145777 (accessed on 25 June 2016).

Radio Free Asia. 2015. 'Vietnam Must Better Manage Trade Imbalance with China: Economist', 1 October, http://www.rfa.org/english/ (accessed on 1 September 2016).

Scott, David. 2016. 'India-China Competition Across the Indo-Pacific', *Asia Pacific*, http://www.realcleardefense.com/articles/2016/04/27/india-china_competition_across_the_indo-pacific_109303.html (accessed on 25 June 2016).

Sokinda, Sanjive. 2015. 'India's Strategy for Countering China's Increased Influence in the Indian Ocean', Indo-Pacific Strategic Papers, The Centre for Defence and Strategic Studies, http://www.defence.gov.au/ADC/Publications/IndoPac/Sokinda_IPS_Paper.pdf (accessed on 3 September 2016).

Suri, Gopal. 2016. 'Vietnam and the South China Sea', Vivekananda International Foundation, http://www.vifindia.org/article/2016/june/13/vietnam-and-the-south-china-sea (accessed on 10 June 2016).

The Economic Times. 2015. 'India's naval diplomacy aims to contain China: Report', 7 October, http://economictimes.indiatimes.com/news/defence/indias-naval-diplomacy-aims-to-contain-china-report/articleshow/49260286.cms (accessed on 25 June 2016).

The Hindu. 2013. 'India, Vietnam to Strengthen Defence Ties', 9 October http://www.thehindu.com/news/national/india-vietnam-to-strengthen-defence-ties/article5214921.ece (accessed on 25 May 2016).

The Indian Express. 2014. 'Vietnam to buy naval vessels from India to patrol disputed South China Sea', 29 October, http://indianexpress.com/article/india/india-others/vietnam-to-buy-naval-vessels-from-india-to-patrol-disputed-waters/ (accessed on 25 May 2016).

The Times of India. 2011. 'Vietnam counters Chinese aggression', 2 September, http://www.timesnow.tv/Vietnam-counters-Chinese-aggression/articleshow/4382852.cms (accessed on 4 June 2016).

The Times of India. 2017. 'Strategic Move': Vietnam Renews India Oil Deal in Tense South China Sea', 6 July, http://timesofindia.indiatimes.com/business/india-business/strategic-move-vietnam-renews-india-oil-deal-in-tense-south-china-sea/articleshow/59478405.cms (accessed on 6 August 2017).

Vietnam Breaking News.com. 2016. 'Vietnam's frigate to attend International Fleet Review 2016 for first time', 21 January, https://m.vietnambreakingnews.com/2016/01/vietnams-frigate-to-attend-international-fleet-review-2016-for-first-time/ (accessed on 1 September 2016).

Vietnam Customs. 2016. 'Preliminary assessment of Vietnam international merchandise trade performance in June and the first half of 2016', 1 September, http://www.customs.gov.vn/Lists/EnglishStatistics/ViewDetails.aspx?ID=605&Category=Scheduled%20analysis&Group=Trade%20news%20%26%20Analysis&language=en-US (accessed on 12 September 2016).

Xinhua. 2005. 'China-Vietnam Bilateral Relations', 28 October, http://english.sina.com/1/2005/1028/51407.html (accessed on 25 May 2016).

Xinhua. 2015. 'China, Vietnam to link development initiatives', 6 November, http://news.xinhuanet.com/english/2015-11/06/c_134789540.htm (accessed on 13 May 2016).

6

The US Rebalancing Strategy: Impact on Relations between Vietnam and China

Nguyen Thi Phuong Hoa

After the global financial crisis, China's rapid rise and transition from economic power to military power along with its increasing political influence have changed the balance of power in the Asia-Pacific, leading to a contentious restructuring of the regional order formed and led by the United States for decades since the end of the Cold War. The situation forced the Obama administration to make strategic adjustments with different names—first the 'return to Asia', then the 'pivot to Asia' and finally, the 'Asian rebalance'. From 2011 to 2016, with both statements and actions, the US rebalancing strategy made a direct impact on its relationship with countries in the region, thereby having indirect effects on their bilateral relations, including that of Vietnam and China. The future of this rebalancing strategy is becoming difficult to predict with the newly-elected American President Donald Trump going in for an 'America first' policy tending towards isolationism. What then will be the impact of the US rebalancing strategy on the Vietnam-China relationship in the coming years?

Review of the US Rebalancing Strategy

Regarding the relationship between the US and the Asia-Pacific region, the former US President Barack Obama and many US officials insisted, first that whether in terms of economics or security, the Asia-Pacific region was becoming more important for the US and that the destiny of the US and the Asia-Pacific region had become more closely linked than ever before, that 'America has been and will always be a Pacific nation' (The White House 2011; *Financial Times* 2009).

Second, the US benefited from closely linking itself with Asia's economy, security and politics. The US interest in the region is to protect the benefits of its markets and citizens, to ensure freedom and security of the sea and to maintain a balance of regional power, to prevent the dissemination of weapons of mass destruction, and to promote democracy and human rights. What happens in the area could directly affect its people's lives, from trade relations to employment to traditional and non-traditional security issues such as terrorism. Thirdly, there are more and more challenges in the Asia-Pacific region, but the rise of China ultimately affects the US interests in Asia and concerns the US most.

Since February 1995, reports from the Department of Defense have confirmed: 'History, geography and demography make the US an integral part of the region', 'The US has been the pre-eminent Pacific power since World War II, but our interests in the region date back more than two centuries' and the US will remain a Pacific power in the twenty-first century. The US interests in Asia in the past two centuries of peace and security, commercial access to the region, freedom of navigation, and the prevention of the rise of any hegemonic power or coalition, thus 'require sustained engagement by the US in this important region' (US Department of Defense 1995). However, for various reasons, previous governments have mainly focused on Europe, and paid less attention to the area. Under George W. Bush, US policies towards Asia focused on maintaining stability with China, strengthening the US-Japan alliance, developing relations with India but 'ignoring' Southeast Asia (Bader 2015: 30). The general perception in Asia was that the US has left the region unattended to cope with terrorism and the economic downturn. Therefore, in addition to the traditional focus on Europe, the Obama administration rebuilt the presence and relationship with previously-neglected regions, conveying the message that it was not a US return to the Asia-Pacific region, since the US has always been a member country, and that the area was associated with American economic, security, and political interests, and thus always a focus in its global strategy.

At the ASEAN Regional Forum (ARF), in July 2009, Secretary of State Hilary Clinton said that the US was back in Southeast Asia and in 2010, confirmed that safety, security and freedom of navigation in the East Sea were US national interests. On January 12, 2010, in a speech in Honolulu, she pointed out the basic content of the US strategy in the Asia-Pacific region. The main strategic goals were to consolidate and strengthen the leadership role within the region and to prevent and contain rivals when the defence budgets were cut down. In the article 'America's Pacific Century' published in the *Foreign Policy* journal on 11 October 2011, for the first time, Clinton introduced the concept of 'axis rotation policy' to the Asia-Pacific region. However, the US authorities often used the term 'rebalancing strategy' instead, since the phrase 'return to Asia' could easily lead to inferences and misunderstandings that would be unfavourable to the US that it had left and now must return to Asia, while the term 'rebalancing' could imply that the US still treasured Asia and only needed to reallocate and redeploy an adequate balance of power in the region.

The main contents of the US' Asia-Pacific strategy include: (1) To strengthen the alliance system and promote US partnership in the Asia-Pacific region; (2) To actively participate in the regional security and economic cooperation mechanism; (3) To emphasise the significance of 'fruitful cooperation'; (4) To enhance the flexibility and creativity of the US in taking part in a multilateral cooperation mechanism; (5) To ensure the mechanisms created by the Asia-Pacific region would include relevant beneficiaries, especially the US.

To implement the rebalancing strategy, the Obama administration implemented the following measures.

First, from 'a party in the balance of forces' it was to become 'the engaged party to balance the forces'; there would be strengthening relationships with existing allies, especially with South Korea, Japan and Australia, and building security and political relations with India, Indonesia and Vietnam. Obama did not completely change Bush's way in using the military to balance China. The US military continued to be stationed in the Asia-Pacific region and focused on enhancing the quality of US troops in Japan, maintaining a missile defence system in the region and strengthening alliances with Japan and Korea. At the same time, the US was trying to build a regional multilateral force to balance China.

Second, the US applied diplomatic approaches by comprehensively intervening in and promoting bilateral and multilateral cooperation mechanisms in the region to divide, separate, and control the related parties.

Finally, the US spread the values of democracy and human rights as public opinion tools to carry out this strategy.

In summary, the key idea in the US rebalancing strategy to the Asia-Pacific region was to intervene. The structural contents of this strategy can be described as: intervention + balance of power + military deterrence, of which 'intervention' accounted for five points, 'balance of power' accounts for three points, and 'military deterrence' accounts for two points. The context of this strategy is not to narrow but to expand, and this was underlined by specific strategic moves as follows: at the East Asia Summit (EAS) in 2011, Obama announced that the US would not only maintain but also strengthen its military presence in the region. Apart from enhancing military ties with the Philippines, in late 2011, the US also announced plans to rotate 2,500 US Marines in Darwin, Australia and deployed four littoral combat ships in Singapore. In June 2012, Secretary of Defense Leon Panetta said that the US would mobilise 60 per cent of its naval forces to the Pacific by 2020.

In 2014, the US Senate Committee on Foreign Relations assessed the rebalancing strategy after three years of implementation; from a rebalance of military resources, intervention in diplomatic, economic and trade, and investment, intervention in regional institutions, strengthening alliances and developing new partnerships, civil society and human rights. In military terms, the US has performed a rebalancing of military resources: plans to transfer forces and equipment to the region have been and will be deployed, for example moving 2,500 US marines to Darwin (Australia); one additional battalion of ground forces to Korea; two missile defence destroyers to Japan; four littoral combat ships (LCS) to Singapore; rotating forces in the Philippines; strengthening defence cooperation with Vietnam, Malaysia and some other countries; intensifying exercises with allies and paying military visits to countries in the region. As regards diplomatic intervention, the US civilian agencies stepped up their presence in the region in the areas of foreign affairs, finance, trade, and energy, but still have not met the expectations yet. The amount of high-level visits by US officials to the region could not prove the shift of focus as well. The number of visits of President Obama, cabinet officials, delegations from Departments of Trade, Finance, Agriculture, and Energy to the region were more or less the same in comparison with previous governments (Committee on Foreign Relations United States Senate 2014: 10).

Despite achieving significant milestones in strategic adjustment towards the Asia-Pacific region and China, the Obama administration faced tremendous challenges in order to continue applying this strategy in the most effective way. This was because of issues such as whether the US could stand up after the global financial crisis and regain its economic strength in the future, the future of the TPP, the US military facing overall budget cuts over the next 10 years, the growth of China's military and its actions in the East Sea and East China Sea. These issues have all challenged the US' stature in Asia.

Small countries will look to the US to deal with other major countries, such as China, Japan and India. The way the US has dealt with China-related issues such as the Impeccable incident or China's provocative declarations and actions in the East Sea signal the US security commitment to the region. At the same time, as China tends to exploit the tension within the US alliance structure, doubts could be cast on the US ability to maintain and implement the rebalancing strategy and its commitment to its allies in the region the coming years.

Impact of the US Rebalancing Strategy on the Vietnam-US Relations

Although Vietnam-US ties had achieved some progress before the rebalancing strategy was applied by the US, they were not as smooth due to the issues of ideology, human rights, democracy and religious freedom. When Southeast Asia region was 'ignored', the position and priority for Vietnam in the US policy were weak. However, since 2009, when implementing the US rebalancing strategy, the Obama administration paid more attention to the Southeast Asia region. Within one year from late 2011 to late 2012, Clinton highlighted the change from her predecessor Condoleezza Rice by visiting all 10 ASEAN member countries and East Timor and attending the ASEAN Regional Forum four times in a row. President Obama attended the East Asia Summit (the first time for the US) and co-chaired a conference of the US-ASEAN leaders. This context, coupled with the resurgence of China, made the US attach greater importance to Vietnam's position. Vietnam is considered to be an important new partner of the US in Asia.

With the recent progress in bilateral relations, US Secretary of State John Kerry talking about Vietnam-US ties, stated that no other two countries 'have put further efforts, done more and better in bilateral approach to change history and the future' like the US and Vietnam (*Vietnam News Agency* 2015). President Truong Tan Sang's visit to the US and the signing of a comprehensive partnership agreement on 25 July 2013 created a turning point in the Vietnam-US relations. The agreement established a new framework, helping Vietnam-US ties to develop both in width and in depth, both bilaterally and multilaterally, especially in the focus areas of the Vietnam-US dialogue: politics and military. By 2015, the Vietnam-US relationship had achieved a real breakthrough and switched to 'the shaping period'. Secretary General Nguyen Phu Trong's visit to the US in 2015 also proved that both sides had overcome ideological barriers to build a relationship by sharing concerns and common interests in a spirit of mutual institutional respect, and President Obama's visit to Vietnam in 2016 also proved that the two sides had established trust to complete the normalisation process of relations.

In the economic realm, the TPP, one of the three 'cornerstones' of the American pivot to Asia as quoted by the US Secretary of Defense Ashton Carter (*Vietnam News Agency* 2015: 2), had overcome many obstacles, and completed the five-year negotiation process on 5 October 2015. If the agreement is ever adopted, Vietnam will have the opportunity to further export-led growth, participating in the supply chain to be formed in the TPP region, have the opportunity to attract foreign investment and diversify export markets in order to avoid excessive dependence on any one market.

In the military domain, President Truong Tan Sang's visit to the US created a new comprehensive partnership framework and contributed to promoting security and defence cooperation—previously considered as sensitive issues. On 1 June 2015, Minister of Defense Phung Quang Thanh and US Secretary of Defense Carter signed the Joint Vision Statement on Defense Relations between Vietnam and the US. After a process that President Obama called 'relatively tough, with difficult dialogues in many years' (*Viet Anh* 2016) during his visit to Vietnam in May 2016, the US declared the complete removal of the weapon embargo on Vietnam, marking the full normalisation of relations with Vietnam.

To deal with China's U-shaped line territorial claims and actions that violated international law in the East Sea, the US has made several statements and actual actions despite its persistent stance not to take sides in this sovereignty dispute. At the ARF in 2010, Clinton announced that the US national interests were tied to security, freedom of navigation and respect for international law in the East Sea, and the US was, therefore, particularly concerned about the disputes including the dispute over the two archipelagos of Hoang Sa and Truong Sa and would support a solution through negotiations rather than military strength. In late August 2015, the Pentagon published its 'Asia-Pacific Maritime Security Strategy', which referred to the possibility that the US would take action if China started to use its military bases on artificial islands to impede trade or freedom of navigation or aviation, endangering the interests of the US and others. In a joint press conference with Chinese president Xi Jinping on 25 September 2015, Obama said that US troops would patrol the sea and in the air wherever international law allowed. Shortly after Xi's visit to the US, Secretary of Defense Carter again stated on 13 October that the US military forces would operate anywhere international law allowed, including the East Sea. Following this, on 27 October 2015, the *USS Lassen* destroyer started to patrol the area of 12 nautical miles around China's illegal artificial island in Truong Sa despite the 'advice' of Chinese Minister of Foreign Affairs Wang Yi to 'think carefully before you act, do not act without thinking, should not look for trouble for no reason' (Wang 2015). This action showed that the US did not recognise the legal claims, and the artificial island had no legal value of sovereignty, and marked the beginning of the US challenge to Beijing's claims on the East Sea.

During the Obama visit to Vietnam, the US and Vietnam both agreed in favour of the regional order, including in the East Sea, where international laws and regulations are upheld, with freedom of navigation and aviation, lawful trade is unimpeded and disputes are resolved in a peaceful manner, in accordance with the provisions of international law, and reiterated that 'the US planes and ships will continue to move, operate anywhere the international law allows. We will support the right of all countries to do the same' (*Viet Anh* 2016). These actions could prompt China to be more cautious in the East Sea, but also be an excuse for China to increase its infringement upon the sovereignty of Vietnam and further complicate the situation, thereby negatively impacting the Vietnam-China relations.

Impact on Vietnam-China Relations

Vietnam is situated in an important location in Southeast Asia, and has previously become the object of competition for influence of the leading power countries during the Cold War. China is extremely concerned with every single move of Vietnam in the Vietnam-US relations since Vietnam lies on the southern border of China, and is similarly under the leadership of the Communist Party to follow socialism. Thus, the US rebalancing strategy has a direct impact on Vietnam and Vietnam-US ties, thereby indirectly affecting the Vietnam-China relations. Chinese scholars have evaluated that the close Vietnam-US relationship 'has increasingly affected the favorable development of China-Vietnam ties' (Li 2012: 22). However, in fact, we think that the US presence in the region as well as the development of the Vietnam-US relations in recent years have had not only negative impacts but also positive effects on the Vietnam-China relationship. We will focus below on influences in key areas including diplomacy and politics, economics and security.

Impact on Diplomatic and Political Relations

The positive effects of the development of Vietnam-US relations have become an important factor in helping Vietnam and China quickly break the 'cold politics' after incidents in the East Sea region. Diplomatic and political relations between Vietnam and China in 2015 were improved by high-level visits and many other activities. These include Secretary General Nguyen Phu Trong's visit to China in April 2015 and Xi's visit to Vietnam in November 2015. In 2015, three out of the four Vietnamese senior leaders (Secretary General, President, National Assembly Chairwoman) paid official visits or attended important celebrations in China, in addition to another three Deputy Prime Ministers' visits to China. In the other direction, it was the first visit by China's highest-ranking officials to Vietnam in nine years. Vice-Premier Zhang Gaoli also visited. These visits showed both sides' efforts to stabilise the situation, bringing Vietnam-China relations back to the normal direction following the severe impact of the East Sea dispute. Secretary General Nguyen Phu Trong's visit was considered as a 'healing visit' (Browne 2015), while Xi's visit to Vietnam was considered a 'reset with Vietnam', part of a 'relationship revitalization among China and Vietnam, Singapore and ASEAN' (Phuong Vu 2015).

This improvement is understood to be related to a series of positive changes in Vietnam-US relations and the US rebalancing strategy. Secretary General Nguyen Phu Trong's visit to China took place before his US visit, and the Chinese President's visit to Vietnam took place after the news that the US President would likely pay a visit to Vietnam in late 2015. Through the visits, China wanted to convey a message: China and Vietnam have much in common, having a close and special relationship. Before Secretary General Nguyen Phu Trong's visit to China, its official news agency *Xinhua* commented that the two countries would not allow anyone to come between them. Despite the disputes between Vietnam and China it would be naive to think about the collapse of deep-rooted relations between the two countries just because of the East Sea disagreements. Le Dang Doanh has said, 'The enthusiasm and the words of friendship and goodwill of China should be considered in the context where they want to … prevent Vietnam from moving towards the US side' (*BBC* 2015). Thus, quickly stabilising Vietnam-China relations is a way to prevent Vietnam leaning towards the US.

However, the US rebalancing strategy may also have negative impacts on Vietnam-China ties as the development of relations between Vietnam and the US can make trust-building more difficult between Vietnam and China. Most Chinese scholars think that the US is a negative factor for Vietnam-China relations, for example,

> 'The US used economics as a springboard, bringing their strategic interests to Vietnam, interfering in the East Sea issue, creating new challenges and complications for China-Vietnam relations. The close relationship between Vietnam and the US has affected the favorable development of China-Vietnam ties' (Liu 2012: 22).

Similarly, another commentator writes that under the influence of the US rebalancing strategy, 'the political trust between China and Vietnam would be tested' (Sun 2012: 36). Some even pointed out that the US factor would make Vietnam rely on the US and that this would allow Hanoi to show a tougher attitude and standpoint in its foreign policy towards China, that the US and Vietnam could combine to contain China as part of the US 'China encirclement policy' (Wang 2011: 44).

Vietnam and China have experienced troubles in trust-building owing to historical burdens, from the 'imbalanced' relationship, and from the existing problems. Although, as two neighbouring countries, there are many similarities, developing trust between Vietnam and China is more difficult than any between other countries, even with those who had invaded Vietnam like the US, France, and Japan. The longstanding relationship between Vietnam and China was by default considered the relationship between a big country or 'celestial empire' and a small country or a 'vassal' with many ups and downs in history, in which Chinese feudal dynasties repeatedly wanted to assimilate and take over Vietnam. Vietnam meanwhile put in every effort to avoid war while at the same time, being ready to cope with aggressive wars to protect its sovereignty and independence.

Moreover, although the two socialist countries are under the leadership of the communist parties and share the same ideology, in modern times, China has always actively started aggressive wars with Vietnam such as the border war in 1979, the Paracel Islands conflicts in 1956 and 1974 and the Spratly Islands incident in 1988. The historical past, together with the imbalanced relationship, can easily create incorrect perceptions on both sides. Usually, the smaller countries are more vulnerable; they will usually look back on the past when certain issues occur in the present and this leads to vigilance and suspicion and the issues are 'politicized'. The East Sea dispute is heating up and creating negative impact on all aspects, especially the people's psychology and emotions in each country while Vietnam-US relations are significantly improved. This in turn decreases the level of trust and increases scepticism between Vietnam and China.

China pays special attention to the US factor, considering it as one of the divisive and hindering factors in the healthy development of relations between Vietnam and China. Chinese leaders have quite frequently implied that the two countries need to maintain appropriate progress, and remove interference. On 19 June 2013, during the talks with President Truong Tan Sang, President Xi Jinping stressed: 'the two sides should firmly have correct directions to develop relations between the two parties, the two countries...do not let China-Vietnam relations deviate from the right direction'. On 28 August 2014, when meeting Le Hong Anh, the Special Envoy of the Vietnamese Communist Party's Secretary General, Xi said, 'The two sides should persistently start from important issues to maintain traditional friendship and Vietnam-China relations, removing interferences...' (*People's Daily Online* 2015b). On another occasion, he also stressed that in the future, despite changes in the international situation, the two sides will have to be patient and consider the strategic and long-term perspective in handling their bilateral relationship, building a common understanding, taking the proper political direction, strengthening strategic communications and enhancing political trust to ensure that the relationship moved forward in the right direction (*People's Daily Online* 2015a).

Chinese mainstream newspapers have directly mentioned the US factor and the Vietnam-US relationship. Shortly after Secretary General Nguyen Phu Trong's visit to China, on 13 April 2015, the *Global Times* accused Vietnam of taking advantage of the US-China relationship to benefit from and to play one party against the party. Vietnam-US military cooperation has always been inferred as being aimed at China. Vietnamese Defense Minister Phung Quang

Thanh clearly defined Vietnam's balancing policy in relations with the US and China: 'Vietnam is not in collusion with a country to go against another country. Vietnam pinpoints China as a comprehensive cooperation partner in the spirit of the '16 golden words'. Vietnam also looks forward to strengthening national defense, friendship, stability, and comprehensive cooperation with the US for mutual benefits of both countries' (The Kha 2015).

At the 4th National Defense Strategic Dialogues in 2013, at a press conference, Deputy Minister of Defense Nguyen Chi Vinh stressed: 'Vietnam will pursue and follow the principles of independence and autonomy, never collude with a country to go against another country' (*Laodong* 2013). During his visit to Vietnam, US President Obama too stated in a joint press conference with his Vietnamese counterpart Tran, 'The decision to lift the weapons embargo to Vietnam does not depend on the China factor or other considerations, but it is based on our wish to complete the connection points in the normalization process of relations with Vietnam' (Viet Anh 2016). However, in fact, the Chinese government still considers the US removal of weapon embargo to Vietnam as an action to contain China noting that closer Vietnam-US military cooperation would reinforce Vietnam's capacity to challenge China in the East Sea and that this was a strategic signal on the part of Washington to strengthen its alliances across the Pacific Ocean and the Indian Ocean to counter China (Hong Thuy 2016).

The Chinese side claims that strategic meetings between the US and Vietnam to deal with China is an important platform to promote the relationship. The US wants to implement its rebalancing strategy in Asia to contain China, and Vietnam also wants to rely on the US to deal with China in the East Sea dispute. Southeast Asia expert, Xu Liping of the Chinese Academy of Social Sciences, says,

> 'No doubt, Vietnam has become one of the US' strategic fulcrums in rebalancing towards Asia. President Obama hopes Vietnam will further contain China on the South China Sea issue... From its strategic perspective, Vietnam hopes for US involvement in the dispute, increasing security forces in the Sea, and especially the US' strong support to Vietnam including weapon sales' (*China National Radio* 2015).

Impact on Economic Relations

In terms of economic relations, Chinese scholars believe the development of Vietnam-US economic relations has affected Vietnam-China economic ties and even has a certain political impact. The biggest influence is to demote the status of China in the external economic relations of Vietnam, creating an impact also on China's politics towards Vietnam as the economic dependence on China decreases (Li 2012: 23).

However, in reality, economic ties between Vietnam and the US have no clear negative effects yet on the economic relations between Vietnam and China; in fact, to some extent, it shows the opposite trend. While Vietnam-US economic ties have no sudden developments and Vietnam is enjoying trade surplus with the US, Vietnam-China economic and trade ties maintain their upward trend and Vietnam still suffers a massive trade deficit with China. It is said that Vietnam's surplus from the US market somehow returns to the Chinese market. According to data from the General Statistics Office of Vietnam (2015), the total Vietnam-China trade turnover in 2015 was US$66.67 billion, an increase by 13.7 per cent over the previous year. Vietnam's imports and exports to China account for about one-third of that with Asia and higher than with the whole of the ASEAN. China continues to be the largest export market for Vietnam with an import value of US$49.53 billion, an increase by 13.3 per cent in comparison with 2014. The trade deficit from China is estimated at US$32.3 billion, an increase of 12.5 per cent in comparison with 2014. In 2016, Vietnam overtook Malaysia to become China's largest trading partner in the ASEAN with a US$28 billion trade deficit with it at the same time.

Total investments from China into Vietnam in 2015 reached US$665.5 million with 169 projects, accounting for 4.3 per cent of total investment in the country, and ranked 9th among 58 countries and territories with newly-approved projects in 2015 (General Statistics Office of Vietnam 2015). Vietnam's negotiations to conclude the TPP has become the push for Chinese businesses to increase investments in Vietnam. The early wave of investment in the field of textile and dyeing started in 2014 and continued to increase in 2015. At present, in the north of Vietnam, China has three major projects in the textiles sector including a US$400 million project in Nam Dinh, a US$300 million project in Quang Ninh, and a US$200 million project in Hai Duong. In Ho Chi Minh city, over 70 per cent of all newly-licensed FDI within the year is in the textile sector, in which the largest project also belongs to China with a total investment of US$300 million (*Vietnamnet* 2015). China's shift of textile and dyeing factories to Vietnam has helped to reduce the imports of textile raw materials, thereby reducing the trade deficit, but this does not change the dependence of Vietnam on Chinese raw materials. The most influential factor in the Vietnam-China economic relationship is the East Sea dispute, not the US factor.

Impact on the East Sea Dispute

On the East Sea issue, the US has repeatedly declared that it has its national interests here and has the responsibility to ensure freedom of navigation in the region. American patrol and exploration activities in the East Sea are all to this purpose. However, the standpoint is not to take sides in the sovereignty dispute, and in fact, the US is not ready to interfere in the dispute over sovereignty issues, including those of allies unless China unilaterally changes the conditions, militarising the entities in the East Sea.

The US rebalancing strategy has become an excuse for China to conduct a series of actions that completely change the balance of power and the context in the East Sea disputes, thereby creating a negative impact on Vietnam-China relations. At the same time when the US announced its rebalancing strategy, China implemented a series of actions in the East Sea. Since 2009, China's marine surveillance ships have continually intruded into Vietnam's continental shelf and exclusive economic zone to destroy equipment and impede normal exploration operations of the Vietnam Petroleum Corporation—the incidents of 26 May and 9 June 2011, for example. The situation became extremely serious when China moved its Haiyang Shiyou 981 oil rig to the exclusive economic zone and continental shelf of Vietnam for exploration in 2014.

China also repeatedly launched international tenders for petroleum blocks in the East Sea, including several lots located in Vietnam's exclusive economic zone, very close to the central and southern coasts of Vietnam. Since late 2013, and especially from mid-2014 to the present, China has carried out a lot of actions to change the present conditions in the Spratly Islands, building 'unsinkable aircraft carriers' and 'the Great Wall' in the sea, thus stepping up dangerous and long-term strategic military activities. The US actions in the East Sea were exploited by China to create the 'impact-response' cycle. The impact of the US actions was not much, but the responses (actually, the consistent intentions) from China, were quick and strong.

China has pointed out the consequences of the US return to Asia and Vietnam's exploitation of the US to contain China on the East Sea issue, including firstly, that the East Sea sovereignty dispute will become more complicated. The US stance has changed from non-intervention to an anti-war position implying a multilateral resolution by the concerned parties in the East Sea dispute. This, in essence, is to multilateralise and complicate the East Sea issue, and China's bilateral approach to resolving the East Sea dispute will face substantive challenges. The US interest in the issue has encouraged countries to have higher expectations for the multilateralisation of the East Sea dispute, and this has forced the Chinese to respond with appropriate policies.

Second, China-US relations will collide with China-ASEAN relations. Third, the US' East Sea policy and its implementation in practice will test the Vietnam-China relationship in the future. Fourth, the political trust between China and Vietnam too, will come under the scanner (Sun 2012: 36). According to Maj. Gen. Luo Yuan, Vice Chairman and Secretary General of the Chinese Strategic Culture Promotion Association, the US involvement in the East Sea dispute has three goals, including support for the 'little guys' so as to help them form a group and fight against China, with the ultimate goal to contain the rise of China (*China Youth Daily* 2016).

However, in fact, it is China's own actions that have caused the tension of the East Sea dispute. Chinese scholars have themselves acknowledged, 'The incident of Haiyang Shiyou 981 oil rig has marked policy changes in the South China Sea' (Bi 2015: 223). China had to respond in the Scarborough incident, but it was China that took the lead in the Haiyang Shiyou 981 drilling rig incident, both starting and concluding it in an unpredictable manner (Bi 2015: 223).

Since 2009, and especially after the Haiyang Shiyou 981 drilling rig incident, Chinese actions have influenced all areas of cooperation in Vietnam-China relations. Sovereignty disputes in the East Sea between Vietnam and China have created negative impacts on all parts of Vietnam-China relations. Bilateral relations are constantly hitting the bottom and appear to be getting worse. The East Sea dispute has not only forced the two countries to be diplomatically opposed, but also explained the lack of high-level visits, with both sides sometimes ceasing to exchange delegations. From 2009 to 2013, the leaders of the two countries maintained their mutual visits, but in comparison with the previous years, this was the period with the minimum number of high-level visits (only three visits in five years). In 2014, senior leaders did not have any official visits, but only meetings on the sidelines in international conferences, and from May to August, both sides did not exchange delegations. The impact of the dispute was not only reflected in political and diplomatic relations but also spread to economy and trade, culture, education and tourism. This was also revealed in the wave of protests and boycotts in each country, seriously affecting the general atmosphere and the people's feelings and attitudes in each country towards the other.

While the US rebalancing strategy is facing many difficulties and is yet to create a firm belief for the countries in the region due to the US' slow economic recovery, a tightened defence budget and change in administration, its impact on the region and Vietnam as well as on the Vietnam-China relations has become obvious. For the relationship between Vietnam and China, there are direct and indirect, positive and negative impacts, partly from the effectiveness of the rebalance itself but mostly from the 'inflation and exaggeration' of the Chinese. Although Vietnamese leaders have frequently affirmed their foreign policies and the position of China in those policies, China still continues to feel sceptical and insecure over the development of Vietnam-US relations, including national defence and security ties, and considers Vietnam's ties with the US as part of efforts to contain China. While the US still continues to implement its 'take-no-sides' policy in sovereignty disputes and only takes actions to protect the freedom of navigation, China sees the US rebalancing strategy towards the East Sea issue as an excuse to carry out a series of actions to implement its sovereignty claims. It thus plays the role of a victim, of a passive and innocent party in the East Sea dispute. It could therefore, be said that the US rebalancing strategy has had a negative indirect impact on the Vietnam-China relationship.

* *This research was funded by the Vietnam National Foundation for Science and Technology Development (NAFOSTED) under grant number V1.2-2013.06.*

REFERENCES

Bader, J. A. (2012). Obama and China's Rise: An Insider's Account of America's Asia Strategy. National Politics Publishing House, 2015, Hanoi.

BBC. 2015. 'Quan he Viet - Trung: Y kien tu Bac Kinh va Ha Noi' [Vietnam-China relations: Ideas from Beijing and Hanoi], 8 April, http://www.bbc.com/vietnamese/vietnam/2015/04/150408_trong_xi_talks (accessed 12 January 2017).

Bi Li (薛力). 2015. '21 shijie haishan sichou zhilu jianshe yu nanhai xin xingshi' (21世纪海上丝绸之路建设与男孩新形势) [21st Century Maritime Silk Road Construction and the Boy's New Situation], Zhang Jie (张洁) (ed.) *'Zhongguo zhoubian anquan xingshi pinggu 2015: 'yidai yilu' yu zhoubian zhanlue'* (中国周边安全形势评估 2015: '一带一路'

与周边战略) [The Assessment of China's Peripheral Security Situation 2015: 'One Belt One Road' and the Peripheral Strategy], Beijing: Social Science Literature Publishing House.

Browne, Andrew. 2015. 'Vietnam's Impossible Bind: How to Stand Up to Beijing', *The Wall Street Journal*, 7 April, https://www.wsj.com/articles/chinas-world-vietnams-impossible-bind-how-to-stand-up-to-beijing-1428397027 (accessed 12 January 2017).

China National Radio (央广网). 2015. 'Yue gongzhong zongshuji shou ci fang meifenxi cheng liang guo you gongtong zhanlue qihe dian' (越共中央总书记首次访美分析称两国有共同战略契合点), [Maiden visit of Vietnamese Communist Party General Secretary to the US: both countries have common strategic agreement, say analysts] http://world.huanqiu.com/hot/2015-07/6938541.html (accessed 12 January 2017).

China Youth Daily (中国青年网). 2016. 'Luo Yuan tan nanhai zhongcai an: baochi zhanlue dingli qianghua zhuquan cunzai' (Luo Yuan on South China Sea arbitration case: maintain strategic force to strengthen the existence of sovereignty) [罗援谈南海仲裁案：保持战略定力强化主权存在] http://www.chinanews.com/mil/2016/07-13/7937440.shtml (accessed 12 January 2017).

Financial Times. 2009. 'Full text: Barack Obama's speech in Tokyo', 14 November, https://www.ft.com/content/9e985a46-d0c2-11de-af9c-00144feabdc0 (accessed 12 January 2017).

General Statistics Office of Vietnam. 2015. 'Tinh hinh kinh te - xa hoi nam 2015' [Socio-economic conditions in 2015], http://www.gso.gov.vn/default.aspx?tabid=621&ItemID=15507 (accessed 12 January 2017).

Hong Thuy. 2016. 'Viet Nam kien Trung Quoc thi quan he se "mot di khong tro lai"?' [If Vietnam starts legal proceedings against China, will the relationship reach a point of 'no-return'?], 16 June, http://giaoduc.net.vn/Quoc-te/Viet-Nam-kien-Trung-Quoc-thi-quan-he-se-mot-di-khong-tro-lai-post168735.gd (accessed 12 January 2017)

Laodong. 2013. 'Viet Nam khong lien minh voi nuoc khac de chong nuoc thu ba' [Vietnam never collude with a country to go against another country], 7 June, http://laodong.com.vn/doi-ngoai/viet-nam-khong-lien-minh-voi-nuoc-khac-de-chong-nuoc-thu-ba-120417.bld (accessed 12 January 2017).

Li Jing (李婧). 2012. 'Zhong yue guanxi zhongde meiguo yinsu' (中越关系中的美国因素) dongnanyazhichaung《东南亚之窗》[The U.S factor in Sino-Vietnam Relations] *Window of Southeast Asia*, Issue 19, No. 2.

People's Daily Online (人民网). 2015a. 'Xi Jinping huijian yuenan zongli Ruan Jinyong' (习近平会见越南总理阮晋勇) [Xi Jinping meets Vietnamese Prime Minister Nguyen Tan Diung], 5 November, http://politics.people.com.cn/n/2015/1105/c1001-27782528.html (accessed 12 January 2017).

People's Daily Online. 2015b. 'Xi Jinping shi juhua tan zhongyue guanxi: linguo ban buzou youha fuhe shuangfang liyi' (习近平十句话谈中越关系：邻国搬不走友好符合双方利益) [Xi Jinping's Ten Statements on Sino-Vietnamese Relations: Neighboring countries do not move away, but must talk friendly for the common interests], 5 November, http://cpc.people.com.cn/xuexi/n/2015/1105/c385474-27778930.html (accessed 12 January 2017).

Phuong Vu. 2015. 'Bao chi quoc te binh luan ve chuyen tham Viet Nam cua ong Tap' [International press' comments on Mr. Xi Jinping's visit to Vietnam], 3 November, http://vnexpress.net/tin-tuc/the-gioi/phan-tich/bao-chi-quoc-te-binh-luan-ve-chuyen-tham-viet-nam-cua-ong-tap-3305697.html (accessed 12 January 2017).

Sun Xiaoling (孙晓玲). 2012. 'Zhong-Yue Nanhai zhengduan zhong de meiguo yinsu' (中越南海争端中的美国因素) [The U.S. Factor in the South China Sea Dispute between China and Vietnam], *Dongnanya yanjiu* (东南亚研究), Issue 3, 32-37.

The White House. 2011. 'Remarks By President Obama to the Australian Parliament', 17 November, https://obamawhitehouse.archives.gov/the-press-office/2011/11/17/remarks-president-obama-australian-parliament (accessed 12 January 2017).

United States Department of Defense. 1995. *US Security Strategy for the East Asia Pacific Region*, Washington, University of California, https://babel.hathitrust.org/cgi/pt?id=uc1.31822021409347;view=1up;seq=7 (accessed 12 January 2017).

Viet Anh. 2016. 'My do bo hoan toan lenh cam van vu khi voi Viet Nam' [The US lifts weapon embargo on Vietnam], 23 May, http://vnexpress.net/tong-thuat/thoi-su/my-do-bo-hoan-toan-lenh-cam-van-vu-khi-doi-voi-viet-nam-3407563.html. (accessed 12 January 2017)

Vietnam News Agency. 2015. 'The US-China economic relations are not life-and-death games', 23 April.

Vietnamnet. 2015, 'Trung Quoc o at dau tu vao Viet Nam: Lanh it, du nhieu' [A huge influx of China's investment to Vietnam: Less goodness and more badness], 11 November, http://vietnamnet.vn/vn/kinh-doanh/trung-quoc-o-at-dau-tu-vao-viet-nam-lanh-it-du-nhieu-272461.html (accessed 12 January)

Wang Xinxin (王鑫欣). 2011. 'Lengzhan hou Meiguo chongfan Yuenan dui Zhong-Mei-Yue sanjiao guanxi de yingxiang' (冷战后美国重返越南对中美越三角关系的影响) [The Return of US to Vietnam after the Cold War: Impact on Sino-US-Vietnam Relations] *Chifeng Xueyuan Xuebao* (*Hanwen Zhexue Shehui Kexueban*), Issue 32, No. 11, November.

Wang Yi (王毅). 2015. 'Fengquan Meifang buyao wushi shengfei' (奉劝美方不要无事生) [(We) Advise the Americans not to be deliberatively provocative], *China News Network* (中国新闻网). 27 October, http://www.chinanews.com/gn/2015/10-27/7590847.shtml (accessed 12 January 2017).

7

Towards a New Geostrategy in the Indo-Pacific: Vietnam in the Quadrilateral Security Dialogue?

Atul Kumar

The Indo-Pacific region is immensely important for global trade and commerce and international stability. If the world's economic gravity is shifting eastwards back to Asia, it is the Indo-Pacific region that is at the forefront of this gravitational attraction (Summer 2015; Tencer 2012). The region consists of Northeast Asian advanced economies, littoral tiger economies and equally important, large emerging economies and markets in southern Asia and Africa. These sub-regions and their connections with resource-producing regions in the Middle East and the Asian hinterland in Central Asia, make the Indo-Pacific region a true economic cauldron.

The Indo-Pacific Conundrum

It is, therefore, not surprising that developments in the Indo-Pacific are affecting the entire international political and economic system in a deeper, system-shaping way. During this transition in the economic centre-of-gravity and the consequent system-shaping process, there is enough space for the emergence of a country, with relatively larger economic and military heft, as the predominant power in the region. One potentially capable country that has strived to achieve this regional predominance is China. It has consistently pushed to expand its economic and military influence over the entire Indo-Pacific region, underwritten by its phenomenal economic growth since 1978. The consistent high economic growth has in turn whetted the Chinese appetite for strengthening its military, the People's Liberation Army (PLA), which has been enjoying a double-digit growth in its budget for more than the last three decades.

Table 1: Chinese Economic Growth vs. Defence Budget Growth 2005-16

Year	*GDP (in US$ trillion) Nominal*	*Growth Rate*	*Defence Budget (in US$ billion)*	*Growth Rate*	*Percentage of GDP*
2005	2.25	11.3	30.6	12.6	2
2006	2.7	12.7	35	15	2
2007	3.5	14.2	44.9	17.8	2
2008	4.5	9.6	58.8	17.6	2
2009	4.9	9.2	70	14.6	2
2010	5.9	10.4	81.3	16	2.1
2011	7.3	9.3	91.5	12.7	2
2012	8.2	7.7	106	11	2
2013	9.2	7.7	114.3	10.7	2.1
2014	10.36	7.4	132	12.2	2.06
2015	11.21	6.8	141.45	10.1	1.26
2016	11.8	6.7	151	7	1.28

Source: World Bank 2012; SIPRI 2015; China National Bureau of Statistics 2000-14; International Monetary Fund 2017; *Xinhua* 2017.

As shown in Table 1, the continued growth in China's economic and military capabilities has shaped the Chinese behaviour towards its neighbours and the major powers active in the region. Since the beginning of the millennium, the PLA has considerably augmented its power projection capabilities, with major accretions taking place in the PLA Navy, the PLA Air Force and the PLA Rocket Force. The PLA has attempted to increase China's influence and dominance in the sea around its mainland, especially in the East China Sea and the South China Sea, with the additional help of Chinese maritime law enforcement agencies, the China Coast Guard and even the maritime militia. Consequently, frequent disputes and disruptions have occurred in these two maritime regions between China and its maritime neighbours, mainly Japan, Vietnam, Philippines, Malaysia and Indonesia (*BBC News Asia* 2014b; Latiff and Blanchard 2016; Mie 2016; Perlez 2012; Murdoch 2016; Ngui and Wee 2015; Suryadinata 2016).

As none of China's maritime neighbours are capable enough to deter China's aggressive actions in the East and South China Seas, they have opted for both external and internal balancing for the purpose. Thus, Japan has changed the scope of Article 9 of its pacifist constitution to conduct military operations when its national interests or the interests of friendly countries are at stake (Ripley, Hanna and Yamamitsu 2015). Vietnam has discarded its apprehensions against the US and become favourable towards receiving military assistance including weapon acquisitions from the US, Russia, India, Japan and other defence suppliers (*BBC News Asia* 2014a; Gokhale 2016; Harris 2016; Minnick 2015). The Philippines has embarked upon the conclusion of a military alliance with the US. It has allowed the US forces to access its five naval bases in exchange for security from the Chinese threat (Katigbak 2016). Malaysia and Indonesia are fortifying their naval borders and increasing their military interactions with other major powers with interests in the Indo-Pacific (Ng 2014; *The Sun Daily* 2014; Vaswani 2014).

A probability of Chinese predominance over the Indo-Pacific creates considerable insecurity for the interests of major powers having stakes in the security and stability of the region. Therefore, the US, Japan, India, Australia and France are increasingly expressing their concerns over Chinese unilateral actions in the region against its smaller neighbours (Lee 2016; Kaye and Siegel 2016; Rahmat 2016; Torode and Kitano 2016). It is here that the idea of Quadrilateral Security Initiative/Dialogue (Quad) has gained and sustained its importance (Ali 2007). Even though the obituary of the Quad was written in 2008 (Chellaney 2008a),[1] the idea has remained beneath the radar, only to resurface in the current increasingly precarious situation in the Indo-Pacific. Here, this chapter argues that the idea needs a slight modification, in which, Vietnam is offered the chance to become a crucial member of the Quad while Australia is given a choice to opt out of the group. As will be explained further, Vietnam would prove to be a worthy Quad member, on account of its geographical proximity to the region, resolute willingness to defend its national interests and in having a respected military capability. On the other hand, Australian ambivalence is not only impeding the growth of the initiative but it essentially undermines the Quad's prospects in the region. The Australian economy is heavily dependent on the Chinese economy and therefore, Australia has a propensity to avoid actions that can improve regional security but which can also go against Chinese interests. Although there is an ongoing discussion in the Australian academic and strategic circles on whether the economic interdependence on China is good or bad for their nation, Australia remains ambivalent on looking for options and consequently, its economy will remain tied closely to China for a considerable period in the future.

Birth of the Quad

The Quad emerged in May 2007 when Japan, Australia, India and the US decided to cooperate in areas of defence and security and towards this, agreed to coordinate their actions in the region and beyond (US-Japan Joint Statement 2007). The Quad was the brainchild of Shinzo Abe in his first inning as the Prime Minister of Japan. He buttressed the idea in his visit to India in August 2007, where he called for a 'confluence of the two seas – Indian and Pacific Oceans' as seas of freedom and prosperity (Abe 2007). Shinzo Abe propounded a broader 'Asian Arc of Freedom and Prosperity' along the outer rim of the Eurasian continent that also included the US and Australia (Abe 2007). US Vice-President Dick Cheney was another enthusiastic supporter of the initiative and the proximity between India and the US during the George W. Bush presidency was another factor pulling India under the Quad umbrella.

The actual development under the rudimentary Quad initiative took place in the form of the Malabar 2007 multinational naval exercise, where navies from the US, India, Japan, Australia and Singapore participated (Garg 2007). The participants conducted coordinated and joint operations on humanitarian disaster/disaster relief missions, anti-surface and anti-submarine operations. The conduct of this naval exercise projected an image of a military alliance. Moreover, the nature and objective of these naval operations had an implied Chinese angle in the Indo-Pacific. Consequently, the Quad and the Malabar-2007 exercise raised concerns in the Chinese media and China's official circles. China had been expressing its concerns, much before the Malabar-2007 took place, over the Quad's central objective, which China interpreted as being a regional forum to 'contain and encircle China' (*People's Daily Online* 2007). The Chinese government issued demarches to each of the member countries and sought clarification (Dikshit 2007; Gupta 2011). China, however, did not have to worry for long as Australia became the first member to withdraw after Kevin Rudd was elected its new premier in 2008 (Medcalf 2008; Chellaney 2008b). The Indian government soon followed suit in January 2008 when Manmohan Singh visited Beijing and assured his hosts that India would not participate in any anti-China coalition (Chellaney 2008b; Poff-Webster and

Chotani 2015). The Malabar series of naval exercises continued annually during 2008-13 but the Indian government restricted its membership to the US only. Finally, with the ouster of Prime Minister Shinzo Abe from power in Japan and the onset of the new American administration under Barack Obama, the Quad began losing its relevance.

Resurrection of the Quad

The Quad as an idea did not vanish completely and has made a return as a consequence of China's unilateral actions in the East and the South China Seas (Chaudhury 2016; Rossow and Watson 2016). The re-election of Shinzo Abe in Japan and the election of an assertive Narendra Modi as Prime Minister in India did play additional roles in its resurrection (Brewster 2010b; Davies 2013; Frossard 2013; Poff-Webster and Chotani 2015). Thus, since 2014, the idea has picked up pace again. There are a number of concrete actions taking place to solidify the initiative, such as the addition of Japan as a permanent member in the Malabar-2015 exercise in a partial redux of the Malabar-2007, the meetings of security officials from member countries and an obvious coordination on issues of major relevance in the Indo-Pacific (Aneja 2015; Chaudhury 2015; Press Information Bureau, Government of India 2015a; Kulkarni 2015; *Kyodo News* 2016). These actions were followed by the Malabar-2016 naval exercises in the Western Pacific where navies from India, the US and Japan participated (Peri 2016, Singh 2016). Even though China yet again raised concerns on the nature of these exercises and the apparent resurgence of an anti-China coalition in the Indo-Pacific, this time all three participants chose to overlook Chinese concerns and went ahead with exercises while further increasing their coordination on regional security issues (Lu 2015; Shan 2016; Yu 2015).

Australia: The Weaker Leg

Australia remains the weakest link in the Quad, whether in the previous iteration or the current resurgence. The cautiousness and ambivalence is prevalent not only in its policymaking circles but even in its academia, media and political groups. In 2015, Kevin Rudd, the architect of Australia's withdrawal and by then no longer Prime Minister, felt that the Quad was being seen in China as the 'rest of the region ganging up on Beijing' (Haidar 2015). He believed that the call for 'freedom of navigation and overflight in the South

China Sea', mentioned in the Indo-US Joint Vision Document (Press Information Bureau, Government of India 2015b) during President Obama's visit, was a strong and apparently unnecessary statement (Haidar 2015). Australia tends to see an ideological dimension to the Quad and the Malabar series of exercises and therefore, remains apprehensive of being seen by China as confrontational (Hayden 2015). Therefore, while the Labour Party governments headed by Kevin Rudd and Julia Gillard stayed away from any re-association with Quad, the Liberal Party Premier Tony Abbott was eager to promote it (Hayden 2015).

Table 2: Australia: Vital Statistics (US$ Billion)

Indicators *Year*	*GDP*	*GDP Growth Rate (%)*	*Defence Budget*	*Defence Budget Growth Rate (%)*
2015	1340	2.26	24.6	4.5
2014	1455	2.5	31.5	14
2013	1564	2.44	28.9	3.6
2012	1537	3.63	29.5	-6.5
2011	1390	2.38	31.5	-4.2

Source: World Bank 2016; Australian Department of Defence 2015a; 2015b.

Abbott saw the Quad as a hedging strategy against any Chinese misadventure in the maritime territory around Australia. He was an enthusiastic supporter of Premier Shinzo Abe's 'proactive contributions to the regional peace' and therefore, considered Japan to be 'Australia's best friend in Asia' (Hornung 2016). Consequently, he strived to improve defence cooperation with Japan by offering it the Sea-1000 submarine contract to replace Australia's Collins-class submarines with the newly-built Japanese Soryu-class advanced submarines (White 2015a). The step would have not only provided one of the most advanced diesel-electric submarines in the world to the Australian Navy but could have knit closely together the Australian, Japanese and the US navies, as they would have shared a large number of internal components and sub-systems in these submarines (Hornung 2016). However, Abbott's enthusiasm has not been shared by his successor Malcolm Turnbull, who looks at China as a crucial business opportunity and therefore, is unlikely to antagonize it. Expectedly, Turnbull chose the safe option of France as the submarine builder and effectively scuttled the budding defence relationship with Japan (Heginbotham and Samuels 2016).

Apart from these concrete pacifist steps, even the Australian discourse on the issue suffers from multiple apprehensions of Japan, India, China, and even the US, if the latter decided to turn isolationist. Australian apprehensions about Japan run deep and even though both countries are bound by the trilateral military alliance with the US, in the event of a crisis between Japan and China, Australia will keep its option open on whether or not to join in the conflict (Igata 2016; White 2016a). In reality, if the US is not involved, Australia would be less enthusiastic of getting involved in a conflict between Japan and China (White 2016a). The entire discourse of strategic partnership, therefore, remains paper-thin between both countries.

In the Indian case, Australia believes that India would either remain strongly non-aligned or prefer to stay with its traditional partners such as Russia and it would not be a reliable partner for the US or its allies against China (White 2015b). Rather, it is also possible that India, Russia and China may make an alliance that would challenge the US-led international order in the future as India considers itself an emerging great power and therefore, has no incentive for sustaining the existing order (Rovere 2015). There is an additional fear in the Australian strategic circles about a probable Indian dominance over the Indian Ocean. Although, Australia does not consider India as a maritime threat in the southeast Indian Ocean, it generally harbours suspicions of any great power increasing its role in the Indian Ocean, other than the US (Brewster 2010a). In the last few years, this apprehension has reduced due to frequent interactions between both the Indian and Australian navies (Kumar 2013; Taylor 2014; Singh 2014); both have frequently interacted in the Indian Ocean Naval Symposium (IONS) and conducted exercises together in multilateral events and in 2015, for the first time, executed a joint naval exercise, the AUSINDEX (Bangara 2015; Indian Navy 2014; *The Hindu* 2015). Nevertheless, the bilateral strategic cooperation remains superficial and it is at the most, a hedging strategy.

The most difficult and delicate balancing emerges in Australian dealings with the US and China. China remains Australia's largest trade partner and the largest market for Australian commodities such as iron ore, coal, milk, gold and wool among other things (Australian Department of Foreign Affairs and Trade 2016). Australia's economic dependency on China is substantial as is evident from the following tables on Australian trade:

Table 3: Australian Trade Relations with China, the US and Others (AU$ Million)

		Rank				*% Growth*	
Rank		*2013*	*2014*	*2015*	*% Share of Total*	*2014-15*	*5-Year Trend*
1.	China	151,050	152,494	155,502	23.2	2.0	8.4
2.	US	55, 569	60,596	70, 201	10.5	15.9	5.9
3.	Japan	71,006	70,149	65,103	9.7	-7.2	-0.6
4.	S. Korea	32,379	34,815	35,854	5.4	3.0	3.2
5.	Singapore	27,036	29,544	25,747	3.8	-12.9	3.1
6.	India	15,281	15,762	19,826	3.0	25.8	-4.4

Source: Australian Department of Foreign Affairs and Trade 2016.

As can be seen in Table 3, the Australian trade with China is almost three times the size of its trade with the US. Moreover, Australian exports to China are almost five times the size of its exports to the US. A similar lead is present in imports as well and therefore, it can be argued that the Chinese dominance in Australian trade figures constrains Australian options in its foreign, economic and security policymaking. Tables 4 and 5 show that the dependency will only grow.

Table 4: Australian Top Five Exporting Destination (AU$ Million)

		Rank				*% Growth*	
Rank		*2013*	*2014*	*2015*	*% Share of Total*	*2014-15*	*5-Year Trend*
1.	China	101,719	98,212	91,297	28.8	-7.0	8.1
2.	Japan	49,536	50,264	42,355	13.4	-15.7	-1.5
3.	US	15,858	18,535	22,114	7.0	19.3	8.4
4.	S. Korea	21,278	21,996	20,014	6.3	-9.0	-2.7
5.	India	11,403	11,252	13,574	4.3	20.6	-9.3

Source: Australian Department of Foreign Affairs and Trade 2016.

Table 5: Australian Top Five Importing Destinations (AU$ Million)

		Rank				*% Growth*	
Rank		*2013*	*2014*	*2015*	*% Share of Total*	*2014-15*	*5-Year Trend*
1.	China	49,332	54,282	64,204	18.2	18.3	8.9
2.	US	39,710	42,061	48,086	13.6	14.3	4.9
3.	Japan	21,470	19,885	22,747	6.4	14.4	1.4
4.	S. Korea	11,101	12,819	15,840	4.5	23.6	16.3
5.	Thailand	13,841	12,877	15,449	4.4	20.0	4.3

Source: Australian Department of Foreign Affairs and Trade 2016.

Nevertheless, Australia maintains close military relations with the US forces and remains a crucial ANZUS alliance partner, providing basing facility to the US Marines in Darwin and retaining extensive military-to-military linkages (*Marine Corps Times* 2016; Schubert and Purtill 2015). It is the only country that has deployed its military officer as the Deputy Commanding General for Operations at the US PACOM (USARPAC) in Hawaii (Johnson 2013). It is one of the major customers of US defence articles including fighter aircraft, transport aircraft, ground systems, radars and score of other sensitive (unavailable to non-NATO allies) equipment (Greene 2015; Pittaway 2016). Australia is also a node in the American FIVE EYES intelligence-sharing programme (Corera 2013). In sum, the strategic and military relations between Australia and the US run quite deep. Cultural and ethnic similarities also increase the bond between both countries.

However, this bilateral bonhomie has limited influence over Sino-Australian trade relations. The Australian government ignored American concerns and went ahead with awarding of the Darwin port development contract to a Chinese company (Murphy 2015; Perlez 2016), even though the port is situated right next to the US Marine base. In addition, it has maintained its manoeuvring space between the US and China on issues of regional security in the Indo-Pacific and has not committed to any military-related venture to safeguard the regional order. Rather, apprehensions about the US role in the Western Pacific run deep in Australian academic circles (White 2016b).

Therefore, the Australian policy regarding China has been of 'engage and hedge' since the Kevin Rudd days and this policy has been reiterated using different semantics by different leaders over the years (Garnaut 2015). Hence, Malcom Turnbull's 'balance and resistance' strategy, Julia Gillard's 'strategic dialogue with China while opening the US Marine base in Darwin' and Tony Abbott's 'Free Trade with China but support to Quad with Japan, India and the US' are different assertions of the same policy. Considering the economic and geostrategic factors, there is a low chance of any paradigmatic change in this Australian security policy in the region, in the near future. Therefore, Australia as a member of the Quad remains the weakest link, driving down the intensity of integration and combined approach.

Vietnam as a Potential Member

In comparison, Vietnam can become an important member of the Quad and can enhance the security and economic cooperation between members to a better level. There are three main drivers for this proposition, namely, Vietnam's geopolitical importance for the Indo-Pacific region, its potential willingness to play a crucial role in the Quad and its strong bilateral relations with Japan, India and the US.

Vietnam's Geopolitical Importance

Vietnam remains one of the crucial states in the Indo-Pacific, especially in Southeast Asia. The following table shows its economic numbers:

Table 6: Vietnam: Vital Statistics (US$ Billion)

Indicators *Year*	*GDP*	*GDP Growth Rate (%)*	*Defence Budget*	*Defence Budget Growth Rate (%)*
2015	191.5	6.68	4.6	7.4
2014	186.20	6.0	4.3	14.2
2013	171.22	5.4	3.7	10.9
2012	155.82	5.2	3.36	24.4
2011	135.53	6.2	2.7	0.5

Source: World Bank 2016, SIPRI 2016.

Table 7: Vietnamese Trade Relations with China, the US and Others (US$ Million)

Rank	*2013*	*2014*	*2015*	*% Share of Total*
1. China	50,210	53,050	66,000[2]	17-19
2. US	29,700	33,600	45,800	11-12
3. S. Korea	25,920	28,800	37,000	9-10
4. Japan	25,260	28,010	28,510	9-10
5. Singapore	13,900	16,300	21,600	5
6. India	5,230	5,600	5,130	2

Source: World Integrated Trade Solutions 2013-14; Vietnam General Department of Customs 2016.

Table 8: Vietnamese Top Five Exporting Destination (US$ Million)

Rank	*2013*	*2014*	*Jul 2015-Jul 2016*	*% Share of Total*
1. US	23,870	28,650	31,990	18-19
2. Japan	13,544	14,675	7,952	10-11
3. China	13,178	14,928	10,854	9-10
4. S. Korea	6,683	7,167	6,033	5-6
5. Other	Malaysia 4,984	Hong Kong 5,265	Hong Kong 3,402	— 3-4

Source: World Integrated Trade Solutions 2013-14; Vietnam General Department of Customs 2016.

Table 9: Vietnamese Top Five Importing Destinations (US$ Million)

Rank	*2013*	*2014*	*July 2015-Jul 2016*	*% Share of Total*
1. China	36,886	43,648	27,329	27-28
2. S. Korea	20,678	21,728	17,502	15-16
3. Japan	11,558	12,857	8,153	6-7
4. Other Asia	9,402	11,064	12,758	7-8
5. Thailand	6283	7,053	4,613	4-5

Source: World Integrated Trade Solutions 2013-14; Vietnam General Department of Customs 2016

As detailed in the above table, Vietnam has a fast-growing economy and an equally fast-growing defence budget. In fact, Vietnam is the strongest military power in Southeast Asia with a large military, and a sizeable navy and air force. Due to its long combat experience during conflicts with the US and China, Vietnam also commands a professional armed force.

Further, Vietnam is located at a crucial place in the Indo-Pacific where it straddles the entire western coast of the South China Sea. Naturally, Vietnam has a crucial stake in the peace, security and economic well-being of the region. It also has claims over island chains in the South China Sea, many of which it already controls and administers. The EEZ of Vietnam contains substantial amount of energy deposits and minerals, which various global companies are interested in exploring (Kaplan 2015). In brief, the size and location of Vietnam makes it a frontrunner for the membership in the Quad.

Vietnam's Relations with Quad Members

Vietnam enjoys close relationship with Japan and India due to its historical proximity with these two states. Japan is the fourth-largest trade partner of Vietnam, with the two-way trade hitting US$28 billion in 2015 (*Vietnam Net* 2016b).

Japan is also the second-largest foreign investor in Vietnam and by January 2015 had invested US$37 billion, behind only South Korea (*Vietnam Net* 2016a). The rate of Japanese investment has been growing over the years with the country investing about US$1.84 billion in 2015 and the conclusion of the Trans-Pacific Partnership (TPP) or its replacement minus the US that could further fuel investment and trade relations (*Thanh Nien News* 2016b).

Apart from trade, Vietnam-Japan military relations have also grown over the years. Following the Chinese placement of an oil rig in the sea near Vietnamese coast in 2014, Japan decided to boost Vietnamese naval capability by providing six naval vessels (Petty 2014). Another two patrol vessels were transferred in 2015 to boost Vietnamese maritime law enforcement authorities (*VOA News* 2015). Vietnam, in return, agreed to allow Japanese ships and submarines to dock in its ports and naval bases, especially in its strategic Cam Ranh Bay base and Japanese naval vessels have begun to avail of the facility (*Kyodo News* 2016b). Japanese maritime patrol aircraft have begun surveillance over the South China Sea and they use Vietnamese facilities for refuelling stops (*Thanh Nien News* 2016a).

Japan and Vietnam have also agreed to design five plans of action for Vietnam's industrialisation towards 2030 and 2050 (Ministry of Foreign Affairs of Japan 2015). They have established an 'Extensive Strategic Partnership for Peace and Prosperity' to develop comprehensive relations. A strategic programme for cooperation in education has been in place since 2014 and Japan is helping to establish the 'Vietnam-Japan University' as well as improving its human resource development programmes (Ministry of Foreign Affairs of Japan 2015). Both countries are cooperating in regional and international institutions and Vietnam is a major recipient of the Japanese Overseas Development Assistance (ODA) (Ministry of Foreign Affairs of Japan 2015). In sum, Vietnam and Japan are increasing their proximity in economic and security aspects and therefore, both have a strong incentive to conclude a collaborative mechanism to institutionalise their ever-growing bilateral relations.

Similarly, India-Vietnam relations are quite strong and India was a strong votary of Vietnam during the Cold War days. In 2016, both countries decided to upgrade their strategic partnership to a 'comprehensive strategic partnership' (Modi 2016). The economic relations have picked up over the years and the bilateral trade stood at US$9 billion in 2014-15, with a target of US$15 billion to be achieved by 2020 (Embassy of India in Vietnam 2016). Indian companies have been heavily investing in Vietnam's food processing, fertiliser, auto component, textile accessory and mineral exploration sectors over the years. India has also established the Cuu Long Delta Rice Research Institute in Vietnam (Modi 2016). In addition, Indian gas and oil companies are exploring the seas around Vietnam for energy deposits, often in the teeth of opposition from China (*DNA News* 2014; *Gulf Times* 2015).

Further, India-Vietnam bilateral relations are strongest in the political and strategic domains. Vietnam has received a copious amount of help in military training from India. Indian naval institutions have trained Vietnamese submariners to operate the Russian Kilo-class diesel submarines at the INS Satavahana training base (Taneja 2016). The Vietnamese Air Force receives spare parts of its Sukhoi-30 heavy fighter aircraft and MiG-21 aircraft from Indian manufacturers while the Vietnamese Navy has also stocked spare parts for its Petya-class frigates and other boats from India (Bedi 2016). Both governments are also negotiating the Vietnamese acquisition of the Brahmos supersonic cruise missile, the fastest cruise missile in the world, which would be a significant boost to Vietnam's defensive capability (Sagar 2016). In addition, there is a major scope for bilateral cooperation in the upgradation of Soviet/Russian equipment in the Vietnamese inventory such as Mi-8/Mi-17 helicopters, T-55 tanks and air defence missiles (Bambha 2016).

Further, India considers Vietnam to be crucial in its 'Look East' and since 2014, 'Act East' policies (*The Hindu* 2014). Vietnam is the ASEAN coordinator for India. Indian naval ships have visited Vietnamese ports and bases for a number of years and the naval deployment is increasing in duration, year by year (*Xinhua* 2016). India has also opened a line of credit for Vietnam to buy Indian naval vessels and other equipment to augment its maritime capabilities (*The Times of India* 2016). In sum, the bilateral relationship between Vietnam and India are multifaceted and deep enough that a larger institutional mechanism for better cooperation in security and economic matters should be welcome to both countries.

Finally, Vietnam-US relations are inching ahead towards normalisation after a long duration of estrangement. The formal normalisation of diplomatic relations came in 1995 but bilateral economic relations boomed after the then US President Bill Clinton's visit in 2000 (Bennett-Jones and Phillips 2000). Thereafter, Vietnam and the US have enjoyed better economic relations with a bilateral trade at US$45 billion in 2015 (White House Press Secretary 2016) and this trade momentum might even increase further under the Donald Trump presidency.

The two countries began their strategic dialogues in 2008 and the US vessels soon resumed their visits to Vietnamese naval bases (US Embassy in Vietnam 2016). Moreover, both have concluded multiple agreements over the years that cover nuclear energy, maritime security capability enhancement and other capacity-building aspects (White House Press Secretary 2016). Finally, President Obama visited Vietnam in 2016 and removed the arms embargo from Vietnam, which may result in major weapons procurements in the future (The Economist

2016). Therefore, all ingredients to build a better economic and security relationship between both the US and Vietnam are present.

Willingness to Play a Role in the Indo-Pacific

As explained in above paragraphs, there is a need for a better assessment over the function and membership of Quad in the Indo-Pacific and it would be better if both Australia and Vietnam are considered on the basis of their capabilities as well as their willingness to play a larger role in the region. Although Australia commands a larger economy and a better-equipped military, the ambivalence of its policymakers on account of close economic relations with China reduces its manoeuvring space in the region. Moreover, the size of the Australian military is quite small (approximately 58,000 personnel compared to above 700,000 troops in Vietnam's military) and inadequate for a nation seeking bigger role in the Indo-Pacific security architecture. It projects an image of defence outsourcing, which does not sit well with the Chinese strategic calculations for the region. In the economic domain, Australia has been trying to diversify and reduce its dependence on the Chinese market, especially after the 2015 slowdown in the Chinese economy (Jericho 2016; *The Australian* 2013). Nevertheless, the size of its trade relations with China are such that any reduction effort will stretch over a longer duration in future and could go either way (Conley 2014).

Almost 10 years since withdrawing from the Quad, Australia requested to rejoin the Malabar naval exercises in 2017 as an observer (Greene 2017). The request put India in a difficult situation, owing to three reasons. First, the Australian ambivalence on the role of Quad has not really changed in the last few years. It may not have as many objections to the central idea of the Initiative but the absence of objections does not amount to welcome either. Second, it would not be unexpected that with a change in the federal government in Canberra or under sustained Chinese economic and diplomatic pressure in the future, Australia would withdraw from the Quad, again. There is a distinct dichotomy between the strategic-academic and economic discourses in Australia. The strategic and academic communities argue for further enhancement of Australia's relations with the US, Japan and India and remain apprehensive of Chinese actions in the Indo-Pacific. In contrast, the business community, to which the Prime Minister Malcolm Turnbull himself belongs, remains a steadfast supporter of China. This sharp division has affected Australian policies significantly. Finally, three members of the Malabar 2017 – India, Japan and the US – command significant naval and other military assets. In comparison, Australian contribution to the exercise would be marginal and a case of too much trouble for little gain. Accordingly, the Indian government decided to play safe and declined Australia's request to join Malabar-2017. Nevertheless, India has kept open the bilateral route of naval exercises between the Indian and Australian navies and if the bilateral trust grows substantially, there may be a rethink on the Australian request in the future.

In comparison, Vietnam is driven to achieve larger economic and security roles for itself in the Indo-Pacific (Linh 2016). Its fast-growing economy is increasing its regional profile and consistent military acquisitions of quiet diesel submarines, frigates and heavy fighter aircraft have boosted its military capability (Goldstein 2015; *Thanh Nien News* 2013; Torode 2015). In addition, Vietnam is willing to contest Chinese claims over the Western Pacific, as Chinese dominance will be detrimental to Vietnam's core national interests (Linh 2016). It will not only restrain Vietnam's fisheries industry, mineral exploration, marine resources and tourism industry, but also dispossess Vietnam from playing any noticeable role in the regional security architecture (*Bangkok Post* 2016; Vu 2016; Nguyen 2016; *South China Morning Post* 2016). Therefore, the maintenance of regional security and stability is an existential question for Vietnam, whereas Australia can take calculated risks to maximise its gains with China in other domains.

Conclusion

The current state of the geostrategic space in the Indo-Pacific has revived the dormant idea of the Quad and enhanced its relevance for regional security and stability. However, this time, the membership of the Quad needs to be tweaked to include Vietnam as a key member of the initiative. Vietnam's importance as a crucial Quad member in the region would grow with increase in its economic and military strength. It enjoys better economic and strategic relations with Japan, India and the US and is willing to contribute constructively to support the regional order. In comparison, Australia is the weakest link in the Quad. Australian ambivalence towards the initiative and its economic dependence on China is reducing the Quad's integration potential. To be effective, Quad members need to enhance their cooperation in crucial areas of intelligence, surveillance and reconnaissance in the region and institutionalise the annual military exercises to increase their interoperability among forces for any eventuality. Therefore, it would be in the larger strategic interest of the group to offer membership to Vietnam while reconsidering Australia's request for renewed membership.

NOTES

1 The Kevin Rudd government in Australia, taking on board the concerns of its largest trading partner, China, decided to withdraw from the Quad Initiative in 2008. This led to a reduced interest in India and the US for the initiative. Finally, the departure of Shinzo Abe in his first tenure as the Japanese Prime Minister brought an end to the discussion on the Quad.

2 Chinese and Vietnamese figures differ on their bilateral trade data. In 2015, Vietnam claimed that bilateral trade stood at US$66 billion while China claimed it to beat US$95 billion. There is rampant smuggling at their border and even companies tend to fudge their data, so the confusion.

REFERENCES

Abe, Shinzo. 2007. 'Confluence of the Two Seas', 22 August, Speech delivered at the Parliament of India, http://www.mofa.go.jp/region/asia-paci/pmv0708/speech-2.html (accessed on 22 March 2016).

Ali, Mahmud. 2007. 'New Strategic Partnership against China', 3 September, http://news.bbc.co.uk/2/hi/south_asia/6968412.stm (accessed on 10 March 2016).

Aneja, Atul. 2015. 'China to take a hard look at Malabar-2015 naval exercises', *The Hindu,* 10 October, http://www.thehindu.com/news/international/china-to-take-a-hard-look-at-malabar2015-naval-exercises/article7747147.ece (accessed on 10 April 2016).

Australian Department of Defence. 2015a. 'Defence Budget 2015-16', 10 August, http://www.defence.gov.au/Budget/15-16/Default.asp (accessed on 10 August 2016).

Australian Department of Defence. 2015b. 'Defence economic trends in the Asia Pacific', 10 March, http://www.defence.gov.au/dio/documents/DET_15.pdf (accessed on 10 August 2016).

Australian Department of Foreign Affairs and Trade. 2016. 'Australia's Trade in Goods and Services 2015', 6 September, http://bit.ly/1WtCNWa (accessed on 7 September 2016).

Bambha, Ruchi. 2016. 'Manohar Parrikar asks Indian private sector to participate in Vietnam's military modernisation', *The Economic Times,* 6 June, http://bit.ly/2c9shkQ (accessed on 12 June 2016).

Bangara, Suresh. 2015. 'Australia-India naval exercise: A long awaited strategic outreach', *The Quint,* 16 September, https://www.thequint.com/india/2015/09/15/australia-india-naval-exercise-a-long-awaited-strategic-outreach (accessed on 10 April 2016).

Bangkok Post. 2016. 'Vietnam warns South China Sea is a test of ASEAN', 25 July, http://www.bangkokpost.com/news/asia/1044125/vietnam-warns-south-china-sea-is-a-test-of-asean (accessed on 20 August 2016).

BBC News Asia. 2014a. 'Japan gives Vietnam six navy ships amid regional tension', 1 August, http://www.bbc.com/news/world-asia-28599397 (accessed 10 April 2016).

BBC News Asia. 2014b, 'Philippines says China 'fired water cannon' on Filipino fishermen', 24 February, http://www.bbc.com/news/world-asia-26320383 (accessed on 10 April 2016).

Bedi, Rahul. 2016. 'India aims to supply Brahmos cruise missiles to Vietnam', *IHS Jane's Defense Weekly,* 1 June, http://www.janes.com/article/60876/india-aims-to-supply-brahmos-cruise-missiles-to-vietnam (accessed on 10 June 2016).

Bennett-Jones, Owen and Jeff Philipps. 2000. 'Clinton's Vietnam visit', *BBC News Asia,* 16 November, http://news.bbc.co.uk/2/hi/asia-pacific/1025169.stm (accessed on 10 March 2016).

Brewster, David. 2010a. 'An Indian sphere of influence in the Indian Ocean?', *Security Challenges,* Vol. 6, No. 3, Spring, pp. 1-20.

Brewster, David. 2010b. 'The Australia-India Security Declaration: The Quadrilateral Redux', *Security Challenges,* Vol. 6, No. 1, Autumn, pp. 1-9.

Chaudhury, Dipanjan Roy. 2015. 'India, US, Japan take on China at first trilateral ministerial meet', *The Economic Times,* 1 October, http://economictimes.indiatimes.com/news/defence/india-us-japan-take-on-china-at-first-trilateral-ministerial-meet/articleshow/49175830.cms (accessed on 10 July 2016).

Chaudhury, Dipanjan Roy. 2016. 'US Pushes for naval quadrilateral between India, US, Japan and Australia to edge out China in Indo-Asia-Pacific Region', *The Economic Times,* 2 March, http://bit.ly/2clcOhw (accessed on 12 April 2016).

Chellaney, Brahma. 2008a. 'Differential Equations', *Hindustan Times,* 12 February, http://www.hindustantimes.com/india/differential-equations/story-o5MEE8DdEUGNMgGAYYy3lJ.html (accessed on 12 April 2016).

Chellaney, Brahma. 2008b. 'Obstacles to overcome in the development of a concert of Asia-Pacific democracies', *The Japan Times,* 20 February, http://www.japantimes.co.jp/opinion/2008/02/20/commentary/obstacles-to-overcome-in-the-development-of-a-concert-of-asia-pacific-democracies/ (accessed on 10 March 2016).

China National Bureau of Statistics. 2000-2014. *China Statistical Yearbook,* Beijing.

Conley, Tom. 2014. 'Australia's China dependence: do we need a plan B?', *The Conversation',* 9 December, https://theconversation.com/australias-china-dependence-do-we-need-a-plan-b-34976 (accessed on 10 January 2016).

Corera, Gordon. 2013. 'Spying scandal: Will the five eyes club open up', *BBC News,* 29 October, http://www.bbc.com/news/world-europe-24715168 (accessed on 20 July 2016).

Davies, Andrew. 2013. 'Some angles on the quadrilateral', *The Strategist,* 11 December, http://www.aspistrategist.org.au/some-angles-on-the-quadrilateral/ (accessed on 20 January 2016).

Dikshit, Sandeep. 2007. 'Biggest joint naval exercise in Bay of Bengal in September', 13 July, http://www.thehindu.com/todays-paper/tp-national/biggest-joint-naval-exercise-in-bay-of-bengal-in-september/article1871738.ece (accessed on 10 March 2016).

DNA News India. 2014. 'India, Vietnam to sign deal for oil exploration in South China Sea despite protest by China', 27 October, http://www.dnaindia.com/india/report-india-vietnam-to-sign-deal-for-oil-exploration-in-south-china-sea-despite-protest-by-china-2029677 (accessed on 10 March 2016).

Embassy of India in Vietnam. 2016. 'Bilateral Relations', 12 September, http://indembassy.com.vn/cms.php?id=8 (accessed on 12 September 2016).

Frossard, Adrien. 2013. 'Is the return of Shinzo Abe good for India', *IDSA Issue Brief,* 8 January, http://www.idsa.in/issuebrief/IstheReturnofShinzoAbeGoodNewsforIndia_AdrienFrossard_080113 (accessed on 10 April 2016).

Garg, Vinay. 2007. 'Exercise Malabar 2007: A major step towards fine tuning maritime capabilities', *Sainik Samachar,* September, http://sainiksamachar.nic.in/englisharchives/2007/sep15-07/h1.htm (accessed on 12 April 2016).

Garnaut, John. 2015. 'Malcolm Turnbull changes direction on foreign policy: China trumps the Islamic State death cult', *The Sydney Morning Herald',* 24 September, http://www.smh.com.au/comment/malcolm-turnbull-outlines-strategy-towards-china-20150924-gjtvts.html (accessed on 10 April 2016).

Gokhale, Nitin. 2016. 'India and Vietnam: Going beyond Brahmos', *ABP Live,* 4 June, http://www.abplive.in/blog/india-and-vietnam-going-beyond-brahmos (accessed on 15 June 2016).

Goldstein, Lyle J. 2015. 'China's nightmare: Vietnam's New Killer Submarines', *The National Interest,* 29 March, http://nationalinterest.org/feature/chinas-nightmare-vietnams-new-killer-submarines-12505?page=show (accessed 10 March 2016).

Greene, Andrew. 2015. 'RAAF to receive two new C-17 Globemaster planes in billion dollar defence purchase', *ABC News,* 11 April, http://www.abc.net.au/news/2015-04-10/raaf-to-receive-two-more-c-17-globemasters-billion-dollar/6384104 (accessed on 10 March 2016).

Greene, Andrew. 2017. 'India blocks Australian bid to join Exercise Malabar naval war games', *ABC News,* 1 June, http://www.abc.net.au/news/2017-05-31/india-rejects-australian-request-to-join-naval-war-games/8577664 (accessed on 2 June 2017).

Gulf Times. 2015. 'ONGC plans to revive drilling off Vietnam, 29 August, http://www.gulf-times.com/story/452968/ONGC-plans-to-revive-drilling-off-Vietnam (accessed on 12 March 2016).

Gupta, Sourabh. 2011. 'US-India Defence ties: The limits to interoperability', *East Asia Forum,* 31 July, http://www.eastasiaforum.org/2011/07/31/us-india-defence-ties-the-limits-to-interoperability/ (accessed on 12 March 2016).

Haidar, Suhasini. 2015. 'Beijing maybe ready for a resolution of the border with India: Kevin Rudd', *The Hindu,* 8 March, http://www.thehindu.com/opinion/interview/interview-with-kevin-rudd-beijing-maybe-ready-for-a-resolution-of-the-border-with-india-kevin-rudd/article6969581.ece (accessed on 12 March 2016).

Harris, Gardiner. 2016. 'Vietnam arms embargo to be fully lifted, Obama says in Hanoi', *The New York Times,* 23 May, http://www.nytimes.com/2016/05/24/world/asia/vietnam-us-arms-embargo-obama.html (accessed 10 June 2016).

Hayden, Shannon. 2015. 'Australia's choice between guns and butter just got a lot messier', *Vice News,* 18 September, https://news.vice.com/article/australias-choice-between-guns-and-butter-just-got-a-lot-messier (accessed on 10 March 2016).

Heginbotham, Eric and Richard J. Samuels. 2016. 'Poor Substitute', *Foreign Affairs,* 3 May, https://www.foreignaffairs.com/articles/australia/2016-05-03/poor-substitute (accessed on 10 May 2016).

Hornung, Jeffery W. 2016. 'Lessons from a sunken submarine deal', *The Wall Street Journal,* 28 April, http://www.wsj.com/articles/lessons-from-a-sunken-submarine-deal-1461861988 (accessed on 12 May 2016).

Igata, Akira. 2016. 'Japan's submarine bid is a first date, not a marriage proposal', 13 April, *The Interpreter,* 13 April, http://www.lowyinterpreter.org/post/2016/04/13/Japans-submarine-bid-is-a-first-date-not-a-marriage-proposal.aspx (accessed on 20 April 2016).

International Monetary Fund. 2017. 'Report for Selected Countries and Subjects', http://bit.ly/2vUylYU (accessed on 20 April 2017).

Indian Navy. 2014. 'IONS: Australia hosts 4th Edition', *Press Release*, 3 April, http://www.indiannavy.nic.in/content/ions-australia-hosts-4th-edition (accessed on 10 April 2016).

Jericho, Greg. 2016. 'Déjà vu for Australian economy as China woes portend another bad year', *The Guardian,* 11 January, https://www.theguardian.com/business/grogonomics/2016/jan/11/deja-vu-for-australian-economy-as-china-woes-portend-another-bad-year (accessed on 10 March 2016).

Johnson, Robert. 2013. 'Why US Appointing an Aussie General to command its Pacific troops is a big deal', *Business Insider India,* 2 February, http://www.businessinsider.in/Why-The-US-Appointing-An-Aussie-General-To-Command-Its-Pacific-Troops-Is-a-Big-Deal/articleshow/21395916.cms (accessed on 10 March 2016).

Kaplan, Robert. 2015. 'Why the South China Sea is so crucial', *Business Insider Australia,* 20 February, http://www.businessinsider.com.au/why-the-south-china-sea-is-so-crucial-2015-2 (accessed on 10 March 2016).

Katigbak, Jose. 2016. 'US, Philippines agree on 5 base locations under EDCA', *Philstar Global,* 20 March, http://www.philstar.com/headlines/2016/03/20/1564662/us-philippines-agree-5-base-locations-under-edca (accessed on 10 April 2016).

Kaye, Byron and Matt Siegel. 2016. 'Australia calls China's South China Sea moves 'counterproductive', *Reuters,* 23 March, http://www.reuters.com/article/us-southchinasea-china-australia-idUSKCN0WP0VS (accessed on 10 April 2016).

Kulkarni, Pranav. 2015. 'Significance of India-US-Japan Malabar naval exercise', *Indian Express,* 21 October, http://indianexpress.com/article/explained/significance-of-the-india-us-japan-malabar-naval-exercise/ (accessed on 20 March 2016).

Kumar, Vinay. 2013. 'India, Australia raise the pitch on maritime cooperation', *The Hindu,* 5 June, http://www.thehindu.com/news/national/india-australia-raise-the-pitch-on-maritime-cooperation/article4783997.ece (accessed on 10 April 2016).

Kyodo News. 2016a. 'Japan, US, India to hold trilateral talks in Tokyo', *The Japan Times,* 20 June, http://www.japantimes.co.jp/news/2016/06/20/national/japan-u-s-india-hold-trilateral-talks-tokyo/ (accessed on 10 July 2016).

Kyodo News. 2016b. 'Japanese destroyers visit Vietnam's Cam Ranh Bay', 12 April, http://www.japantimes.co.jp/news/2016/04/12/national/japanese-destroyers-visit-vietnams-cam-ranh-bay/ (accessed on 10 May 2016).

Latiff, Rozanna and Ben Blanchard. 2016. 'A hundred Chinese boats encroach in Malaysian waters: Minister', *Reuters,* 25 March, http://www.reuters.com/article/us-southchinasea-malaysia-idUSKCN0WR03H (accessed on 10 April 2016).

Lee Seok Hwai. 2016. '5 highlights of Shangri-La Dialogue 2016', *The Straits Times,* 6 June, http://www.straitstimes.com/asia/se-asia/5-highlights-of-shangri-la-dialogue-2016 (accessed on 10 June 2016).

Linh Tong. 2016. 'Vietnam's evolving role in US Asia strategy', *The Diplomat,* 1 June, http://thediplomat.com/2016/06/vietnams-evolving-role-in-us-asia-strategy/ (accessed on 10 June 2016).

Lu Yaodong. 2015. 'Expanded Indo-Japanese military cooperation dangerous for Asia', *Global Times,* 5 August, http://www.globaltimes.cn/content/935616.shtml (accessed on 10 April 2016).

Medcalf, Rory. 2008. 'Chinese Ghost Story', *The Diplomat,* 14 February, http://thediplomat.com/2008/02/chinese-ghost-story/ (accessed on 12 April 2016).

Mie, Ayako. 2016. 'First Chinese Warship to skirt Senkakus triggers protest from Tokyo', *The Japan Times,* 9 June, http://www.japantimes.co.jp/news/2016/06/09/national/chinese-frigate-sails-near-senkakus-russian-military-vessels/ (accessed on 9 June 2016).

Ministry of Foreign Affairs of Japan. 2007. 'Alliance Transformation: Advancing United States-Japan Security and Defense Cooperation', US-Japan Joint Statement, 1 May, http://www.mofa.go.jp/region/n-america/us/security/scc/joint0705.html (accessed on 10 March 2016).

Ministry of Foreign Affairs of Japan. 2015. 'Joint Vision Statement on Japan-Vietnam relations', 18 September, http://www.mofa.go.jp/files/000099707.pdf (accessed on 10 March 2016).

Minnick, Wendell. 2015. 'Vietnam pushes modernization as China challenge grows', *Defensenews.com,* 30 August, http://www.defensenews.com/story/defense/naval/2015/08/30/vietnam-pushes-modernization-china-challenge-grows/32042259/ (accessed on 10 March 2016).

Modi, Narendra. 2016. 'Banquet Speech during visit to Vietnam', Press Information Bureau, Government of India, 3 September, http://pib.nic.in/newsite/PrintRelease.aspx?relid=149504 (accessed on 4 September 2016).

Murdoch, Lindsay. 2016. 'South China Sea dispute: Vietnamese subs deployed as deterrent to China', *The Sydney Morning Herald,* 7 January, http://www.smh.com.au/world/vietnamese-subs-deployed-to-south-china-sea-20160107-gm0z6a.html (accessed on 10 March 2016).

Murphy, Katharine. 2015. 'Malcolm Turnbull shrugs off US concern over Darwin port lease to Chinese firm', 19 November, https://www.theguardian.com/australia-news/2015/nov/19/malcolm-turnbull-shrugs-off-us-concern-over-darwin-port-lease-to-chinese-firm (accessed on 10 January 2016).

Ng, Jason. 2014. 'US, Malaysia pledge cooperation on security, trade', *The Wall Street Journal,* 27 April, http://on.wsj.com/2cFZfrs (accessed on 10 March 2016).

Ngui, Yantoultra and Sui-Lee Wee. 2015. 'Malaysia to protest over Chinese coast guard intruders: WSJ', 9 June, http://www.reuters.com/article/us-southchinasea-malaysia-china-idUSKBN0OP06120150609 (accessed on 12 April 2016).

Nguyen, Mai. 2016. 'Vietnam warns China against rig activity in disputed waters', 19 January, http://uk.reuters.com/article/uk-southchinasea-vietnam-idUKKCN0UX1Y4 (accessed on 10 March 2016).

People's Daily Online. 2007. 'A goodwill joint naval drill', 21 April, http://en.people.cn/200704/21/eng20070421_368521.html (accessed on 10 April 2016).

Peri, Dinakar. 2016. 'Malabar exercises begins near islands contested by China', *The Hindu,* 11 June, http://www.thehindu.com/news/national/malabar-exercise-begins-near-islands-contested-by-china/article8714965.ece (accessed on 10 July 2016).

Perlez, Jane. 2012. 'Philippines and China ease tensions in rift at sea', *The New York Times,* 18 June, http://www.nytimes.com/2012/06/19/world/asia/beijing-and-manila-ease-tensions-in-south-china-sea.html?_r=0 (accessed on 10 April 2016).

Perlez, Jane. 2016. 'US Casts wary eye on Australian port leased by Chinese', *The New York Times,* 20 March, http://www.nytimes.com/2016/03/21/world/australia/china-darwin-port-landbridge.html (accessed on 10 April 2016).

Petty, Martin. 2014. 'Japan offers vessels to Vietnam to boost its sea strength', *Reuters,* 1 August, http://www.reuters.com/article/us-vietnam-japan-idUSKBN0G13EA20140801 (accessed on 10 March 2016).

Pittaway, Nigel. 2016. 'Bogdan: Australian F-35 block buy still possible', *Defense News,* 25 February, http://www.defensenews.com/story/defense/air-space/air-force/2016/02/25/bogdan-australian-f-35-block-buy-still-possible/80920054/ (accessed 15 March 2016).

Poff-Webster, Will and Vindu Mai Chotani. 2015. 'Tapping into Quad potential', *The Pioneer,* 27 March, http://www.dailypioneer.com/columnists/oped/tapping-into-quad-potential.html (accessed on 10 April 2016).

Press Information Bureau, Government of India. 2015a. 'India and Japan hold defence dialogue', 30 March, http://pib.nic.in/newsite/PrintRelease.aspx?relid=117830 (accessed on 10 April 2016).

Press Information Bureau, Government of India. 2015b. 'Joint Statement during the visit of President of USA to India', 25 January, http://pib.nic.in/newsite/PrintRelease.aspx?relid=114955 (accessed on 10 March 2016).

Rahmat, Ridzwan. 2016. 'Shangri-La Dialogue: France proposes for more visible presence of European navies in South China Sea', IHS Jane's Defense Weekly, 6 June, http://www.janes.com/article/60976/shangri-la-dialogue-france-proposes-for-more-visible-presence-of-european-navies-in-south-china-sea (accessed on 10 June 2016).

Ripley, Will, Jason Hanna and Eimi Yamamitsu. 2015. 'Japanese lawmakers ok greater overseas role for military', *CNN,* 18 September, http://edition.cnn.com/2015/09/18/asia/japan-military-constitution (accessed on 10 April 2016).

Rossow, Richard and Sarah Watson. 2016. 'China creates a second chance for the Quad', *AMTI Brief,* 14 March, https://amti.csis.org/4379-2/ (accessed on 12 April 2016).

Rovere, Crispin. 2015. 'India is no ally of the US', *The Interpreter,* 16 March, http://www.lowyinterpreter.org/post/2015/03/16/India-is-no-ally-of-the-US.aspx (accessed on 10 April 2016).

Sagar, Pradip. 2016. 'India plans to export Brahmos to Vietnam', *New Indian Express,* 10 June, http://www.newindianexpress.com/nation/India-plans-to-export-Brahmos-to-Vietnam/2016/06/10/article3475122.ece (accessed on 11 June 2016).

Schogol, Jeff. 2016. 'First of 1250 Marines arrive in Australia for six-month training deployment', *Marine Corps Times,* 13 April, https://www.marinecorpstimes.com/story/military/2016/04/13/first-1250-marines-arrive-australia-six-month-training-deployment/82980622/ (accessed on 16 April 2016).

Schubert, Steven. 2015. 'US marines begin arriving in Darwin in fourth rotation as part of US pivot to the Asia Pacific', *ABC News,* 18 May, http://www.abc.net.au/news/2015-04-13/us-marines-arrive-darwin-us-pivot-amid-concern-tensions-china/6387444 (accessed on 10 April 2016).

Shan Jie. 2016. 'China hopes Us-led naval exercise will not harm the interest of 'third parties', *Global Times,* 3 April, http://www.globaltimes.cn/content/971844.shtml (accessed on 10 April 2016).

Singh, Abhijit. 2014. 'Modi's Australia visit: Maritime cooperation in focus', *IDSA Comment,* 13 November, http://www.idsa.in/idsacomments/ModisAustraliavisitMaritimeCooperation_asingh_131114 (accessed on 10 April 2016).

Singh, Sushant. 2016. 'Four Navy ships to join trilateral Malabar exercise', *Indian Express,* 4 May, http://indianexpress.com/article/india/india-news-india/four-navy-ships-to-join-trilateral-malabar-exercise-2783422/ (accessed on 10 May 2016).

SIPRI. 2015. 'Military Expenditure Database', 10 May, http://www.sipri.org/databases (accessed on 10 May 2015).

SIPRI. 2016. 'Arms Transfers Database', 10 August, https://www.sipri.org/databases (accessed on 10 August 2016).

South China Morning Post. 2016. 'Vietnam's President warns all will lose in any South China Sea war', 30 August, http://www.scmp.com/news/china/diplomacy-defence/article/2011282/vietnams-president-warns-all-will-lose-any-south-china (accessed on 1 September 2016).

Summers, Lawrence. 2015. 'Time US Leadership woke up to new economic era', *Financial Times,* 6 April, https://next.ft.com/content/a0a01306-d887-11e4-ba53-00144feab7de#axzz3WX4sXQ7O (accessed on 10 April 2016).

Suryadinata, Leo. 2016. 'The Natunas Incident and Indonesia-China Relations', *The Straits Times,* 23 June, http://www.straitstimes.com/opinion/the-natunas-incident-and-indonesia-china-relations (accessed 25 June 2016).

Taneja, Kabir. 2016. 'Obama's historic visit to Vietnam and India's Act-East Policy', *DNA News India,* 21 May, http://www.dnaindia.com/world/column-obama-s-historic-visit-to-vietnam-and-india-s-act-east-policy-2215171 (accessed on 10 June 2016).

Taylor, Lenore. 2014. 'Tony Abbott and Narendra Modi agree to hold regular joint military exercises', *The Guardian,* 18 November, https://www.theguardian.com/australia-news/2014/nov/18/tony-abbott-and-narendra-modi-share-high-hopes-for-bright-trading-future (accessed on 10 April 2016).

Tencer, Daniel. 2012. 'World's Economic Center of Gravity Shifting Back to Asia at Unbelievable Speed: McKinsey Institute', *Huffington Post,* 5 July, http://www.huffingtonpost.ca/2012/07/05/world-economic-center-of-gravity_n_1651730.html (accessed on 10 April 2016).

Thanh Nien News. 2013. 'Vietnam to buy dozen Sukhoi fighter planes from Russia', 23 August, http://www.thanhniennews.com/politics/vietnam-to-buy-dozen-sukhoi-fighter-planes-from-russia-1428.html (accessed on 10 January 2016).

Thanh Nien News. 2016a. 'Japanese patrol aircraft to stop at Vietnam naval base', 11 January, http://www.thanhniennews.com/politics/japanese-patrol-aircraft-to-stop-at-vietnam-naval-base-58001.html (accessed on 10 March 2016).

Thanh Nien News. 2016b. '64 percent of Japanese investors in Vietnam see growth', 25 February, http://www.thanhniennews.com/business/64-percent-of-japanese-investors-in-vietnam-see-growth-59585.html (accessed on 10 March 2016).

The Australian. 2013. 'Australia urged to diversify economy', 8 October, http://www.theaustralian.com.au/business/business-spectator/australia-urged-to-diversify-economy/news-story/dad48c19861bac7b93eb3c20faee3a04 (accessed on 10 May 2016).

The Economist. 2016. 'America lifts its arms embargo on Vietnam', 23 May, http://www.economist.com/news/asia/21699323-end-decades-long-ban-will-win-vietnams-trust-and-worry-china-america-lifts-its-arms (accessed on 10 June 2016).

The Hindu. 2014. 'Look East Policy now turned into 'Act East' policy: Modi', 13 November, http://www.thehindu.com/news/national/look-east-policy-now-turned-into-act-east-policy-modi/article6595186.ece (accessed on 12 April 2016).

The Hindu. 2015. 'Three Australian ships arrive in Visakhapatnam for naval exercise', 12 September, http://www.thehindu.com/news/national/three-australian-ships-arrive-in-visakhapatnam-for-naval-exercise/article7642831.ece (accessed on 10 April 2016).

The Sun Daily. 2014. 'Malaysia-US wrap up joint military exercise', 2 September, http://www.thesundaily.my/news/1158127 (accessed on 10 April 2016).

The Times of India. 2016. 'Prime Minister Modi's Vietnam visit: key takeaways', 4 September, http://timesofindia.indiatimes.com/Prime-Minister-Narendra-Modi-Vietnam-visit-Key-takeaways/listshow/53997039.cms (accessed on 4 September 2016).

Torode, Greg and Masayuki Kitano. 2016. 'Countries played diplomatic tag, lined up to criticize China at ASEAN Summit', *The Wire,* 6 June, http://thewire.in/41082/countries-played-diplomatic-tag-lined-up-to-criticise-china-at-asian-summit/ (accessed on 10 June 2016).

Torode, Greg. 2015. 'Vietnamese military grows to face China threat', *The Japan Times,* 20 December, http://www.japantimes.co.jp/news/2015/12/20/asia-pacific/vietnamese-military-grows-face-china-threat/ (accessed on 10 April 2016).

US Embassy in Vietnam. 2016. 'Policy and History', https://vn.usembassy.gov/our-relationship/policy-history/ (accessed on 2 September 2016).

Vaswani, Karishma. 2014. 'The sleepy island Indonesia is guarding from China', *BBC News Asia,* 20 October, http://www.bbc.com/news/world-asia-29655874 (accessed on 10 March 2016).

Vietnam General Department of Customs. 2016. *Statistics of Export by Country/Territory – Main Imports,* July, http://www.customs.gov.vn/Lists/EnglishStatisticsCalendars/Attachments/576/2016-T07T-5X(EN-PR).pdf (accessed 10 August 2016).

Vietnam General Department of Customs. 2016. *Statistics of Import by Country/Territory – Main Imports,* July, http://www.customs.gov.vn/Lists/EnglishStatisticsCalendars/Attachments/577/2016-T07T-5N(EN-PR).pdf (accessed 10 August 2016).

Vietnam Net. 2016a. 'Japanese funding drives Vietnam economic growth', 31 January, http://english.vietnamnet.vn/fms/business/150580/japanese-funding-drives-vietnam-economic-growth.html (accessed on 10 March 2016).

Vietnam Net. 2016b. 'VN-Japan relations witness breakthrough progress', 27 May, http://english.vietnamnet.vn/fms/government/157059/vn-japan-relations-witness-breakthrough-progress.html (accessed on 10 June 2016).

VOA News. 2015. 'Japan donates two more patrol boats to Vietnam amid S. China sea tensions', 3 November, http://www.voanews.com/a/japan-donates-patrol-boats-to-vietnam-south-china-sea-tensions/3035300.html (accessed on 10 April 2016).

Vu Trong Khanh. 2016. 'Vietnam says China's flights to South China Sea a threat to Air Safety', *The Wall Street Journal,* 9 January, http://www.wsj.com/articles/vietnam-says-chinas-flights-to-south-china-sea-a-threat-to-air-safety-1452334018 (accessed on 10 March 2016).

White House Press Secretary. 2016, 'Fact-Sheet: United States-Vietnam relations', 23 May, https:/

/www.whitehouse.gov/the-press-office/2016/05/23/fact-sheet-united-states-vietnam-relations (accessed on 30 May 2016).

White, Hugh. 2015a. 'Abbott's plunge into submarine market is a risk we cannot afford', *The Age,* 17 February, http://www.theage.com.au/comment/abbotts-plunge-into-submarine-market-is-a-risk-we-cannot-afford-20150215-13fmw4 (accessed on 10 April 2016).

White, Hugh. 2015b. 'Obama's India visit reveals weakness of US position in Asia', *the Interpreter,* 16 February, http://www.lowyinterpreter.org/post/2015/02/16/Obama-India-visit-reveals-weakness-of-US-position-in-Asia.aspx?COLLCC=1313358785& (accessed on 10 April 2016).

White, Hugh. 2016a. 'If we strike a deal with Japan, we're buying more than submarines', *The Age,* 15 March, http://www.theage.com.au/comment/if-we-strike-a-deal-with-japan-were-buying-more-than-submarines-20160313-gni3hl.html (accessed on 10 April 2016).

White, Hugh. 2016b. 'Need to face the facts in Asia', *East Asia Forum,* 18 April, http://www.eastasiaforum.org/2016/04/18/need-to-face-the-facts-in-asia/ (accessed on 10 May 2016).

World Bank. 2012. *World Bank Development Indicators Database 2013,* http://data.worldbank.org/indicator/NY.GDP.MKTP.KD (accessed on 15 January 2014).

World Bank. 2016. 'GDP Growth', *National Accounts Data,* http://data.worldbank.org/indicator/NY.GDP.MKTP.KD.ZG (accessed on 10 June 2016).

World Integrated Trade Solutions. 2015. *Vietnam Trade Summary 2014, 2015, World Bank,* http://wits.worldbank.org/CountryProfile/en/Country/VNM/Year/2014/Summary (accessed on 12 July 2016).

Xinhua. 2016. '2 Indian Naval ships start five-day visit to Vietnam', 30 May, http://news.xinhuanet.com/english/photo/2016-05/30/c_135399536_2.htm (accessed on 10 June 2016).

Xinhua. 2017. 'China to raise 2017 defense budget by around 7 pct: Spokesperson', 4 March, http://news.xinhuanet.com/english/2017-03/04/c_136101947.htm (accessed on 5 March 2017).

Yu Jincui. 2015. 'Concurrent India drill sparks unnecessary speculation', *Global Times,* 14 October, http://www.globaltimes.cn/content/947001.shtml (accessed on 10 April 2016).

8

Vietnam-China Economic Relations: Current Situation and Trends

Hoang The Anh

Vietnam and China are two neighbouring countries, sharing common land and sea borders. Since the normalisation of relations in 1991, economic relations between the two countries so far have rapidly developed in the areas of trade relations, investment and tourism. Vietnam–China economic relations have become an important part of Vietnam's economy. On the one hand, these promote socio-economic development, but on the other, these also have limitations and create problems that affect sustainable development in Vietnam.

At present, economic relations between Vietnam and China are widely deployed in many areas. However, within the scope of this article, we will in turn assess the facts in several significant fields that affect the development of Vietnam's economy such as trade relations, investment, project contractors and tourism. At the same time, from the context and the current level of economic development in both countries, we will provide a forecast of the trends in bilateral economic relations in the coming years.

Assessment of Vietnam-China Economic Relations

Trade

It is undeniable that from the normalization of relations until now, trade relations between Vietnam and China have rapidly developed. The trade turnover increased from about US$32 million in 1991 to over US$66 billion in 2015 (Table 1).

Table 1: Vietnam-China Bilateral Trade Relations in the Period 2011-2015

Unit: US$ billion

Year	*Import-Export turnover*	*Export Turnover (from Vietnam)*	*Import Turnover (to Vietnam)*	*Trade Balance*
2011	35,720	11,126	24,593	-13,467
2012	41,172	12,387	28,784	-16,397
2013	50,187	13,233	36,954	-23,721
2014	58,773	14,905	43,867	-28,962
2015	66,668	17,142	49,516	-32,374

Source: General Department of Vietnam Customs (2017).

In recent years, bilateral relations between Vietnam and China have had ups and downs. China's moving its HS-981 drilling rig into Vietnam's exclusive economic zone and continental shelf in 2014 had a negative impact on political trust and cooperation between the two countries and hurt the feelings of the Vietnamese people, but bilateral trade and economic relations still continued to develop. From 2004 to 2015, China has been the largest trade partner of Vietnam (Nam Phong 2016). At the same time, in recent years, Vietnam has turned into the most important partner of China in the ASEAN countries. Statistics show that in the first six months of 2016, Vietnam became the largest trade partner of China in all ASEAN countries (Ha Thang-Le Bao 2016). In the period from 2011 to 2015, a two-way trade turnover gradually increased but Vietnam also increasingly suffered a trade deficit with China (Table 1).

The reasons for trade deficit are attributed to the relatively recent development of Vietnam's economy, the improvement of people's living standards and a large number of Chinese products entering in line with consumer demand in Vietnam. China is the world's factory; Chinese production is large scale, professionalised and economical, and Chinese products are diversified. Meanwhile, Vietnam's production heavily depends on raw materials (up to 90 per cent for some industries) from the Chinese market. At present, China remains the largest import market of Vietnam (Ngo Trang 2015). In textile and garment, footwear, electronics and energy industries, Vietnam still has to import various materials, raw materials, machinery, equipment, etc. including for investment in construction and manufacturing, and even for export processing. Meanwhile, Chinese products, with a cheap price and low-cost transport, have more advantages in entering the Vietnam market (Luong Bang 2014). This also means that Vietnam's auxiliary industries have not developed yet (Ha Thi Hong Van 2015: 24). If the situation remains unchanged in the long term, Vietnamese businesses will lose creativity, only focusing on assembly and processing for export.

Another reason could be that Chinese enterprises have won many contractor projects in Vietnam (see below), and these contractors brought along all materials, spare parts, accessories, etc. that could have been sourced from Vietnam as well as their unskilled workers to Vietnam; the trade deficit in this case was 100 per cent. This can also explain the rapid rise in the Chinese trade surplus in recent years. Annually, Vietnam's trade deficit involving an import of complete sets of equipment reaches US$10 billion (Ha Thi Hong Van 2015: 24).

Also, in recent years, Vietnam has begun to export computers, electronic devices and components, and various types of textile fibres to China. Although the export turnover to China is not high, the number shows that the product structure has improved unlike previously, when export products to China were all agricultural products and raw materials.

Table 2 shows that in 2015, the structure of import and export products between the two countries changed in comparison to the previous years when Vietnam focused on low-tech and agricultural products, raising concerns that Vietnam exported resources, raw and semi-processed products (such as rubber, seafood, etc.), low-tech products (such as garment, footwear, etc.) and could not upgrade its industries or participate in the higher segment of regional and national production chains (Doan Cong Khanh 2014: 22-23). Vietnam has since exported to China machinery, equipment, spare parts, phones and accessories, computers, electronic devices and components. This change is due to the rise of labour costs in China in recent years; multinational companies from East Asian countries such as Japan and South Korea have changed their location and investments from China to the Southeast Asian countries, including Vietnam, to form the model of 'China plus one'. These companies invest in production in Vietnam and then export to China.

Investments between the Two Countries

In terms of investment, up to March 2016, China (excluding Hong Kong, Macau, and Taiwan) has invested in a total of 1,346 projects in Vietnam, with

Table 2: Top 10 Import-Export Products between Vietnam and China in 2015

Unit: US$

No.	*Export Items*	*Value*	*%/Total Export to China*	*Export Items*	*Value*	*%/Total Import from China*
1	PCs, electronic devices and components	2,646,617,551	15.47	Machinery, equipment, accessories	9,019,327,928	18.22
2	Various types of fibre and thread	1,365,410,176	7.98	Phones and accessories	6,900,886,813	13.94
3	Fruits and vegetables	1,194,832,067	6.98	Fabric	5,223,210,460	10.55
4	Cassava and products from cassava	1,168,309,797	6.83	PCs, electronic devices and components	5,205,352,762	10.52
5	Cameras, camcorder and spare parts	1,016,112,115	5.94	Iron and steel	4,155,923,126	8.40
6	Wood and wooden products	974,539,189	5.70	Materials and auxiliary materials for textile, garment and footwear	1,777,854,191	3.59
7	Rice	855,742,579	5.00	Products from iron and steel	1,320,345,717	2.67
8	Crude oil	810,271,437	4.74	Other metals	1,280,285,090	2.59
9	Rubber	763,369,565	4.46	Products from plastic	1,151,067,587	2.33
10	Footwear	754,088,470	4.41	Automobiles	1,046,032,261	2.11
	Total Value of Export	17,109,303,862	100%	Total Value of Import	49,498,692,669	100%

Source: General Department of Vietnam Customs (2017).

the total value of registered investment of US$10.4 billion, ranking 9th out of the 102 countries and territories investing in Vietnam. The average investment for each project is US$7.7 million, equivalent to 50 per cent of investment in Vietnam from other countries and territories.

First, China has invested in a total 916 projects, mainly in processing and manufacturing, with a registered capital of US$5.38 billion—about 52 per cent of the total investment. Second, China's investment in power generation, natural gas and air conditioning accounts for 20 per cent of the total investment; the remainder is invested in other areas. In terms of location, Chinese investment projects are present in 54 out of Vietnam's 63 provinces and cities, especially in Binh Thuan (with a total investment of US$2 billion) and Tay Ninh (with a registered investment of US$1.2 billion), followed by Ha Giang, Lao Cai and Binh Duong. In terms of investment methods, China's investment in Vietnam is mainly in 100 per cent foreign-invested enterprises, and now there are 1,058 projects of 100 per cent Chinese-invested companies, with a total investment of US$5.6 billion, accounting for 78.6 per cent of the total number of investment projects, i.e., 54.3 per cent of the total registered investment. Of these, only three projects are under BOT, BT and BTO structure, with a total investment of US$2.06 billion, accounting for 20 per cent of the total investment turnover. The remainder of the Chinese investment in Vietnam is in the form of joint ventures and contractual joint-venture enterprises (Tri Lam 2016).

Although increasing, the number of direct investment projects in Vietnam is still limited with a small scale of investment, and most are in low-tech processing. Therefore, compared to developed countries like Japan, Korea, and the United States, the effect of China's investment in Vietnam remains relatively low (Nguyen Dinh Liem 2013: 11-12).

Based on the facts of the Chinese investments in Vietnam, diverse studies have shown that Chinese investors have likely misjudged Vietnam's consumer market. This then makes China's investment in Vietnam ineffective and also dents the image and reputation of the Chinese enterprises. Chinese businessmen did not understand the context and customs in Vietnam; some considered Vietnam underdeveloped and backward, and that its consumers could not afford high quality products. Thus, they brought along outdated technologies and products to Vietnam. As a result, the Vietnamese consumers rated Chinese products as low-quality products while, other countries like Japan and South

Korea, which had a relatively good understanding of Vietnam's consumer perceptions, entered the Vietnamese market with high-quality products, and thus became favorites (Lu Jue Xuan 2013: 52).

There is also another reason: since the auxiliary industry and the processing industry in Vietnam are still underdeveloped, the Chinese investors need to import raw materials and equipment from China and other countries. This has also increased the cost of production and reduced the competitiveness of the Chinese products manufactured or produced in Vietnam. Even in the context where China tries to implement its 'one belt, one road' strategy, if the Chinese enterprises cannot build their own image and establish their brands, then it would be difficult to improve the situation of China's investment in Vietnam.

In recent years, Vietnam has also begun to invest in China. By the end of 2015, Vietnam had invested in 15 projects in China, with a registered amount of US$16 million mainly in manufacturing and services (Tri Lam 2016). Although the scale of Vietnam's investment in China is very small, it shows nevertheless that Vietnamese businesses have started to enter the Chinese market.

Project Contractors

China has won many projects related to infrastructure, iron and steel production, mining, thermal power plants, hydropower plants, etc. According to statistics published in early April 2014 by the National Research Institute of Mechanical Engineering (Ministry of Industry and Trade), Vietnam now has 20 thermal power projects, and 15 of them are contracted to Chinese contractors. Although it is not specifically mentioned, in the field of cement production, the localisation rate is being determined at 0 per cent for Chinese contractors (in a total of 24 projects). Figures previously provided by the Finance and Budget Committee-National Assembly also show that till 2010, 90 per cent of the EPC projects (consulting, design-equipment supply-construction and installation, operation; or in other words, projects implemented under the turnkey method) in Vietnam had been contracted to Chinese contractors, with the majority being in the fields of oil and gas, chemicals, electric power and textile industries (Hoang Lan 2014).

Chinese contractors are chosen owing to their cheaper bidding prices in comparison with other countries. However, in reality, some projects are prolonged, along with low quality and poor management, and thereby damaging the image of the Chinese contractors. In fact, many projects performed by Chinese contractors in Vietnam have been delayed from at least three months to up to three years. Other frequent issues include unequal equipment quality, altered or low quality auxiliary equipment, altered material standards, altered or additional suppliers, etc. (Nguyen Van Thu 2014).

With the above-mentioned models deployed by the Chinese contractors in Vietnam, Vietnamese industries too, have no chance to participate as sub-contractors for the EPC projects. This has affected the development of some Vietnamese industries and reduced the competitiveness of Vietnam's own industries (Le Kim Thoa and Ngo Hoang Dai Long 2014: 72).

In order to overcome these adverse effects, Vietnam amended the Law on Bidding with effect from 1 July 2014. According to this Law on Bidding (new amendment), technical quality requirements have been increased and pricing methods are no longer included in the original construction price but for the whole lifecycle of projects (including operation and maintenance) to easily and correctly make comparison and assessment. In addition, successful bidders will be forced to prioritise the use of Vietnamese labour as well as local materials, equipment and services (Le Kim Thoa and Ngo Hoang Dai Long 2014: 72).

Tourism

Both Vietnam and China possess a lot of well-known tourist attractions in the world. In recent years, foreign visitors to Vietnam have always been outnumbered by Chinese tourists: 1.4 million people in 2012, 1.9 million people in 2013, and 1.9 million in 2014, respectively (Manh Nguyen 2015). According to the General Statistics Office of Vietnam, Chinese visitors to Vietnam in 2016 reached 2.7 million people; about twice the number of people in 2012 and 1.5 times the number of people in 2015 (Ky Duyen 2016). A lot of Vietnamese tourists also choose to visit China with about two million Vietnamese people travelling to China each year (Minh Khoa 2016).

The increased number of Chinese tourists to Vietnam will create employment for local people and at the same time contribute to the state budget, bringing back economic benefits for Vietnam. However, Chinese tourists also pose many problems for Vietnam's tourism industry, especially in some attractive regions like Khanh Hoa where at present there are only 11 registered tourist guides who can speak Chinese. Local businesses are thus forced to recruit tourist guides from Hanoi, Quang Ninh and Ho Chi Minh City. Some businesses have taken advantage of this and created difficulties for local authorities by using unregistered tourist guides (Giang Dinh 2016).

Another outstanding issue is that now there are more and more Chinese travellers attempting to work illegally in Nha Trang city, Khanh Hoa province. Nevertheless, to catch them in the act is not so easy because they often mix with tourist delegations and change their roles when coping with the Vietnamese authorities. As far as immigration is concerned, immigration desks are usually overcrowded due to entry and exit procedures at airports. It is because with the flow of 20 flights per day, and 150 to 170 passengers per trip from China, that there are times when the entry and exit passengers reach a thousand in number and the immigration procedures get therefore, prolonged and some businesses take advantage of this to evade taxes by changing hotel bookings (Giang Dinh 2016).

Trends in Vietnam-China Economic Relations

Currently, most of the world's largest economies are enduring slow growth. Although protectionism and nationalism seem to be on the rise around the world, interdependent economies and globalisation still remain the world's dominant trends.

Currently, Vietnam and China are both enjoying rapid economic growth in the Asia-Pacific area. Both are members of the World Trade Organization (WTO) and of the China-ASEAN free trade area and the Greater Mekong Sub-region (GMS) cooperation that bring opportunities and challenges for economic collaboration between the two countries within multilateral and bilateral cooperation frameworks. Vietnam not only benefits from these free trade regimes but also faces competition from Chinese products at home and abroad.

Vietnam and China are both entering a new period. At present, Vietnam's economy is approaching an important development stage with the GDP per capita surpassing US$2,000. Based on the experience of China and other foreign countries, Vietnam will rapidly develop and promote industrialisation, urbanisation, marketisation, and internationalisation in the next 10 years. At the same time, to increase the effectiveness of economic development, Vietnam is strengthening and promoting economic structural adjustment, transforming economic growth patterns and enhancing global integration efficiency. While Vietnam has concluded the Trans-Pacific Partnership (TPP) negotiations with

11 countries, this agreement is presently in a difficult situation since the US President Donald Trump announced that his country would no longer take part in the agreement.

Whether the TPP agreement is approved or not, Vietnam's standpoint will remain unchanged. Currently, Vietnam is also a member state negotiating the Regional Comprehensive Economic Partnership (RCEP), and therefore increasingly needs to cooperate with other countries, including economic cooperation for mutual benefit with China.

China's population is around 1.4 billion people, and thus, it is the largest market in the world. Nowadays, it is also speeding up its economic development transformation, trying to improve quality and efficiency, minimising environmental pollution, accelerating urbanization and domestic consumption, etc. China's GDP per capita has reached US$8,000, and might reach US$10,000 in some developed cities in the eastern region before long. As a middle class with high demand expands on China's eastern coast, Vietnam and other countries could take the opportunity to export specialty products to China. Since the 18th Congress of the Communist Party of China, China has continued to implement its going-out strategy, especially with the 'one belt, one road' strategy, encouraging Chinese businesses to invest abroad, strengthening cooperation and exchange, and negotiating mechanisms with other countries. In theory, this will create both opportunities and challenges for cooperation among developed and developing countries, including Vietnam and China.

From the context of current economic relations between Vietnam and China, the two countries are entering a new development stage with several likely trends as highlighted below.

First, in the coming years, Vietnam-China economic relations will inevitably be affected by multidimensional international economic relations. However, relations between the two countries will still remain 'half-cooperating, half-struggling' because the trend of globalisation and economic integration is still mainstream, and countries will continue to take part in international competition and division of labour and resources in economic development and commodity markets. Vietnam and China as two neighbouring countries are partners in both bilateral and multilateral economic cooperation, and thus always need and still have to cooperate with each other. However, China's intention to monopolise most of the East Sea in recent years and in the long run is not expected to change. Therefore, Vietnam and China will remain distrustful as long as the East Sea issue remains unresolved. To protect its maritime sovereignty and interests, Vietnam will resort to peaceful means to deal with China, including the latter's policy of using economic benefit as bait to annex Vietnam's territory. This will no doubt, somewhat affect trade and economic relations between the two countries.

Second, Vietnam has always considered China as a major market, seeking to export Vietnamese specialties and products to the Chinese market, and thereby resolving the bilateral trade imbalance and reducing the deficit. As mentioned above, the high and diverse demands of China's middle class in the developed eastern coast area offer opportunities for Vietnam to penetrate the Chinese market with some advantageous cultural products. To do this, in the coming years, Vietnam will need to guide businesses to convert to high-quality processing and refined products, and to reduce raw materials exports. At the same time, Vietnam has to encourage businesses to increase innovation, research and development, to advance manufacturing techniques and improve their position in the value chain, and to enhance competitiveness of traditional industries. Besides, Vietnam can also attract Chinese enterprises to invest in Vietnam and set up factories, thereby reducing imports from China, using local human resources and available natural resources in Vietnam, and encouraging Chinese businesses to export back to China and to third countries (Zhu 2012).

Third, after nearly 40 years of applying its reforms and open door policy, China's economy after years of growth at high speed has now reached a certain level of development, with the reliance on natural resources and cheap labour declining. In the context of increasing costs for labour and natural resources, many foreign businesses in China will move to adjacent countries following the China+1 model mentioned above. Vietnam could thus, be receiving investment from multinational companies. However, due to its underdeveloped auxiliary industries, there will be space for Chinese businesses to participate in the international division of labour in Vietnam. Chinese enterprises can invest, process and sell raw materials, spare parts, equipment and machinery to those multinational companies in Vietnam. For example, auxiliary industries have been formed to support major companies such as Canon and Foxconn in the QueVo Industrial Zone, BacNinh. Most spare parts and component suppliers for these companies come from countries of origin or from China (Hoang Van Hoan 2011: 59).

Fourth, Vietnam and China are seeing changes in their economic growth pattern and economic development methods, seeking to improve the efficiency of economic growth and environmental protection, and focusing on solving welfare issues. In particular, China is now in the transition phase of its economic development, and the implementation of its 'going out' strategy will lead to a shift of industries, technologies and products that cause environmental pollution to other countries. The tendency to move outdated technologies to the countries China invests in may hamper the long-term development of these countries. As a result, Vietnam should restrict outdated technologies and polluting production businesses from China and simultaneously, constantly improve its investment environment, focusing on advantageous industries, worker training and fostering talents.

Fifth, the Vietnamese and Chinese governments should continue to encourage the development of the tourism industry. According to data from the World Tourism Organization, there were 120 million Chinese people travelling abroad in 2015, and this number could probably reach 220 million in 2025. China is an important tourism source market of the world and also for Vietnam. Therefore, Vietnam has always maintained promotion and marketing activities in this potential market (Minh Khoa 2016). The Vietnamese government can support and guide the tourism industry to further promote specific tourist products of Vietnam to China, combining characteristics of Vietnamese ethnicity and culture, while improving material and nonmaterial environments of tourist attractions, and creating greater appeal for the Chinese tourists to Vietnam. This could also be an important factor that can compensate for Vietnam's trade deficit.

Conclusion

This study shows that, at present, economic relations between Vietnam and China have the following main characteristics: China is now the largest trading partner of Vietnam; Vietnam has the largest trade deficit with China; and China (excluding Hong Kong, Taiwan, and Macau) is the 9th largest investor in Vietnam, with relatively low-tech and small scale of investments, scattered across most cities and provinces of Vietnam. China is currently the largest contractor in Vietnam but its contracted projects are often inefficient and behind schedule. Currently, the numbers of foreign visitors to Vietnam are being overwhelmed by the influx of Chinese tourists even as more and more

Vietnamese tourists also travel to China. Thus, we can say that Vietnam-China economic relations have both positive and negative features and offer both opportunities and challenges.

From the above facts and trends in economic relations between the two countries, it remains very important for Vietnam to maintain good economic ties with China, especially in the context of international and regional integration. However, given that there also exist many problems such as the trade imbalance and the inefficiency of Chinese projects in Vietnam and if the situation does not improve or gets worse, there may be potential risks and hazards in the long run. To solve these problems, both governments need to raise the awareness of businesses and people through the market mechanism, thereby strengthening step-by-step bilateral economic relations in a healthy and sustainable way. Besides, maritime sovereignty disputes over the East Sea should be settled to avoid a negative impact on the trust between the political leaders, people and businesses of the two countries, and thereby also on economic relations between Vietnam and China.

REFERENCES

Doan Cong Khanh. 2014. 'Vietnam-China Economic Relations: Facts, Issues and Solutions', *Chinese Studies*, No. 8.

General Department of Vietnam Customs. 2017. https://www.customs.gov.vn/default.aspx (accessed 7 January 2017).

Giang Dinh. 2016. 'Khach du lich Trung Quoc tang truong manh: Vua mung vua lo' [A strong growth of Chinese tourists: half joy half sorrow], 25 March, http://baokhanhhoa.com.vn/phong-su/201605/khach-du-lich-trung-quoc-tang-truong-manh-vua-mung-vua-lo-ky-2-nhung-bat-cap-trong-quan-ly-2436181/ (accessed 7 January 2017)

Ha Thang-Le Bao. 2016. 'Chuyen tham cua Thu tuong toi Trung Quoc co y nghia quan trong' [The Prime Minister's visit to China and its important implications], 10 September, http://vcci.com.vn/chuyen-tham-cua-thu-tuong-toi-trung-quoc-co-y-nghia-quan-trong (accessed on 7 January 2017).

Ha Thi Hong Van. 2015. 'Fundamental Characteristics of Vietnam-China Trade Relations in the Current Period', *Chinese Studies*, No. 1.

Hoang Lan. 2014. '10 du an lon cua nha thau Trung Quoc tai Viet Nam' [10 major projects of Chinese contractors in Vietnam], 12 May, kinhdoanh.vnexpress.net/tin-tuc/doanh-nghiep/10-du-an-lon-cua-nha-thau-trung-quoc-tai-viet-nam-2989807.html (accessed on 7 January 2017).

Hoang Van Hoan. 2011. 'Phat Trien Cum Nganh Congo Viet Nam Trong Dieu Kien Toan Cau Hoa Va Hoi Nhap Kinh Te Quoc Te' [Development of industry clusters in Vietnam in the context of globalization and international economic integration], *Kinhte & Phattrien* [*Journal of Economics and Development*], No. 172/2011, 54-61, http://www.cantholib.org.vn/Database/Content/3073.pdf (accessed on 7 January 2017).

Ky Duyen. 2016. 'Du khach Trung Quoc đen Viet Nam đong chua tung co' [An unprecedented influx of Chinese tourists to Vietnam], 31 December, http://kinhdoanh.vnexpress.net/tin-tuc/vi-mo/du-khach-trung-quoc-den-viet-nam-dong-chua-tung-co-3521925.html (accessed 7 January 2017)

Le Kim Thoa and Ngo Hoang Dai Long. 2014. 'The East Sea Issue and its Impacts on Vietnam-China Trade Relations and Vietnam Economy', *Chinese Studies*, No. 7

Lu Jue Xuan. 2013. 'Initial Analysis of How to Create Business Images for Chinese Investors in Vietnam Market, in *Culture and Business*, Hangzhou, China-Vietnam Trade and Economic Forum Proceedings

Luong Bang. 2014. 'Hon 10 nam nhap sieu tu Trung Quoc - Vi sao?' [Suffered trade deficit with China for over 10 years - Why?], 8 May, http://www.baohaiquan.vn/Pages/Nhap-sieu-tu-Trung-Quoc-Bao-gio-cho-den-ngay-xua.aspx (accessed on 7 January 2017).

Manh Nguyen. 2015. 'Quan he thuong mai Viet-Trung qua nhung con so' [Vietnam-China Trade Relations by Numbers], *BaoMoi.com,* 21 January, http://www.baomoi.com/quan-he-thuong-mai-viet-trung-qua-nhung-con-so/c/15788488.epi (accessed on 7 January 2017).

Minh Khoa. 2016. 'Viet Nam xuc tien du lich tai 4 thanh pho cua Trung Quoc' [Vietnam tourism promotion in 4 cities in China], 16 December, http://www.bvhttdl.gov.vn/vn/tin-hd-dv-tt/viet-nam-xuc-tien-du-lich-tai-4-thanh-pho-cua-trung-quoc.html (accessed 7 January 2017)

Nam Phong. 2016. 'Trung Quoc tiep tuc la doi tac thuong mai lon nhat cua Viet Nam' [China continues to be the largest trading partner of Vietnam], 7 March, http://enternews.vn/trung-quoc-tiep-tuc-la-doi-tac-thuong-mai-lon-nhat-cua-viet-nam.html (accessed on 7 January 2017).

Ngo Trang. 2015. '32 ty USD Viet Nam nhap sieu tu Trung Quoc nam 2015' [Vietnam suffered US$32 billion trade deficit with China in 2015, 26 December, http://vne-conomy.vn/thoi-su/32-ty-usd-viet-nam-nhap-sieu-tu-trung-quoc-nam-2015-20151226021543133.htm (accessed on 7 January 2017).

Nguyen Dinh Liem. 2013. 'Awareness and Assessment on Chinese Direct Investment in Vietnam', in *Culture and Business*, Hangzhou, China-Vietnam Trade and Economic Forum Proceedings.

Nguyen Van Thu. 2014. 'Diversification of Machinery and Equipment Suppliers and Opportunities for Mechanical Engineering Industry, Economic Autonomy in an Interdependent World', Hanoi, VCCI workshop.

Tri Lam. 2016. 'Trung Quoc dau tu hon 10 ti USD vao Viet Nam don TPP', *BaoMoi.com*, 20 March, http://www.baomoi.com/trung-quoc-dau-tu-hon-10-ti-usd-vao-viet-nam-don-tpp/c/18925092.epi (accessed on 7 January 2017).

Zhu Jianjun. 2012. 'Vietnam's Trade Deficit Analysis and Counter-Tactics Study', in *Vietnam-China Business Forum: Cooperation Opportunities and Potentials*, Hanoi, Vietnam Academy of Social Sciences and Zhejiang University of Industry.

9

Growing Economic Integration of China and India with ASEAN: Glancing through Select Trade Indicators

Debashis Chakraborty and Anushree Chakraborty

The Association of Southeast Asian Nations (ASEAN) countries moved towards trade liberalisation since the late sixties and early seventies. The outward-orientation received support through the 'flying geese' model of investment, where Japanese capital boosted manufacturing sector productivity across recipient countries (Hayter and Edgington 2004). The initial wave of Japanese foreign direct investment (FDI) and technology in Hong Kong, South Korea, Taiwan and Singapore gradually shifted to Indonesia, Malaysia, Thailand and the Philippines. Since the late 1990s, the FDI from Japan and South Korea came to increasingly target newer entrants to the bloc, namely Vietnam, Cambodia and Lao PDR (Menon and Bhandari 2006). The FDI flows created a pool of skilled workforce in the ASEAN countries, aided by which ASEAN export in general and, in high-technology products in particular, increased considerably (UNESCAP 2014).

The rising prominence of the ASEAN countries in world trade has been aided by several factors. First and foremost, the group was able to create a comprehensive framework through appropriate leadership roles played by major players, move towards collective identity building and create an efficient conflict management framework (e.g., the 'ASEAN Way' principle), all of which enhanced the cohesiveness of the bloc (Chakraborty and Chakraborty 2015). They have also been able to complement their economic strengths to specialise in various segments of production and enhance the competitiveness of the region as a whole. As a result, several key international production networks (IPN) emerged, particularly involving the small and medium enterprises (SMEs) from the region, through the contract manufacturing model (Chakraborty 2016). The smaller players became an integral part of the value chain, performing the necessary tasks (e.g., parts and component manufacturing) given by the local leaders as well as multinational corporations (MNCs) from Japan and South Korea, and the associated interactions enhanced their technology absorption, competitiveness and managerial efficiency. Third, a number of infrastructure development initiatives were implemented involving East and Southeast Asian countries, and this deepened connectivity linkages promoted ASEAN exports further (Plummer et al. 2016). Finally, the inception of the ASEAN Free Trade Area (AFTA) reduced trade barriers on one hand and introduced several trade facilitation measures on the other (Calvo-Pardo et al. 2009).

Aided by rising export competitiveness and urge to expand market reach, the ASEAN countries have entered into a number of regional trade agreements (RTAs) over the last decade, both bilaterally and collectively as a bloc (Wignaraja 2013). Two forthcoming mega-regional initiatives, given their coverage, deserve particular attention in this regard. The first is the Regional Comprehensive Economic Partnership (RCEP), also known as ASEAN+6, i.e., trade integration involving six bilateral RTA partners of ASEAN, namely Australia, China, India, Japan, New Zealand and South Korea. The second is the Trans-Pacific Partnership (TPP), which involves four ASEAN countries (Brunei, Malaysia, Singapore and Vietnam) with several developed and developing countries situated at both sides of the Pacific.

The current analysis intends to understand the growing ASEAN association with two Asian partners, namely China and India. Both economies have entered into RTAs with ASEAN and are presently involved in the ongoing RCEP negotiations. Through use of important trade indices, the current analysis attempts to find out whether the integrations of China and India with ASEAN are moving along divergent paths. The analysis is arranged along the following lines. First, the trade balance scenario for China and India with ASEAN is observed, followed by the depth of their respective trade integrations. The extent of the IPN integration for the Chinese and Indian firms with ASEAN across three major sectors is undertaken next. Finally on the basis of the results, the policy conclusions are drawn.

Understanding the Effects of ASEAN–China and ASEAN-India FTAs on the Trade Balance

China joined the World Trade Organisation (WTO) in 2001, but with a 'non-market economy' (NME) status (Chaise and Chakraborty 2005). This paved the way for all WTO member countries to subject Chinese exports to anti-dumping investigations (Panitchpakdi and Clifford 2002). Moreover, the WTO members were also able to specifically target Chinese exports up to 31 December 2013 by a special provision (WTO 2001). To counter the negative influence of these provisions on exports, China actively followed a RTA policy where the demand for market-economy status was matched by a supply of greater access to the Chinese market (Xiao 2010). This was a major negotiating agenda during the ASEAN–China FTA negotiation, and finally by Article 14 of the Agreement, all the ten ASEAN countries agreed to recognise China as a market economy (ASEAN Secretariat, undated). The FTA came into force from 2005 onwards. Subsequently, the Service Trade Agreement between ASEAN and China was signed on January 14, 2007, and came into effect from 1 July of the same year, with certain flexibilities for new ASEAN members (Xiao 2010). However, the growing trade deficit with China, especially in absence of the NME instrument, subsequently emerged as a concern in several ASEAN economies (Chakraborty and Kumar 2012).

For India meanwhile, its 'Look East Policy' has, since 1991, been an integral part of its outward-oriented export strategy and interaction with the ASEAN countries (Saint-Mezard 2003). In 1992, India became a Sectoral Dialogue Partner of ASEAN, and FTA negotiations started from 2004 onwards. However, concerns over trade repercussions in the post-bloc period delayed the negotiation for a long period (Chakraborty and Sengupta 2010). Although the India-ASEAN FTA came into force from 2010 onwards, trade growth continues to be modest vis-à-vis initial expectations (Chakraborty 2014). After a long negotiation, India's agreement on Trade in Service and Investments with seven ASEAN countries has entered into force from 1 July 2015 onwards (GoI 2015). With the introduction of the 'Act East Policy' (AEP) at the India-ASEAN Summit in November 2014, India has pledged to deepen engagements with the region further, underlining a more action-oriented policy towards Southeast and the wider East Asia.

Tables 1 and 2 describe the merchandise export and import scenario of China and India with ASEAN partners over 2001-15, respectively. In Table 1, for understanding the evolving export pattern of China and India, the entire period is divided in two sub-periods, namely, 2001-10 and 2011-15. The corresponding figures for imports are reported in Table 2. To put things in perspective, the percentage share of the ASEAN countries in the overall export basket of China and India are also noted in addition to the average trade figures.

Table 1: Export Scenario for China and India with ASEAN Partners

Partner	*China*				*India*			
	Export Value (USD Million)	*Export Share (%)*	*Export Value (USD Million)*	*Export Share (%)*	*Export Value (USD Million)*	*Export Share (%)*	*Export Value (USD Million)*	*Export Share (%)*
	2001-10 Average		*2011-15 Average*		*2001-10 Average*		*2011-15 Average*	
China	-	-	-	-	7152.87	6.084	14174.95	4.695
India	16357.91	1.862	51825.73	2.404	-	-	-	-
Brunei	188.63	0.021	1237.43	0.057	13.80	0.012	203.43	0.067
Cambodia	667.10	0.076	3095.58	0.144	33.53	0.029	127.17	0.042
Indonesia	10136.35	1.154	34774.40	1.613	1884.91	1.603	5058.75	1.676
Lao PDR	102.45	0.012	1371.82	0.064	6.08	0.005	43.49	0.014
Malaysia	12919.90	1.471	40178.02	1.863	1780.40	1.514	4524.23	1.498
Myanmar	1462.77	0.167	7326.22	0.340	144.31	0.123	690.82	0.229
Philippines	5823.41	0.663	20204.53	0.937	529.06	0.450	1267.24	0.420
Singapore	9091.58	1.035	48400.62	2.245	5011.73	4.263	12170.18	4.031
Thailand	9322.49	1.061	32442.65	1.505	1286.73	1.094	3395.59	1.125
Vietnam	19880.98	2.263	44840.65	2.080	1030.68	0.877	4999.21	1.656
ASEAN	69595.64	7.923	233871.92	10.847	11721.24	9.969	32480.09	10.758

Source: Calculated by the authors from Trade Map (undated) data.

Several interesting observations emerge from the two tables. First, the trade volumes of both China and India increased with all ASEAN partners in 2011-15 over 2001-10, signifying a deepening of trade relationships. Second, while China enjoys a positive trade balance with all ASEAN countries with the exception of Malaysia over 2001-15, the scenario for India is quite modest, with a trade surplus only with Cambodia, Philippines, Singapore and Vietnam in the corresponding period. Third, China has generally enhanced its trade surplus with the ASEAN partners; for India the trade deficit fluctuates in the second period, which is a major area of concern. This implies that while post-2010, India's exports to ASEAN have increased, the imports have often grown at a higher rate. However, the reverse is true for Chinese exports. Finally, while

ASEAN's importance in China's export basket has gone up, the reverse is true with respect to its import basket. For India, however, ASEAN's importance is rising in both the export and import baskets. The observation indicates that there may be scope for deepening the trade facilitation measures between India and ASEAN countries, so as to enhance the trade flows further (Wong and Pellan 2012).

Table 2: Import Scenario for China and India with ASEAN Partners

Partner	*China*				*India*			
	Import Value (USD Million)	*Import Share (%)*	*Import Value (USD Million)*	*Import Share (%)*	*Import Value (USD Million)*	*Import Share (%)*	*Import Value (USD Million)*	*Import Share (%)*
	2001-10 Average		*2011-15 Average*		*2001-10 Average*		*2011-15 Average*	
China	-	-	-	-	16794.42	9.600	56218.78	12.396
India	10538.27	1.414	17778.90	0.971	-	-	-	-
Brunei	265.80	0.036	263.34	0.014	148.41	0.085	792.14	0.175
Cambodia	39.81	0.005	382.29	0.021	2.11	0.001	18.15	0.004
Indonesia	10064.77	1.350	27801.35	1.519	4173.36	2.386	14420.79	3.180
Lao PDR	130.51	0.018	1143.21	0.062	2.17	0.001	105.56	0.023
Malaysia	23491.26	3.151	57901.31	3.164	3785.67	2.164	9883.90	2.179
Myanmar	381.25	0.051	5347.52	0.292	668.54	0.382	1276.70	0.282
Philippines	12186.23	1.635	19163.67	1.047	205.38	0.117	454.43	0.100
Singapore	15108.86	2.027	29020.31	1.586	4400.27	2.515	7488.94	1.651
Thailand	16904.79	2.268	38332.24	2.094	1640.04	0.937	5472.27	1.207
Vietnam	3039.79	0.408	17853.11	0.975	240.06	0.137	2357.64	0.520
ASEAN	81613.06	10.948	197208.34	10.775	15266.00	8.726	42270.52	9.321

Source: Calculated by the authors from Trade Map (undated) data.

Integration Scenario: Synergy in the Trade Pattern?

Given the difference in the trade balance pattern for the ASEAN countries involving China and India, it is important to identify the underlying determinant, i.e., whether India's poorer export performance is the result of a demand-supply incompatibility. To understand this perspective, the current analysis calculates the bilateral *Trade Complementarity Index* (TCI) between China and India with individual ASEAN countries over 2005, 2010 and 2015 and the results are summarised in Table 3. TCI indices are calculated by considering the export pattern of China/India and imports of another ASEAN country (say, Thailand), and vice versa. The higher values of TCI over time indicate increasing similarities between the export (import) basket of a country

(China/India) and the import (export) basket of its ASEAN trade partner (say, Singapore). The TCI is calculated by using the following formula:

$$TCI_{ij} = 100 - \frac{(\sum |M_{jk} - X_{ik}|)}{2}$$

where X_{ik} is share of commodity k in country i's total exports, and M_{jk} is share of commodity k in country j's total imports. The data for the analysis is obtained from the Trade Map database (ITC, undated), with Harmonized System (HS) classification at 2-digit level (i.e., HS 1 – live animals, HS 2 – meat products and so on).

Several conclusions emerge from Table 3. First, export TCI for China has risen over 2005-15 for all the economies, indicating that China's export supply pattern has adjusted itself in tune to the ASEAN import demand pattern. In contrast, India has witnessed a declining export TCI for two ASEAN countries, namely, Brunei and Vietnam. The fall in export TCI is caused by the divergence in the export pattern of India and the import pattern of Vietnam in several commodities, including petroleum products (HS 27), organic chemicals (HS 29), pharmaceutical products (HS 30), gems and jewelry products (HS 71), machinery and equipment (HS 84), electrical equipment (HS 85), ships and boats (HS 89), optical and other instruments (HS 90). Second, the import TCI for China went down only for Thailand over the two terminal years. India witnesses a similar drop in the import TCI for Vietnam. The fall in import TCI is caused by the divergence in the import pattern of India and the export pattern of Vietnam in several commodities, including animal or vegetable fats (HS 15), petroleum products (HS 27), organic chemicals (HS 29), fertilisers (HS 31), plastic products (HS 39), leather products (HS 42) and electrical equipment (HS 85). Hence, the ASEAN countries have generally been able to align their exports in line with the import demands of China and India. Third, over 2010-15, the change in export TCI between China and ASEAN countries has been positive, but for India the corresponding figure has been negative for five countries. In other words, the Indian export basket, after the formation of the FTA with ASEAN, has become dissimilar with demand patterns of several ASEAN partners. Finally, over 2010-15 the change in import TCI has been quite strong for several ASEAN countries. This indicates that the exports of ASEAN countries have increasingly realigned themselves with the demand pattern of China and India in the recent years.

Table 3: Trade Complementarity Index for China and India with ASEAN Countries

Partner	*China-ASEAN Trade*						*India-ASEAN Trade*					
	China Export – ASEAN Partner Import			*China Import – ASEAN Partner Export*			*India Export – ASEAN Partner Import*			*India Import – ASEAN Partner Export*		
	2005	*2010*	*2015*	*2005*	*2010*	*2015*	*2005*	*2010*	*2015*	*2005*	*2010*	*2015*
Brunei	50.04	51.21	52.50	12.82	18.39	18.81	46.48	49.23	50.54	35.76	36.48	33.43
Cambodia	37.99	39.08	44.89	4.40	9.01	33.31	43.60	46.49	54.53	3.20	7.54	15.63
Indonesia	46.13	55.50	63.56	49.20	49.32	48.10	51.57	63.18	60.33	59.51	58.89	60.11
Lao PDR	47.56	45.35	48.28	19.28	33.34	37.83	47.63	54.65	54.02	20.94	23.78	38.26
Malaysia	66.76	66.15	69.00	70.41	70.78	71.94	44.52	50.59	55.22	49.84	51.45	58.85
Myanmar	-	43.97	57.09	-	20.29	26.73	-	53.11	56.26	-	37.87	52.84
Philippines	58.42	60.92	65.42	57.77	56.45	59.82	42.95	54.68	54.94	32.66	35.48	38.40
Singapore	64.94	62.16	65.38	71.16	69.85	75.64	40.48	48.34	46.91	47.89	52.89	53.72
Thailand	63.59	60.80	64.82	62.98	57.61	54.30	53.54	62.62	58.91	43.30	44.41	47.84
Vietnam	51.03	56.30	68.68	31.29	43.54	51.73	55.10	54.28	52.73	46.01	42.85	34.08

Source: Calculated by the authors from Trade Map (undated) data.

In addition, the *Trade Intensity Index* (TII), which reveals whether a region exports more (as a percentage) to a given destination than the world does on average or not, has been reported between China, India and the ASEAN countries for 2005, 2010 and 2014. The value of TII above 1 indicates that the trade relation is 'intense', while a value less than '1' indicates otherwise. The formula of calculating TII is as follows below. In the numerator, X_{sd} refers to the bilateral exports of a given country pair, while X_{sw} indicates their global exports. In the denominator, X_{wd} and X_{wy} represent the world's exports to a country pair and to the world, respectively.

$$TII = \frac{\sum_{sd} X_{sd} / \sum_{sw} X_{sw}}{\sum_{wd} X_{wd} / \sum_{wy} X_{wy}}$$

The summarised results for the country-pairs in Table 4, as obtained from ADB (undated), indicate that in 2014, China has TII figures greater than 1 for all ASEAN partners. In other words, China and the ASEAN partners' bilateral trade flows as a share of the world trade is relatively more and is generally increasing. Stated alternatively, it can be said that the rising TCI has contributed to the 'intensity' of the trade relationship in the post-FTA formation period. On the other hand, for India in 2014, the trade relation is 'non-intense' for four countries, namely, Cambodia, Lao PDR, the Philippines and Thailand. The deeper reach of Chinese exports in the ASEAN market as compared to India is clearly observed.

Table 4: Trade Intensity Index for China and India with ASEAN Countries

Partner	*China*			*India*		
	2005	*2010*	*2014*	*2005*	*2010*	*2014*
Brunei	0.507	0.862	1.000	0.398	1.014	2.814
Cambodia	1.184	0.957	1.179	0.293	0.236	0.295
Indonesia	1.343	1.359	1.414	2.045	2.354	2.423
Lao PDR	1.127	2.024	2.642	0.250	0.285	0.499
Malaysia	1.604	1.738	1.669	1.101	1.159	1.410
Myanmar	2.582	2.891	4.667	7.751	4.701	2.349
Philippines	2.242	1.850	2.051	0.532	0.415	0.469
Singapore	1.487	1.174	1.136	2.205	1.748	1.326
Thailand	1.431	1.445	1.384	0.846	0.861	0.969
Vietnam	1.776	1.847	2.122	1.008	1.107	1.306

Source: Obtained by the authors from ADB ARIC (undated) data.

Integration Scenario: Deeper Association in Production Networks?

A major part of the growth in the trade flows between China, India and ASEAN countries can be explained by the rise in trade in raw materials, intermediate products and parts and components, given the growing IPN integration across firms. The rising IPNs will be reflected through the reported simultaneous export and import flows between any given country pairs across product categories—a phenomenon known as 'intra-industry trade' in trade literature. For understanding the intermediate production integration between the FTA partners, the bilateral IIT indices among them have been calculated with help of the *Corrected Grubel and Lloyd index* (1975), which adjusts for the aggregate trade imbalance. The Grubel-Lloyd formula for calculating the IIT index of country j for industry i could be written as follows:

$$GLC = \frac{\sum_i (X_{ij} + M_{ij}) - \sum_i |X_{ij} - M_{ij}|}{\sum_i (X_{ij} + M_{ij}) - \left|\sum_i X_{ij} - \sum_i M_{ij}\right|} \times 100$$

Here X_{ij} and M_{ij} denote the value of export and imports of country j (China and India, in the current context) with the ASEAN partners at HS 4-digit level respectively. The IIT index could vary between 0 and 100. It is evident from the formula that when exports are exactly equal to imports, i.e., the entire trade is explained by IIT, the value of the index is 100. A higher IIT implies intense trade flows between two countries in final products as well as in parts and components and intermediate products, thereby signifying deepening of IPNs.

On the other hand, when either the export or import is zero, then the index is also zero, which means that the IIT no longer exists. In other words, the entire proportion of trade is then explained by 'inter-industry trade', signifying that the two countries are rather specialising in complementary sectors.

The calculated IIT indices are summarised in Table 5 and the following conclusions emerge. First, both China and India generally witnessed a rise in bilateral IIT indices over 2005-2015 with ASEAN partners, indicating a greater volume of trade within product categories, including in intermediate products and parts and components. This indicates a deepening reach of the ASEAN IPNs in China and India as well. Second, Brunei, Cambodia, Lao PDR and Myanmar displayed lower IIT indices with both China and India, signifying that their integration in the value chains is still at a moderate level. Third, the bigger economies, namely, Indonesia, Malaysia, the Philippines, Singapore and Thailand are characterised by a higher level of bilateral IIT. Interestingly, India's IIT has increased over the period for Indonesia and Thailand, while the IIT figures for these countries have declined with respect to China. Finally, Vietnam has witnessed a rise in IIT with both China and India, which reflects its growing integration in value chains with Chinese and Indian firms.

Table 5: Intra-Industry Trade Index for China and India with ASEAN Countries

Partner	*China*			*India*		
	2005	*2010*	*2015*	*2005*	*2010*	*2015*
Brunei	0.01	0.04	0.87	2.17	0.16	0.36
Cambodia	11.25	9.92	23.94	8.96	0.22	4.57
Indonesia	24.58	13.88	15.96	11.71	10.07	18.63
Lao PDR	1.68	0.65	1.30	1.37	0.22	1.33
Malaysia	40.97	36.63	24.98	20.15	19.66	24.07
Myanmar	1.02	1.41	7.95	0.24	1.24	0.47
Philippines	34.15	24.31	21.80	9.67	14.29	18.53
Singapore	43.28	51.45	51.76	21.00	52.27	33.42
Thailand	39.18	37.10	29.39	19.77	31.96	32.18
Vietnam	10.25	27.68	37.68	10.55	9.10	13.75

Source: Calculated by the authors from Trade Map (undated) data.

The overall IIT indices reported in Table 5 however mask the dynamics at the sectoral level. Hence, there is a need to understand whether China and India have been able to effectively participate in the ASEAN IPNs in recent times. UNESCAP (2011) notes that Asian IPNs have considerably deepened in engineering and machinery sectors in general, and in automobile and transport equipment, IT products, textile and garments sectors in particular.

In Tables 6-8, the regional contribution in exports for three major industries witnessing IPN integration (electrical machinery and apparatus, transport equipment and textile, garments and leather) are compared for 2000 and 2011 by drawing data from the Organisation for Economic Co-operation and Development (OECD) Trade in Value-Added (TIVA) database on origin of value added in gross exports (OECD, undated). While exporting a final product, a country may source the necessary raw materials, parts and components and support services either from within the nation or from abroad and undertake the necessary value addition on them before exporting the final product in a due course of time.

A rise in the domestic value added contribution by the home country (i.e., percentage contribution of a country in own exports) implies strengthening of the domestic supplier network (backward integration) in that sector, while a decline implies that the exporters are increasingly relying on imported raw materials, parts and components and service link supports from abroad. The latter then indicates greater integration with regional IPNs. The database arrives at the TIVA figures by comparing and matching the trade and input-output related data for more than 60 countries across the world. The TIVA data, thus arrived at, is reported for seven years, namely, 1995, 2000, 2005, 2008, 2009, 2010 and 2011.

In the present context, the Chinese and Indian export scenario in 2000 and 2011 is compared with five ASEAN countries (Indonesia, Malaysia, Singapore, Thailand and Vietnam), and the source country of value addition for their exports provides interesting insights. As noted earlier, the analysis has been conducted for three manufacturing sectors, which witness significant incidence of IIT and extended IPNs. 2000 represents a period before the formation of ASEAN-China and ASEAN-India FTAs, while the integration effects can be observed in 2011.

In the table, the figures for exporting countries in columns represent the source of value addition in percentage terms either in the home country or in partner countries (arranged in rows). So, in Table 6, the interpretation for China's entries reveal that while in 2000, domestic producers in China contributed 31.80 percent of value addition in the country's total export of electrical machinery and apparatus, the corresponding figure in 2011 had increased to 51.38 percent.

Table 6 reveals the scenario for the electrical machinery and apparatus sector.

First, domestic contribution has increased in China, Indonesia, Singapore and Thailand while declining in India, Malaysia and Vietnam. Second, the share of ASEAN in China's total export has declined in percentage terms, while the same has increased for India. Third, the value-addition contribution of Japan has declined in ASEAN countries and China, while it has increased in India. Fourth, the contribution of South Korea has increased in India, Malaysia, Singapore, Thailand and Vietnam, but declined in China and Indonesia. Finally, the share of China's value addition has sharply increased in the exports of all ASEAN countries, while the value addition from India has been relatively modest.

Table 6: Origin of Value Added in Gross Export from Electrical Machinery and Apparatus Sector (in per cent)

Source Country	*Exporting Countries*						
	2000						
	China	*India*	*Indonesia*	*Malaysia*	*Singapore*	*Thailand*	*Vietnam*
Brunei	0.04	0.00	0.04	0.04	0.04	0.14	0.04
Cambodia	0.01	0.00	0.00	0.01	0.01	0.01	0.01
China	31.80	0.38	1.06	1.53	1.81	2.16	1.93
India	0.34	80.51	0.69	0.52	0.44	0.43	0.48
Indonesia	0.96	0.12	68.79	1.60	3.46	0.94	0.90
Japan	15.23	0.86	5.36	16.01	10.27	15.20	13.14
Malaysia	0.97	0.21	1.15	39.38	3.24	1.94	1.14
Philippines	0.31	0.02	0.08	0.67	0.46	0.54	0.20
Singapore	0.78	0.25	2.02	3.71	45.64	2.07	3.46
South Korea	4.99	0.33	1.46	2.67	1.38	1.87	3.84
Thailand	0.82	0.12	0.82	1.43	1.81	45.87	1.53
Vietnam	0.18	0.02	0.13	0.24	0.14	0.87	51.07
ASEAN	4.07	0.74	73.03	47.09	54.80	52.39	58.36
	2011						
Brunei	0.04	0.05	0.16	0.08	0.04	0.07	0.15
Cambodia	0.01	0.00	0.00	0.01	0.02	0.03	0.02
China	51.38	3.52	3.53	8.07	6.38	7.94	14.03
India	1.04	66.04	1.07	1.45	1.48	0.88	1.13
Indonesia	0.82	0.58	74.23	3.12	3.96	1.89	1.64
Japan	7.98	1.39	2.71	9.20	4.72	10.42	8.89
Malaysia	0.94	0.43	1.14	37.78	2.28	1.91	1.54
Philippines	0.42	0.13	0.17	0.47	0.59	0.66	0.54
Singapore	0.66	0.46	1.22	3.03	47.45	0.93	1.17
South Korea	3.68	0.89	1.42	2.65	1.66	2.20	6.13
Thailand	0.67	0.34	1.00	1.93	0.87	46.58	2.72
Vietnam	0.20	0.09	0.16	0.44	0.27	0.43	33.61
ASEAN	3.75	2.08	78.09	46.86	55.48	52.50	41.39

Source: Constructed by the authors from OECD TIVA database (undated).

Table 7 depicts the scenario for textiles, leather and footwear products. First, domestic contribution has increased in China, Indonesia and Vietnam while the same has declined in India, Malaysia, Singapore and Thailand. Second, the share of value addition by ASEAN has increased in both China and India's total exports in percentage terms. Third, the share of Japan has declined in the exports of ASEAN countries and China, while it has increased for India. Fourth, the contribution of South Korea has declined in the exports of China and all ASEAN countries, but has increased in India. Finally, the share of China's value addition has sharply increased across all ASEAN countries, while the same for India has been relatively lower.

Table 7: Origin of Value Added in Gross Export from Textiles, Textile Products, Leather and Footwear Sector (in per cent)

Source Country	*Exporting Countries*						
				2000			
	China	*India*	*Indonesia*	*Malaysia*	*Singapore*	*Thailand*	*Vietnam*
Brunei	0.02	0.00	0.02	0.03	0.28	0.12	0.03
Cambodia	0.01	0.00	0.00	0.02	0.41	0.01	0.02
China	61.82	0.32	0.96	2.52	4.69	1.44	2.11
India	0.55	90.40	0.49	1.35	1.67	0.57	0.41
Indonesia	0.65	0.10	78.15	2.54	5.31	0.51	0.86
Japan	7.26	0.30	2.65	6.61	3.93	3.27	6.92
Malaysia	0.51	0.13	0.69	55.86	7.66	0.58	0.57
Philippines	0.08	0.01	0.07	0.23	0.22	0.09	0.09
Singapore	0.39	0.16	1.09	3.06	44.83	0.74	0.89
South Korea	6.47	0.24	2.75	2.04	2.51	1.16	11.31
Thailand	0.50	0.11	0.53	1.83	1.74	78.26	1.33
Vietnam	0.13	0.01	0.12	0.33	0.42	0.18	53.32
ASEAN	2.27	0.53	80.67	63.91	60.86	80.48	57.09
				2011			
Brunei	0.02	0.02	0.19	0.05	0.03	0.03	0.15
Cambodia	0.02	0.00	0.01	0.04	0.07	0.04	0.08
China	73.52	2.57	2.80	10.61	11.91	3.76	7.12
India	0.86	80.17	0.57	2.23	2.40	1.14	0.99
Indonesia	0.66	0.39	81.75	2.66	3.41	0.91	1.03
Japan	2.62	0.65	1.04	4.25	2.43	2.38	3.33
Malaysia	0.45	0.30	0.78	50.76	2.88	0.77	0.99
Philippines	0.13	0.13	0.11	0.32	0.26	0.19	0.33
Singapore	0.35	0.51	0.75	2.28	44.23	0.88	0.90
South Korea	2.08	0.49	1.94	1.34	1.27	0.84	3.90
Thailand	0.58	0.32	0.52	1.82	1.00	74.13	1.68
Vietnam	0.28	0.05	0.17	0.79	0.46	0.30	62.53
ASEAN	2.49	1.73	84.29	58.72	52.34	77.24	67.68

Source: Constructed by the authors from OECD TIVA database (undated)

Table 8 summarises the scenario for the transport equipment sector. First, domestic contribution has increased in China, Indonesia and Singapore while the same has declined in India, Malaysia, Thailand and Vietnam. Second, the share of ASEAN in China's total export has declined in percentage terms, while the same has increased for India. Third, the value-addition contribution of Japan has declined in the exports of all ASEAN countries and China, while it has increased in India. Fourth, the contribution of South Korea has increased in India, Indonesia, Singapore and Thailand, but has declined in China, Malaysia and Vietnam. Finally, the share of China's value addition has sharply increased across all ASEAN countries, while once again, India's value addition has been relatively modest.

Table 8: Origin of Value Added in Gross Export from Transport Equipment Sector (in per cent)

Source Country	*Exporting Countries*						
				2000			
	China	*India*	*Indonesia*	*Malaysia*	*Singapore*	*Thailand*	*Vietnam*
Brunei	0.02	0.00	0.05	0.04	0.03	0.13	0.06
Cambodia	0.01	0.00	0.00	0.01	0.01	0.01	0.02
China	57.38	0.40	0.87	1.14	1.04	1.16	8.50
India	0.18	80.81	0.32	0.45	0.26	0.37	0.34
Indonesia	0.38	0.11	72.54	1.06	1.53	0.70	0.91
Japan	10.18	1.04	6.34	12.20	8.77	21.50	9.28
Malaysia	0.52	0.19	0.95	53.69	1.94	1.22	0.89
Philippines	0.15	0.02	0.10	0.25	0.19	1.01	0.16
Singapore	0.48	0.26	2.04	2.46	56.23	1.32	2.29
South Korea	2.48	0.32	0.92	3.20	3.93	1.39	7.12
Thailand	0.39	0.12	0.38	0.95	0.50	48.75	1.73
Vietnam	0.11	0.01	0.20	0.17	0.09	0.26	45.78
ASEAN	2.05	0.71	76.26	58.63	60.54	53.41	51.84
				2011			
Brunei	0.02	0.04	0.06	0.06	0.02	0.08	0.14
Cambodia	0.00	0.00	0.00	0.02	0.01	0.04	0.02
China	70.03	3.67	3.04	6.61	3.47	5.46	10.55
India	0.52	68.00	0.72	1.22	1.15	0.98	0.98
Indonesia	0.45	0.52	75.91	2.74	0.92	2.33	1.58
Japan	5.16	1.49	4.50	8.28	2.57	13.48	7.99
Malaysia	0.43	0.39	0.69	46.79	1.05	1.30	1.38
Philippines	0.17	0.12	0.27	0.38	0.24	1.04	0.44
Singapore	0.38	0.51	0.92	2.01	60.73	1.22	1.08
South Korea	2.01	0.99	1.11	2.10	4.17	2.23	5.14
Thailand	0.33	0.32	1.65	2.24	0.26	45.12	2.03
Vietnam	0.10	0.07	0.14	0.47	0.09	0.34	41.99
ASEAN	1.89	1.98	79.65	54.69	63.32	51.47	48.66

Source: Constructed by the authors from OECD TIVA database (undated).

Conclusion

Both China and India entered into FTAs with ASEAN with the objective of merchandise trade promotion. China got the beginner's advantage with an early conclusion of the negotiations, with the entry of the ASEAN-China FTA into force in 2005. Bilateral trade also received a boost from the Trade in Services agreement subsequently, as the service link costs could effectively be integrated. The aggressive negotiating strategy for the Chinese has been to secure a 'market economy' status on the one hand, and to capture a vibrant market like ASEAN on the other. To gain the desired access, China did not shy away from 'front-loading' deep commitments for ASEAN exports in its market.

India conversely, proceeded cautiously in the negotiations, given the perceived threat from ASEAN to several key sectors (e.g., palm oil, fisheries) and the negotiations took a long time to conclude. By the time the ASEAN-India FTA came into force in 2010, Chinese players were already established in the ASEAN market. The Trade in Services and Investment Agreement between seven ASEAN countries and India came into force in 2015, while the corresponding agreement between China and ASEAN has been in effect since 2007. Finally, the fact that China had moved along the path of liberalisation a decade before India, differentiates the efficiency level and outward-orientation in the two countries. Chinese firms, which were already present in the ASEAN market from the early 1990s, were both efficient and able to benefit the most and to consolidate their positions from the formalised FTA, i.e., from the ASEAN cutting down tariff barriers and introducing various trade facilitation measures.

A couple of observations can be drawn from the analysis. First, while both China and India have improved their trade relationship with ASEAN, the flow dynamics has differed. While China witnessed an overall trade deficit vis-à-vis ASEAN over 2001-11, it started enjoying a widening trade surplus from 2012. On the other hand, India has witnessed a trade deficit with ASEAN throughout 2001-15, and it has widened from 2013 onwards. Second, the TCI value for China with ASEAN is relatively higher vis-à-vis the corresponding figures for India, highlighting the underlying reason for the sharp rise of Chinese exports in the ASEAN market. As a result, the TII for China has also turned greater than 1 for all ASEAN countries. Third, the level of IIT is generally increasing between China and ASEAN, especially because it has gradually replaced Japan and South Korea in the value chains of the three sectors considered here. It has been noted that similar results follow in several other manufacturing sectors as well (Chakraborty 2016). This has been partly facilitated by the widespread presence of the Chinese diaspora and business community in Southeast Asia and successful harnessing of the resultant business links. Moreover, the enhanced physical connectivity linkages between China and ASEAN also facilitated the former's export flows. All these factors collectively enabled China to 'mature' its presence in the ASEAN IPNs.

By contrast, while India has been able to expand its presence in ASEAN IPNs across sectors, the participation level looks moderate in comparison with China in 2011. One underlying reason might be that the year signifies a period shortly after formation of the India-ASEAN FTA in 2010, and hence the full integration effects are perhaps not yet reflected in the trade data. The paucity of data points beyond 2011 therefore might be a reason behind the moderate 'deepening' trend for India with ASEAN, and the actual scenario might be rosier. It is expected that as in the case of China, with a full implementation of the FTA provisions, the conclusion of the Trade in Services agreement with ASEAN and the introduction of stronger trade facilitation measures, India's contributions to the ASEAN IPNs will rise further. However, it is less likely that India will be able to replace China in the ASEAN IPNs, the way China had replaced Japan earlier. One reason behind this modest expectation is that Indian firms on the average are relatively smaller compared to their Chinese counterparts, and therefore, advantages of scale are likely to remain in favour of the Chinese firms, at least in the medium run. Indian gains in the ASEAN market are, therefore, expected to come at the cost of Japan and South Korea, against whom the country can compete on the basis of cost advantages including labour. The verification of this hypothesis will be an interesting research question, once the TIVA data for 2012 onwards is released by the OECD.

REFERENCES

ASEAN Secretariat. n.d. 'Agreement on trade in goods of the framework agreement on comprehensive economic co-operation between the Association of Southeast Asian Nations and the People's Republic of China', http://www.asean.org/16646.htm (accessed 5 May 2016).

Asian Development Bank. n.d. 'Integration Indicators', Asia Regional Integration Center (ADB-ARIC), https://aric.adb.org/integrationindicators (accessed 5 May 2016).

Calvo-Pardo, Hector, Caroline Freund and Emanuel Ornelas. 2009. 'The ASEAN Free Trade Agreement: Impact on Trade Flows and External Trade Barriers', World Bank Policy Research Paper No. 4960, Washington DC.

Chaisse, Julien and Debashis Chakraborty. 2005. 'Identifying Mutual Interest Areas at WTO: A Sino-Indian Joint Perspective', *China Report*, Vol. 41, No. 3, 267–88.

Chakraborty, Anushree and Debashis Chakraborty. 2015. 'What SAARC can learn from ASEAN: Past Experiences and Future Strategies', *Indonesian Quarterly*, Vol. 43, No. 1, 55-76.

Chakraborty, Debashis. 2016. 'Deepening of International Production Networks in ASEAN Countries: An Overview of the Integration Indicators', in M. Kaul and A. Chakraborty (Eds), *India's Look East to Act East Policy: Tracking the Opportunities and Challenges in The Indo-Pacific*, pp. 42-67, New Delhi: Pentagon.

Chakraborty, Debashis. 2014. 'The Upcoming Indo-ASEAN CECA: Of Great Expectations and Areas of Concern', *China Report*, 50(3): 259-276.

Chakraborty, Debashis and Anmesh Kumar. 2012. 'ASEAN and China: New Dimensions in Economic Engagement', *China Report*, 48(3): 327–349.

Chakraborty, Debashis and Dipankar Sengupta. 2010. 'Integration Experience and Trade Performance of the Indo-ASEAN FTA: A Review of Issues', in P. Gugler and J. Chaisse (Eds.), *Competitiveness of the ASEAN Countries: Corporate and Regulatory Drivers*, Cheltenham: Edward Elgar, pp. 207-237.

Government of India. 2015. 'Reply of the Minister of State for the external Affairs Gen. Dr. V.K. Singh (Retd.) to a question in Lok Sabha', Press Information Bureau, 23 December, http://pib.nic.in/newsite/PrintRelease.aspx?relid=133837 (accessed on 19 June 2016).

Grubel, Herbert G and P.J. Lloyd. 1975. *Intra-industry Trade: The Theory and Measurement of International Trade in Differentiated Products*, The Macmillan Press Limited.

Hayter, Roger and David W. Edgington. 2004. 'Flying Geese in Asia: The Impacts of Japanese MNCs as a source of industrial learning', *Tijdschrift voor Economische en Sociale Geografie*, 95(1): 3–26.

International Trade Centre. n.d. 'Trade Map database', http://www.trademap.org/Index.aspx (accessed on 8 May 2016).

Menon, Jayant and Sharad Bhandari. 2006. 'The Mekong Region Foreign Direct Investment', Manila: Asian Development Bank.

Organization for Economic Cooperation and Development. n.d. 'Trade in Value Added (TIVA) database', http://stats.oecd.org/Index.aspx?DataSetCode=TIVA_OECD_WTO (accessed on 5 May 2014).

Panitchpakdi, Supachai and Mark L. Clifford. 2002. *China and the WTO: Changing China, Changing World Trade*, Singapore: John Wiley & Sons (Asia) Pvt. Ltd.

Plummer, Michael, Peter J. Morgan and Ganeshan Wignaraja (eds). 2016. *Connecting Asia: Infrastructure for Integrating South and Southeast Asia*, Cheltenham: Edward Elgar.

Saint-Mezard, Isabelle. 2003. 'The Look East Policy: An Economic Perspective', in Frederic Grare and Amitabh Mattoo (Eds.). *Beyond the Rhetoric: The Economics of India's Look East Policy*. New Delhi: Centre de Sciences Humanines and Manohar.

United Nations Economic and Social Commission for Asia and the Pacific. 2014. 'Asia-Pacific Trade and Investment Report 2014: Recent Trends and Developments', New York: UNESCAP.

United Nations Economic and Social Commission for Asia and the Pacific. 2011. 'Fighting Irrelevance: The Role of Regional Trade Agreements in International Production Networks in Asia', New York: UNESCAP.

Wignaraja, Ganeshan. 2013. 'Regional Trade Agreements and Enterprises in Southeast Asia', Tokyo: Asian Development Bank Institute.

Wong, Marn-Heong and Marie Isabelle Pellan. 2012. 'Trade Facilitation: The Way Forward for ASEAN and Its FTA Partners', ERIA Policy Brief No. 2012-04, Jakarta: Economic Research Institute for ASEAN and East Asia.

World Trade Organisation. 2001. 'Protocol of Accession: Accession of the People's Republic of China, Document No. WT/L/432, 23 November, Geneva: WTO.

Xiao, Jun. 2010. 'ASEAN–China FTA: A Pragmatic Approach to Regulating Services and Investment', in Philippe Gugler and Julien Chaisse (eds), Competitiveness of the ASEAN Countries: Corporate and Regulatory Drivers, Cheltenham: Edward Elgar, 237–58.

10

Vietnam's Economic Relations with India and China: The Impact of the Coming Mega FTAs

Aravind Yelery

Mega Free Trade Agreements (FTAs) are underway in the Asia-Pacific that are set to affect regional integration. While Europe and Africa are left out of these major trade arrangements, Asia occupies the centre-stage and within Asia emerging economies like India, China and Vietnam are leading the whole momentum. It is also important to notice that the already existing regional set-ups such as ASEAN are set to play a critical role. The two prominent mega FTAs, which are about to change the definition of regional economic integration, include the Trans-Pacific Partnership (TPP)[1] and the Regional Comprehensive Economic Partnership (RCEP).[2] Both the trade frameworks are conceptualised around the idea of synergising trade complementarities and facilitating the vertical movements of goods and services without any reference to the globalisation of production and supplies. While there is now uncertainty over the TPP following the victory of Donald Trump in the United States and Vietnam's National Assembly has itself put the ratification on hold, it is nevertheless important to understand whether these mega FTAs and their guiding principles are going to help integration or disturb the existing trade set-up by dividing them in overlapping zones of new arrangements and new standards of trade and commerce. Vietnam's potential participation in the TPP and RCEP are likely to build and re-adjust existing trade relations in the region and economies like China are among the first to notice the big change.

Vietnam's Rise as an 'Asian Tiger' and its Role in the Regional Economy

Vietnam's rise as one of the 'rising tigers' is a fairly new phenomenon, but something long overdue. National independence and reunification, economic development and a series of complex reforms have transformed Vietnam into a country with phenomenal socio-economic development, industrialisation and modernisation. Post-unification, the country progressed rapidly irrespective of having 90 per cent of the population employed in agriculture. The reforms which started soon after the unification, had to mainly deal with the problems associated with land management, outdated technology and underdeveloped fiscal policies. Vietnam faced problems, which it inherited from the past involving the divide between a vertically spread geography and economic activity, and between North and South Vietnam resulting from colonialism. The long war also brought about the destruction of natural resources, infrastructure, population and social structure and delayed the post-war recovery and reconstruction, making them arduous and difficult at times. The economic crisis helped Vietnam to look beyond the narrow foreign policy perspective and pursue a wider and much effective economic statecraft. In order to solve the economic crisis, the Communist Party of Vietnam (CPV) started pursuing economic reforms and stressed more on state regulations, pursuing its own version of socialism, which also included the socialist transformation of southern Vietnam. The comprehensive reforms started after 1986, when the 6th CPV Congress put forward a comprehensive reform policy, which also included diversifying the ownership of the economy.

While carrying out the spatial economic reforms, Vietnam followed China's model of reforms. Primarily relying on a rapidly growing population, cheap labour and free trade agreements, Vietnam became a part of the global supply chain. Vietnam's rapid growth comes from its economic competitiveness and innovation policies and an open attitude towards economic challenges as opportunities. Vietnam's rapid rise in economic competitiveness also benefited its neighbours as well as the region.

The Chairman of the Global Trends research and advisory organisation, Patrick Dixon, explains that among the most common reasons—Vietnam's large population, low labour costs, promotion of urbanisation policy—there developed a strong capacity to absorb foreign direct investments (FDI) which, in other words, facilitated Vietnam's rise as the world's factory (Dixon 2012). This was not confined only to industrial machineries but proliferated into areas of sophisticated brands, which moved their production bases to Vietnam. For example, Samsung's Vietnam facility has become one of the most important mobile phone production bases for the company. The 2013 World Economic Forum (WEF) released the '2013-2014 Global Competitiveness Report' in which Vietnam's global competitiveness ranking rose to 5th among 148 countries. The report applauded Vietnam's macroeconomic environment and the efforts by the government (Klaus 2013: 15). In the last few years, inflation returned to single-digit level, the quality of transport systems and energy infrastructure improved substantially and as a result, the WEF indicator for macro environment upgraded Vietnam to the 19th rank (in 2012, Vietnam was 87th) (Klaus 2013: 15). With an economy of US$191.5 billion (Trade Administration 2016) and a strategic location, Vietnam has turned into a centre of dynamic economic activity. For Vietnam, the experiment with the reform process resulted in something bigger and bolder. But there is something more which comes along in the form of baggage, competition and conflict.

Vietnam's Trade Ties with India and China

Vietnam developed its economic model by largely following what the Chinese did soon after they opened up the economy in 1991. It is, therefore, not a surprise that the Vietnamese economy is often called 'little China' to underline the imprint of China on Vietnam. In Southeast Asia, the Vietnamese economy stands strong and is ahead of many other regional economies attracting the bigger economies trading in and out of the region. For example, in 2015, Vietnam's GDP growth was 6.7 per cent, which was higher than that of Indonesia (4.8 per cent), Thailand (2.8 per cent), Malaysia (5 per cent), Singapore (2 per cent), and Philippines (5.9 per cent) (ADB 2016: 22). Hence, it is not a surprise that other developing economies in Asia are trying to find ways to source growth by aligning with Vietnam. Both India and China have considerable engagement with Vietnam and both view Vietnam as a potential partner in their growth trajectories.

India-Vietnam

India and Vietnam have developed their partnerships in areas beyond defence cooperation. Especially in recent times, India's policies towards Southeast Asia remained consistent with its overall interests. India being a Free Trade Agreement (FTA) partner of ASEAN, which also includes Vietnam, the Indian market turned accessible as well as offered a wide range of opportunities. Today, India and Vietnam cooperate with each other through a number of regional and sub-regional mechanisms which include regional forums such as ASEAN, East Asia Summit (EAS) and a sub-regional set-up under the Mekong Ganga Cooperation as well as at a larger global networks of organisations such as the Asia Europe Meeting (ASEM) besides the United Nations (UN) and the World Trade Organization (WTO) (MEA 2016a).

India has consistently supported Vietnam's efforts to reach out to various world forums. To note a special case, while Vietnam is being treated as a Non-market Economy (NME) by the WTO and its member countries, India accepted Vietnam as a Market Economy. This means that India accepted Vietnam's commitment towards meeting guidelines consistent with the WTO and helping global trade. Moreover, commercial engagements are on the rise and India is among the top ten trading partners of Vietnam while Vietnam is ranked 28th among India's trading partners (MEA 2016a). Since India and Vietnam became strategic partners in 2007, the economic ties between the two countries have multiplied quickly. For example, within five years of the economic partnership, the total trade volume between India and Vietnam touched US$3.7 billion in 2012; an increase by 270 per cent compared to the 2007 trade volume of US$1 billion (Export-Import Bank of India 2013). In 2014, the total trade turnover amounted US$5.6 billion (India's export US$3.1 billion, import US$2.5 billion) (MEA 2016a). In 2015, the trade between two countries grew significantly with the total trade amounting to US$7.8 billion (Xuan 2016b).

Overall, the trade between India and Vietnam reflects balanced growth with neither country being threatened by trade deficits. Vietnam seems to be an ideal destination for Indian commercial engagements with options such as investments, services and manufacturing. Due to the price factor, Indian imports i.e. soybean, corn and pharmaceutical products are competitive in the Vietnamese market as compared to imports from other markets around the world (Ngo 2016: 115). India also perceives Vietnam as one of the important markets for its innovative products which include Information Communication Technologies (ICT), aircrafts, spacecraft and parts thereof, electrical, electronic equipment, machinery and instruments, biotechnology, thermal and nuclear energy, etc. (Export-Import bank of India 2013).

The economic relationship between India and Vietnam was further shaped by the present policies of the Indian government under the 'Act East' policy. During 2014—2016, high-ranking leaders including the President, the Prime Minister and Foreign Minister of India visited Vietnam, which indicates the rising importance of engagement between the two states. Indian Prime Minister Narendra Modi's visit to Hanoi in September 2016 was the first official trip to Vietnam by any Indian Prime Minister since Atal Bihari Vajpayee's 2001 visit. The official visit helped both countries to explore bilateral cooperation in the field of finance and capital. India has been instrumental in developing Vietnamese infrastructure and has consistently used lines of credit (LoC) as a prime medium of effective cooperation. During his visit, Prime Minister Modi formalised the cooperation between M/s Larsen & Toubro and Vietnam Border Guards, utilising the US$100 million LoC extended by India to Vietnam. In addition, he also announced a grant of US$5 million for the construction of an Army Software Park at the Telecommunications University in Nha Trang (MEA 2016b). So far, India has extended 17 LoCs worth more than US$165 million to Vietnam. The last major LoC extended by India was in July 2013 for US$19.5 million for the execution of a Nam Trai-IV hydropower project and the Binh Bo Pumping station (MEA 2016a).

China-Vietnam

China is the biggest trading partner of Vietnam and the initial experiments in Vietnam's tryst with the economic reform were openly derived from the Chinese experiences. Since the normalisation of relations between China and Vietnam in 1991, bilateral trade cooperation has gradually deepened. The total trade turnover between Vietnam and China increased more than 1,930 times, from US$30 million in 1991 to US$58.6 billion in 2014 (Na 2015) and further US$66.3 billion in 2015 (Xuan 2016a). It is expected that the China-Vietnam trade may surpass US$100 billion in 2016, and Vietnam will overtake Malaysia, becoming China's biggest trading partner in Southeast Asia (Xuan 2016a).

Although China influenced Vietnam's economy, mainly through trade and the influence varied depending on the period, economic relations have largely remained stable (Na 2015). Vietnam also showed interest in keeping the economic relations safe despite strategic differences over the issue of South China Sea. In 2008, Vietnam proposed the Comprehensive Strategic Cooperative

Partnership. The CPV's Central Committee General Secretary Nong Duc Manh even visited China to propose wider trade arrangements between the two countries (CARIGU 2015). In 2010, after arduous discussions of eight years and positive steps by Vietnam, the ASEAN–China Free Trade Area (ACFTA) came into reality. Though the ACFTA was collective, Vietnam's leadership showed more motivation in pursuing the agreement.

As far as the trade profile is concerned, Vietnam exports rice, coal, natural rubber, crude oil, and some agricultural products like vegetables, cassava, etc. to China but it earns less forex for Vietnam as it is increasingly paying against imported raw materials, machinery, and consumer goods from China. China is also the major source of imports in Vietnam and this includes machinery and equipment, textiles, building materials, household appliances, automobiles and agricultural products (Observatory of Economic Complexity-MIT 2014). Despite the gains brought by economic relations with China, there are still some problems that continue to persist. Trade deficit, which has increased since 2001, is a big problem directly affecting Vietnam's economy. Apart from the trade figures, in the first decade (1991-2001) of their bilateral economic relationship, China's FDI in Vietnam remained limited and does not show a substantial rise. Ha Thi Hong Van and Do Tien Sam in their empirical study 'China's Trade, FDI and Official Development Assistance (ODA) assistance to Vietnam', explain that the average value of China's FDI projects in Vietnam is US$2.7 million per project, while the average value of all FDI projects (against the total investments) in Vietnam is US$8.7 million per project (Ha and Do 2009). It is also pointed out that China's FDI projects involve minimum research and development and technological capability, and thus bring little effect on the technological advancement of Vietnamese industries (Ha and Do 2009). Chinese investments in Vietnam have remained relatively low compared to other regions where China invests. For example, as of December 2001, China had 110 projects with a total value of US$221 million in Vietnam. Currently, this number has gone up to 1,346 with a total registered capital of US$10.4 billion, making China the 9th largest investor in Vietnam (*Vietnam Plus* 2016).

China is still the largest trading partner of Vietnam and while there is a growing trade imbalance, the situation is also changing quite rapidly as Vietnam is acquiring comparative advantage against Chinese companies over the issue of labour, cost and accessibility to markets. On the other hand, the Chinese engagement with Vietnam is getting more mature as the Chinese companies compete in Vietnam and the Vietnamese companies become aware of information on markets, consumption needs and the international legal systems and raise the standards of doing business with Chinese companies.

Mega FTAs and Vietnam

Mega FTAs in the larger Asia-Pacific are set to affect the existing trade relations within and beyond Asia. Countries like Vietnam and other ASEAN members with high levels of growth values have the potential to shape these mega FTAs. These mega FTAs are selective in their partnerships and include countries from the top end of manufacturing and consumption as well as middle and lower rung countries struggling to adapt to the global architecture of finance, production and supply. It is not a surprise that the resurgent Southeast Asian economies are at the centre of these arrangements and countries like Vietnam, whose competitive minimum wage and low costs of utilities boosted foreign direct investment in the manufacturing sector, play a vital role. While Europe and Africa are left out of these major trade arrangements, some of the Asian economies like India, China and Vietnam will be subject to impacts. The two prominent mega FTAs, i.e., the TPP and the RCEP, aim at synergising the trade complementarities and facilitating the vertical movements of goods and services without being compromised by trade protectionism (ADB 2015). While both the mega FTA set-ups look beyond the immediate neighbourhood and create a large geography being synchronised across the value and production chains, there will certainly be challenges for the existing models of trade between countries from both the RCEP and the TPP.

The summary of the negotiations among the TPP countries' ministers spells out intent to promote 'economic growth; support the creation and retention of jobs; enhance innovation, productivity and competitiveness; raise living standards; reduce poverty; and promote transparency, good governance, and enhanced labor and environmental protections' (Office of the United States Trade Representative 2015). This would eventually bring in stricter guidelines in trade arrangements among member countries.

In this context, it is important to understand whether these mega FTAs and their guiding principles are going to help integration or disturb the existing trade set-up by dividing them in overlapping zones of new arrangements and new standards of trade and commerce. Vietnam is a good example of how the economies from the RCEP will be worried in the wake of TPP-related norms. The TPP would require Vietnam to treat its member countries equal and give preference to them over the other non-TPP competitors. For example, the 30 broad categories of cooperation—trade in goods continuing thorough customs and trade facilitation; sanitary and phytosanitary measures; technical barriers to trade; trade remedies; investment; services; electronic commerce; government procurement; intellectual property; labour; environment, among others—would require Vietnam to respect the TPP agreements to lower or eliminate the tariffs, remove protective policies, end subsidies and accept the competition from future member countries based on the ethics of standardisation of rules and treatments.

With the conclusion of TPP negotiations in October 2015, Vietnam received a much-needed momentum to pursue liberalisation policies and help the government to monetise it for political benefits. TPP brings Vietnam both opportunities as well as challenges for its economy, but experts and industry insiders are upbeat about the benefits that will follow from what has been called the most ambitious trade pact in a generation (*Tuoiyre News* 2015). It is estimated that the TPP will expand Vietnam's Gross Domestic Product (GDP) by US$23.5 billion in 2020 and US$33.5 billion in 2025 (*Vietnam News* 2015). As it is claimed, once completed, the TPP will cover 40 per cent of the global economy and can potentially add US$300 billion to the global GDP per year (Dang 2015). Meanwhile, Vietnam's economy has developed stronger relations with the regional countries and utilised these to grow consistently. From 2010 to 2015, Vietnam's exports have doubled in the manufacturing sector. At present, Vietnam's main exports include telephone and spare parts (19 per cent of the total shipments) and textiles (14 per cent) and the US is the major export market for Vietnam while in 2015, US$7.1 billion worth of goods were exported from the US to Vietnam (International Trade Administration 2016). As far as its export markets are concerned, it is clear that Vietnam's top export market is the US (20.7 per cent of the total exports) followed by China (10.6 percent) and Japan (8.7 per cent) (Trading Economics 2016). Vietnam looks forward to pursuing the export-oriented strategy to bolster its economic performance. In addition to agriculture and manufacturing sectors, Vietnam's textiles and apparel industry is also looking for expanding access to developed economies including the US and Japan. Vietnam's relations with the TPP economies are expected to yield larger economic benefits, especially to the country's manufacturing sector. To put it in context, as the TPP signatory countries account for around 40 per cent of Vietnam's total exports, the TPP will not only accelerate Vietnam's exports to the TPP member countries, but also increase the country's total export by an additional US$68 billion by 2025 (Sieburg 2016).

At present, the trade deficit is moderate and Vietnam is interested in keeping it under control as it finds multiple ways to forge economic partnerships. But just as Vietnam expects to expand its export basket, the TPP member countries would also expect duty-free exports to Vietnam in the sectors like chemicals, information and communication technologies, machinery, forest products and textile and apparel etc. (International Trade Administration 2016).

Impact of Mega FTAs on Vietnam's Economic Relations with India and China

The mega FTAs have potential to rearrange existing regional trade engagements and affect the traditional links that Vietnam, India and China enjoy at present. Since Vietnam is a part of both TPP and RCEP, China and India may find it difficult to keep their trade interests secured in the wake of full-blown trading alignments under these mega FTAs. Although, neither mega FTA restricts its member countries from trading outside the pool of members, the trading agenda does affect the trading abilities of its member countries by implying restrictive boundaries of trade under a preferential set-up.

While the TPP concluded its initial discussion over tariff rates and had plans to intensify trade within the bloc, RCEP is still stuck with tariff conflicts. Moreover, other issues involving different levels of development of the participating countries as well as debates regarding the forms of flexibility including provision for special and differential treatment, plus additional flexibility to the least-developed ASEAN member states, consistent with the existing ASEAN+1 FTAs, as applicable, is seen as a reason for reaching the consensus (Australian Department of Foreign Affairs and Trade 2012). Although, RCEP guidelines over negotiations do clearly stipulate that 'the ASEAN+1 FTAs and the bilateral/plurilateral FTAs between and among participating countries will continue to exist and no provision in the RCEP agreement will detract from the terms and conditions in these bilateral/plurilateral FTAs between and among the participating countries', it also implies that integrations be synced within the bloc. The above guideline also ensures that the existing set of trade ties between Vietnam-India and Vietnam-China remains the same and additionally facilitates developing regional supply chains aligned with the global network of production.

Looking at Vietnam's present trade strategies, it gives importance to developing export-oriented economic relations with countries which benefit it directly such as the US. As far as China-Vietnam trade is concerned, Vietnam may rethink its trade policies with China. Given its increasing trade deficit with China, it is not a surprise that Vietnam finds it more meaningful to do business with the US and engage in TPP negotiations. Even though the RCEP may help Vietnam to better integrate in the region, in the long run, due to the need to look for markets away from the ASEAN and in order to diversify its pool of business, Vietnam may prefer to align more actively with the non-RCEP trade set-ups and obligations mentioned.

India, which has improved its engagement with Vietnam over the last decade, is also facing pressure to maintain stable economic relations with Vietnam. In the wake of preferential treatment among TPP countries, the non-TPP countries, which are dependent or integrated with the TPP economies, might be pushed away. Moreover, in order to diversify the businesses, the pre-TPP or -RCEP economies would engage in intense competition instead of cooperating and reciprocating with each other. To better illustrate these complexities further, let us look at the textile industry as a case. India's dominant exports to the West have been textiles – the textile sector in India is one of the largest contributors to its exports with approximately 11 per cent of total exports (India Brand Equity Foundation 2016). The textiles industry is also labour-intensive and is one of the largest employers. Meanwhile, Vietnam's textile sector is currently selling 70 per cent of its products to the TPP countries and the share, it is hoped, will be doubled after the TPP trade pact is in place (*Tuoiyre News* 2015). Hence, the TPP could disturb India's prospects as it would end up competing with Vietnam for the US market since when it comes to the export of readymade garments and made-ups, the US alone accounts for over 30 per cent of India's total exports (Singh 2016) and as per TPP negotiations, the TPP member countries will get preferential access in the US market vis-à-vis exporters from non-TPP member countries like India. This will put India's apparel exports (to the US) at a disadvantage as the US import duties on apparels are quite high with the average duty ranging around 7.9 per cent (Kumar 2016).

The negotiation over the provision of 'yarn forward' is also a factor of worry not only for India but also for China. As per the proposed format of the 'yarn forward', only the fabric produced from yarn made by a TPP country would qualify for the trade agreement's duty-free status (Barbour-Lacey 2015). Interestingly, Vietnamese factories use Chinese-made fabrics in their products and the rule has already left Chinese yarn manufactures and other textile producers in deep shock. On the one hand, the provision will ensure that the trade benefits of the TPP only apply to signatory countries and not the outside players (non-TPP) such as China; on the other hand, the US is seeking to expand its exports of cotton/yarn/fabric to Vietnam where the present share of exports is just US$403 million (Office of the United States Trade Representative 2014).

Conclusion

Mega FTAs are set to bring major changes in the way Vietnam does business and make it another hotspot for trading and investments. Vietnam is potentially a part of both the TPP and the RCEP and this makes it unique by having benefits from both. In short, Vietnam will be having preferential access to countries responsible for about 70 per cent of the world's trade and around 50 per cent of the world's GDP. Nevertheless, accepting the WTO plus proposals on intellectual property, investment protection, services and state-owned enterprises as envisaged under the TPP, will be extremely difficult for the Vietnamese. While the RCEP is composed of countries with varied growth rates and is diverse in nature, most of the TPP member countries are economically developed and Vietnam being an agriculture-based economy, the challenges to maintain standards while keeping the trade volume intact are arduous. As a result, if the TPP were ever to come into force, Vietnamese agriculture products will face fierce competition from advanced agricultural economies. To make sure the mega FTAs benefit the economy, Vietnam has to improve and re-adjust its institutions especially towards stabilising the macro-economy and developing the system of laws and policies to create an open, transparent business environment and ensure that the balance is maintained throughout various economic sectors.

So far, with the present set of standards and tariff levels, Vietnam remains an important trade partner for India and China. However, whenever FTAs such as the TPP or another version of it come into force, the compliances, rules and agreements will prevent members from pursuing traditional ways of doing business. For example, China remains a big market for Vietnam's agricultural products and Vietnam's agriculture exports to China help the country earn valuable forex. In the past five years, agricultural exports to China accounted for about 35 per cent of the country's total exports. In 2015, the export turnover from agricultural products was about US$5 billion (*Vietnam News* 2016). In the absence of stricter 'standardisation', Vietnam could export a large amount of primary products to China as the latter does not specify a high quality for imported products from Vietnam.

For Vietnam, the issue is how access to wider markets and preferential treatment can be pursued aggressively while not losing control over markets like China (*Vietnam News* 2016). The process of importing the raw material and integrating it with the value chain and supplying to a third country was never streamlined strictly as per the required compliances and standards. In the long run, Vietnam may gear up to adapt to the new framework of mega FTAs and that too preferably to the TPP or its equivalent by innovating and adopting newer ways to upgrade its businesses. At the same time, Hanoi also needs to look beyond and engage with conventional partners like India to pursue its economic integration with emerging markets. For Vietnam, there is still a long way to go in ratifying the several mega FTAs and to begin the process of stage-wise tariff eliminations. In the meantime, Vietnam, India and China could work on exploring multiple ways to add value to their intra-regional businesses.

* *The author acknowledges financial support from the Indian Council Social Science Research (ICSSR) and Renu Rana for research support.*

NOTES

1. The 12 potential TPP countries include Australia, Brunei Darussalam, Canada, Chile, Japan, Malaysia, Mexico, New Zealand, Peru, Singapore, United States and Vietnam. However, the agreement cannot come into effect if either Japan or the US stays out.
2. The potential RCEP membership includes 16 countries—the 10 ASEAN members, Brunei Darussalam, Cambodia, Indonesia, Laos, Malaysia, Myanmar, the Philippines, Singapore, Thailand and Vietnam plus the six countries with which ASEAN has free trade agreements, Australia, China, India, Japan, Korea and New Zealand.

REFERENCES

Asian Development Bank. 2015. 'Regional Comprehensive Economic Partnership', https://aric.adb.org/fta/regional-comprehensive-economic-partnership (accessed on 28 November 2016).

Asian Development Bank. 2016. *Asian Development Outlook 2016*. https://www.adb.org/sites/default/files/publication/182221/ado2016.pdf (accessed on 3 October 2016).

Australian Department of Foreign Affairs and Trade. 2012. 'Guiding Principles and Objectives for Negotiating the Regional Comprehensive Economic Partnership', http://dfat.gov.au/trade/agreements/rcep/Documents/guiding-principles-rcep.pdf (accessed on 26 September 2016).

Barbour-Lacey, Edward. 2015. 'Yarn Forward's Effect on the Trans-Pacific Partnership and Vietnam', Vietnam Briefing, 8 May, http://www.vietnam-briefing.com/news/yarn-forwards-effect-transpacific-partnership-vietnam.html/ (accessed on 26 September 2016).

China-ASEAN Research Institute of Guangxi University (CARIGU). 2015. 'Qingting zhongyue jingmao guanxi fazhan zhong de yuenan shengyin' (倾听中越经贸关系发展中的越南声音) [The Sino-Vietnamese Economic and Trade Relations and the echos of development], 26 March, http://cari.gxu.edu.cn/info/1087/6468.htm (accessed on 26 September 2016).

Dang Kim Khoi. 2015. 'Vietnam joins Trans-Pacific Partnership (TPP): Challenges and Opportunities for Agricultural Production', The Centre for Agricultural Policy (CAP), http://en.cap.gov.vn/news/tID454_Vietnam-joins-TransPacific-Partnership-TPP-Challenges-and-Opportunities-for-agricultural-production.html# (accessed on 26 September 2016).

Dixon, Patrick. 2012. 'Future of Vietnam—Economy, Banking, Manufacturing, Digital, Green Tech', Global Change, http://www.globalchange.com/future-of-vietnam-economy-banking-manufacturing-digital.htm (accessed on 28 November 2016).

Export-Import Bank of India. 2013. 'India's Trade and Investment Relations with Cambodia, Lao PDR, Myanmar, Vietnam (CIMV): Enhancing Economic Cooperation', *Occasional Paper* 161, September, p. 22, http://www.eximbankindia.in/sites/default/files/Full%20OP/CLMV%20OP%20NEW%20REVISED.pdf (accessed on 23 September 2016).

Ha Thi Hong Vani and Do Tien Sam. 2009. 'Vietnam-China Trade, FDI and ODA Relations (1998-2008) and the Impacts upon Vietnam', http://www.ide.go.jp/English/Publish/Download/Brc/pdf/01_vietnamandchina.pdf (accessed on 26 September 2016).

India Brand Equity Foundation. 2016. 'Brand India>>Industry>>Textile Industry in India', http://www.ibef.org/industry/textiles.aspx (accessed on 23 September 2016).

International Trade Administration. 2016. 'Trans-Pacific Partnership', September, http://trade.gov/fta/tpp/countries/pdf/vietnam.pdf (accessed on 23 September 2016).

Ministry of External Affairs. 2016a. 'India-Vietnam Relations', January, https://www.mea.gov.in/Portal/ForeignRelation/Vietnam_13_01_2016.pdf (accessed on 21 September 2016).

Ministry of External Affairs. 2016b. 'Joint Statement between India and Vietnam during the visit of Prime Minister to Vietnam', 3 September, http://www.mea.gov.in/bilateral-documents.htm?dtl/27362/Joint_Statement_between_India_and_Vietnam_during_the_visit_of_Prime_Minister_to_Vietnam (accessed on 21 September 2016).

Na Son. 2015. 'Vietnam-China economic relations after 25 years', *Vietnamnet*, 6 November, http://english.vietnamnet.vn/fms/business/145683/vietnam—china-economic-relations-after-25-years.html (accessed on 21 September 2016).

Ngo Xuan Binh. 2016. 'Vietnam–India Economic Ties: Challenges and Opportunities since 2007', *China Report*, Vol. 52, No. 2, May 2016, 112-28.

Observatory of Economic Complexity-MIT (OEC-MIT). 2015. 'What does China export to Vietnam (2014)?' http://atlas.media.mit.edu/en/visualize/tree_map/hs92/export/chn/vnm/show/2014/ (accessed on 30 September 2016).

Office of the United States Trade Representative. 2015. 'Summary of the Trans-Pacific Partnership Agreement', https://ustr.gov/about-us/policy-offices/press-office/press-releases/2015/october/summary-trans-pacific-partnership (accessed on 30 September 2016)

Office of the United States Trade Representative. 2014. 'Vietnam', 5 August, https://ustr.gov/countries-regions/southeast-asia-pacific/vietnam (accessed on 30 September 2016).

Schwab, Klaus. (ed.). 2013. *The Global Competitiveness Report 2013–2014*. World Economic Forum, http://www3.weforum.org/docs/WEF_GlobalCompetitivenessReport_2013-14.pdf (accessed on 28 November 2016)

Sieburg, Michael. 2016. 'How the Trans-Pacific Partnership benefits Vietnam's economy', *Thanh Nien News*, 28 March, http://www.thanhniennews.com/commentaries/how-the-transpacific-partnership-benefits-vietnams-economy-60650.html (accessed on 21 September 2016).

Singh, Ritesh Kumar. 2016. 'TPP threat looms over Indian textiles', *The Hindu Business Line*, 11

August, http://www.thehindubusinessline.com/opinion/tpp-threat-looms-over-indian-textiles/article8974989.ece (accessed on 1 October 2016).

Trading Economics. 2016. 'Vietnam Exports', 1 September, http://www.tradingeconomics.com/vietnam/exports (accessed on 2 October 2016).

Tuoiyre News. 2015. 'Vietnam hails Trans-Pacific Partnership agreement', 10 June, http://tuoitrenews.vn/business/30827/vietnam-hails-transpacific-partnership-agreement (accessed on 30 September 2016).

Vietnam News. 2015. 'TPP offers VN opportunities', 7 October, http://vietnamnews.vn/economy/276733/tpp-offers-vn-opportunities.html#IvHrvXjYGjIIVzYd.97 (accessed on 30 September 2016).

Vietnam News. 2016. 'Agriculture must be restructured', 16 August, http://vietnamnews.vn/opinion/300920/agriculture-must-be-restructured.html#qtoOMzPYhhjZWyR6.99 (accessed on 30 September 2016).

Vietnam Plus. 2016. 'Chinese businesses sharply increase investment in Vietnam', 27 March, http://en.vietnamplus.vn/chinese-businesses-sharply-increase-investment-in-vietnam/90943.vnp (accessed on 26 September 2016).

Xuan Loc Doan. 2016a. 'Vietnamese PM's China visit significant', 16 September, http://atimes.com/2016/09/vietnamese-pms-china-visit-significant/ (accessed on 26 September 2016).

Xuan Loc Doan. 2016b. 'Why India, Vietnam upgraded their ties', *Asia Times,* 10 September, http://atimes.com/2016/09/why-india-vietnam-upgraded-their-ties/ (accessed on 21 September 2016).

11

China–Cambodia Relations: From 'Number One Friend' to 'Strategic Partnership'

Pham Cao Cuong

While Cambodia gained its independence from France in November 1953, it was only five years later in July 1958 that the People's Republic of China (PRC) recognised and established diplomatic relations with Cambodia. During the period 1958-1965, bilateral relations were closely developed and Cambodia regarded China as its 'number one friend'. These relations were maintained based on close personal ties between Prince Norodom Sihanouk and China's Premier Zhou Enlai, since both leaders took part in the Bandung Conference held in Indonesia in 1955. In 1965, after the US deployment of its military forces in Vietnam, Sihanouk cut his country's ties with the United Kingdom and the US but enhanced them with China and the Democratic Republic of Vietnam (DRV). However, during the 1960s following the outbreak of the Chinese Cultural Revolution, bilateral ties saw upheaval as Sihanouk became concerned that China would export its comuminism to his country. At the same time, Cambodia also found that China was backing the Khmer Rouge in its insurgency against Sihanouk and susptected that the Chinese schools in the country were engaged in propaganda for Mao Zedong and his ideology (Heder 2007: 300).

After the military coup d'état led by Lon Nol with support of the American Central Intelligence Agency in March 1970, Sihanouk lived in exile in China.

During the 1960s, on the one hand, China supported Pol Pot and the Khmer Rouge but on other hand also still maintained a good relationship with Sihanouk. Soon however, Sihanouk sided with the Khmer Rouge with the intention of removing Lon Nol.

In 1975, Pol Pot overthrew the Lon Nol regime, took control over the Khmer Rouge and engaged in a brutal genocide in Cambodia. From 1975 to 1977, China provided the Khmer Rouge military weapons, including 200 tanks, 300 armoured cars, 300 artillery pieces, 30,000 tons of ammunition, six naval vessels, six jet fighters and two bombers (Kiernan 1996: 132-133). During the 1980s, China continuously supported the Khmer Rouge to maintain hostilities against the newly-established government in Cambodia supported by Vietnam. By using its veto at the United Nations, China along with the US and Thailand supported the seat for the Khmer Rouge at the UN. And to support this force, China also provided about US$80 million in economic and military aid to the Khmer Rouge. At the same time, China also called for the support of the opposition forces in Cambodia (Haas 1991: 15). Among other things, it was no doubt also the persistent support of Beijing that enabled the Khmer Rouge to conduct one of biggest genocides in history: under Pol Pot's regime from April 1975 to January 1979, about 1.7 to 2.2 million people were killed (Hunt 2011).

After the Paris Peace Agreement in 1991, Sino-Cambodian bilateral ties were quickly transformed. China is today the biggest aid provider for Cambodia, especially in infrastructure, transportation and energy projects. Prior to 1996, China had patronised Prince Norodom Ranariddh, but due to his close relationship with Taiwan, China soon ended this patronage. In 1997, after a bloody coup d'état to oust Ranariddh, Hun Sen became Cambodia's Prime Minister. Despite the opposition of international community, China still recognised the coup and resumed economic and military aid to Cambodia. From 1997 to 2001, China provided to Cambodia US$40 million in aid, more than US$200 million in loans and at least US$3 million for military support (Kosal 2009: 8).

Trade and Investment Relations

After the Cold War, bilateral trade relations have developed quickly and strongly. China is Cambodia's biggest trading partner – about 60 per cent of products selling in Cambodia's market originate from China. In 2006, bilateral trade turover reached US$732 million in which Cambodia's trade deficit with China totalled about US$662 million. After the ASEAN–China Free Trade Agreemet (ACFTA) came into effect in 2010, the trade turnover between ASEAN and China increased seven times from US$232 billion in 2000. Meanwhile, the bilateral trade turnover between China and Cambodia rose three times from US$791 million in 2009 to US$2.5 billion in 2011 (Xu 2012). In 2013, China's exports to Cambodia reached about US$3.4 billion, accounting for 32.6 per cent of the total Cambodian imports of which Cambodia's exports to China only reached US$361 million and it had a trade deficit of US$3.05 billion (Salidjanova 2015: 34). For the 2015-2016 period, the bilateral trade volume amounted to US$4.2 billion and was expected to reach about US$5 billion at the end of 2017 (Mishra 2016: 3).

In terms of tourism, in 2011 there were about 2,47,197 Chinese tourists that visited Cambodia. In 2012, China was ranked as the third-largest source of tourists for Cambodia after Vietnam and South Korea (*Xinhua* 2013); in 2017, China became the largest source (Ngamsangchaikitm 2017). The enhancement of bilateral ties was also the result of the contribution of the Chinese community of over 5,00,000 people living and doing business in Cambodia. Indeed, Chinese Cambodians have played an important part in business and political activities in Cambodia. After English, Mandarin is the most popular foreign language in Cambodia and according to statistics, there are about 56 Chinese schools for about 30,000 students nationwide (*The Phnom Penh Post* 2016).

In terms of foreign investment, since the middle of the 1990s, China's investment in Cambodia has increased rapidly. In just the 1997-1998 period, China's investment in Cambodia rose by three times and by about 40 per cent more in 1999. China soon became the biggest foreign investor in Cambodia. Following the visit of Cambodia's Prime Minister Hun Sen to China in 1999, the two sides agreed to establish a specialised zone not far from Sihanoukville and called the Sihanoukville Special Economic Zone (SSEZ). This zone is now the biggest SEZ in Cambodia and the government has plans to double its capacity and open 300 factories by 2020 (Whitehead 2016). Almost all of the Chinese projects are concentrated mainly in infrastructure and steel industries. In 2012, China began a steel factory in the Preah Vihear province and in 2013, the Cambodian Steel Corporation and the Chinese Railway Corporation signed a contract worth US$9.6 billion to construct a railway system in Cambodia with 11 stations. In 2015, China's aid package to Cambodia amounted to

US$320 million, accounting for 30 per cent of the total aid received. From 2012 to 2016, the total registered investment in Cambodia significantly increased from US$2.9 billion in 2012 to US$3.6 billion in 2016, of which 90 per cent of the total foreign investment came mainly from the Asian region, and about 72 per cent of which was mainly in the industry and infrastructure sectors (Council for the Development of Cambodia 2015). In total investment, the proportion of Chinese investment increased from 20.69 per cent in 2012 to 29.92 per cent in 2016. In 2015 alone, China's FDI in Cambodia reached US$857 million, accounting for 61.1 per cent of the total FDI in Cambodia (Chhoeun 2017). In 2016, this figure amounted to US$1.08 billion, accounting for 41.3 per cent of the total FDI in Cambodia.

However, the increase of Chinese investment in Cambodia also triggered many negative issues for Cambodia. It is estimated that there are about 23 Chinese companies involved in the exploitation of natural resources and mining in Cambodia. There are five companies managing hydro-electronic plants and a hundred other companies investing in the garment industry (*Xinhua* 2011). About half of the land concessions granted since 1994 (about 4.6 million hectares) are in the hands of Chinese companies. According to Ouch Leng, Land Reform Project Coordinator of the Cambodian Center for Human Rights – some 107 Chinese-owned firms control about a quarter of the 17 million hectares of agricultural land and forest available in Cambodia. Because of these concessions, many villagers have lost their homes and land (Titthara 2012). And, Cambodia has been under political pressure from Beijing to attract more trade and investment from China. For example, Cambodia agreed to close the representative office of Taiwan at Phnom Penh. In 2010, China put more pressure on the Hun Sen government to deport 20 Uighur asylum seekers from Cambodia to China. For these and other forms of support, Cambodia has received much economic aid from China (Carmichael 2010b).

Economic and Development Aid

China is now the main provider of economic and development aid to Cambodia in the forms of loans and favorable assistance. From 1992 to 2014, China provided a total 2.85 billion in loans to Cambodia to build infrastructure and industrialise agriculture (Mishra 2016: 2). The rise of China as a regional power to some extent has an impact on Cambodian perceptions. Indeed, in the past, China was regarded by the Cambodian Prime Minister as 'the root of everything that is evil' (Hutt 2016) for its support to the Khmer Rouge, but now due to his own strategic interests, Hun Sen has reconsidered his relations with China and made a u-turn in Cambodia's foreign policy. In 2000, following Chinese President Jiang Zemin's first-ever visit to Cambodia since 1963, Hun Sen's position changed. After this visit, bilateral ties were quickly enhanced with increasing Chinese aid to Cambodia. When talking about China, Hun Sen has said, 'China respects the political decisions of Cambodia.... They are quiet, but at the same time they build bridges and roads, and there are no complicated conditions' (Strangio 2009). In 2006, Hun Sen still maintained that 'China is a trustworthy friend of Cambodia' (*The Economist* 2017). To further strengthen its relations with Cambodia, in April 2006 Chinese Premier Wen Jiabao visited Cambodia; there was a joint communiqué expressing the intention of the two countries to establish a 'Comprehensive Partnership of Cooperation' (*Gov.cn* 2006). As a result, in December 2010, China and Cambodia upgraded their bilateral relations to 'Comprehensive Strategic Partnership of Cooperation'. At that time, China became the biggest foreign investor and loan provider in Cambodia. In February 2009, at a meeting with Jia Qing, Chairman of the National Committee of the Chinese People's Political Consultative Conference, King Norodom Sihamoni expressed his thanks to China, calling it as the '"most reliable friend" of Cambodia for its economic assistance and its contribution to Cambodia's national conciliation, peace and development' (*China News* 2009).

In 2013, China signed agreements with Cambodia worth over US$500 million in loans and grants (*Reuters* 2013), and more such support has followed. China also helped Cambodia build six hydro plants at the Lower Mekong worth US$1.6 billion. These projects were supported by Chinese banks and built under the BOT form with a duration of 30 to 45 years. To support China, in August 2010, Prime Minister Hun Sen warned Cambodia's provincial governors to close Taiwan's governmental offices in their districts or face dismissal from their posts. Phnom Penh has also supported Beijing's initiatives, including the Asian Infrastructure Investment Bank and the 'one belt, one road' or 'belt and road' initiative.

Cambodia has also actively supported China's position in territorial claims in the South China Sea. At the ASEAN Foreign Ministers' Meeting (FMM) held in Cambodia in July 2012, Cambodia as chairman of the meeting did not agree to criticise China's activities in the South China Sea and refused to acknowledge China's assertive behavior in the final statement. Consequently, for the first time in its 45-year history, the ASEAN failed to work out a joint statement of the meeting (*BBC News* 2012). Cambodia stated during the discussions that these were bilateral issues and therefore, could not be mentioned in the joint statement. A few days later, China committed to providing an aid package of about US$600 million to Cambodia. Similarly, at the FMM 2016 held in the Lao capital of Vientiane, Cambodia once again persuaded the ASEAN Ministers to not use rhetoric against China's behaviour in the South China Sea. Cambodia was the only country opposing the proposed wording in the final statement (Baliga and Sokheng 2016). As a result, the section titled 'South China Sea' was left blank in the final statement draft. The joint communique finally did not mention China's assertive activities and behaviour in the South China Sea.

In June 2016, Sihamoni paid a state visit to China and in return, in October 2016, Chinese President Xi Jinping visited Cambodia where he signed 31 cooperative agreements with the Cambodian Prime Minister Hun Sen. During this visit, Xi also promised to provide Cambodia an aid package of US$237 million, further strengthening bilateral ties. Speaking about the importance of bilateral relations, a spokesperson for the Cambodian Council of Ministers stated: 'Cambodia-China relations are the best they've been this year. Our bilateral ties should be viewed as a gold standard of relations between country and country' (Xue and Sovan 2016).

In December 2016, China began the construction of a deep-sea port in Cambodia in the Gulf of Thailand. This project is based on a 99-year lease worth US$3.8 billion, covering about 90 km length and about 20 per cent of total coastline length and run by the Tianjin Union Development Group (UDG) of China (Kotoski and Kimsay 2016). When the project is completed, it would be of political and economic significance for both countries. Further, in early January 2017, a joint venture of two Chinese companies won a bid to build Cambodia's and Southeast Asia's twin highest building worth US$2.7 billion at the Mekong riverside in Phnom Penh, with 133 floors and about 560 meters in height (*China Daily* 2017). In April 2017, Cambodian Prime Minister Hun Sen thanked China for its economic aid of US$150 million to build a new stadium in Phnom Penh (Naren and Sovuthy 2015); the stadium is to host the Southeast Asian (SEA) Games in 2030. At the same time, the Chinese government also provided an additional US$57 million to build a bridge crossing the Mekong River at Krouch Chhma, Tboung Khmum province. In April 2015, the Mekong River bridge was opened by Hun Sen and the Chinese Ambassador to Cambodia, Bu Jianguo. This project was built by the Shanghai Construction Company under a Chinese concessional loan of US$116 million (Li 2015). Following Xi's visit in 2016, China pledged to provide about US$180 million of financial aid to Cambodia. This will support among other things a new bridge, worth US$57 million, and a new road namely National Road 11, worth US$98 million (Manet 2016).

Bilateral Military Cooperation

In January 2017, under pressure from China, Cambodia suspended a joint military exercise with the United States known as 'Angkor Sentinel'. This exercise had begun in 2010 with a concentration on humanitarian assistance and relief. However, Cambodia decided to postpone this military exercise for two years until 2019. In addition, Cambodia also cancelled a planned military exercise with Australia.

The decision to cancel the exercises with the USA was made soon after Cambodia had finished a joint military exercise with China, the 'Golden Dragon', in December 2016.

Their military cooperation therefore, manifests a clear example of a close relationship between Beijing and Phnom Penh. Through military cooperation, Beijing has been trying to draw the smaller country into its sphere of influence, serving its long-term strategic goals in the region.

Firstly, as an emerging regional power, China would like to have more allies to expand its sphere of influence to the overall Southeast Asian region. This will be also used to serve China's interests in case of conflicts in the Taiwan Strait and on the Korean Peninsula. Secondly, China's strengthening of its relations with Cambodia is to promote bilateral trade cooperation because Cambodia is also a potential market for China in the region. Moreover, it also creates favourable conditions for Beijing to access Cambodia's natural resources such as oil and gas and even agricultural lands to serve the demand of its economic development. Thirdly, China's engagement with Cambodia will allow Beijing to access the Gulf of Thailand and the South China Sea in the context of the strengthening of the US relations with its allies and friends in the region. Based on this, China can access the Sihanoukville port and also realise its 'one belt, one road' strategy (Carmichael 2010a).

In fact by the end of the 1990s, China had begun to provide massive military aid to Cambodia, including the building and transference of military schools, hospitals and transportation vehicles and facilities. In 1999, China built an Infantry Institute at Kampong Speu in Cambodia. This was the starting point for a long-term strategy of China to strengthen its influence over the Royal Cambodian Armed Forces (RCAF). By October 2006, there were about 1,000 Cambodian officers trained at this institute (Amaro 2016). At the same time, the Chinese People's Liberation Army (PLA) also conducted a lot of exchange visits with its Cambodian counterpart. The 2013—2017 period especially saw numerous high-ranking visits to promote bilateral military ties.

Specifically, in January 2013, Gen. Qi Jianguo, PLA's Deputy Chief of General Staff, visited Cambodia. At the meeting with Gen. Moeung Samphan, Secretary of State for National Defense, the two sides signed a MOU on military human resources development (Sophirom 2013). This MOU was processed following a plan for Cambodia to buy 12 Zhi-9 helicopters from China under concessional loans. In April 2013, Cambodia's Deputy Prime Minister and Minister for National Defense of Cambodia Tea Banh visited China and had talks with the State Councilor and Minister of National Defense of China Gen. Chang Wanguan (*China Military Online* 2013). In November 2013, Tea Banh visited China again on an 'imperative mission' (Bopha and Woods 2013). The military cooperation between the two countries was further strengthened by the subsequent visit of Admiral Sun Jianguo, PLA's Deputy Chief of General Staff, to Cambodia in March 2014 who was received by Gen. Eth Sarath, Deputy Commander-in-Chief of the RCAF. He also had separate meetings with the RCAF's commander-in-chief Gen. Pol Saroeun and the Deputy Prime Minister and Defense Minister Gen. Tea Banh. At the meeting, Gen. Pol asked the Chinese side to provide long-term training for RCAF's officers, and expressed his commitment to further consolidate and expand the cooperation between the two armies (*Khmer Times* 2014).

In May 2014, Gen. Xu Qiliang, Vice-Chairman of China's Central Military Commission (CMC), made a visit to Cambodia where he met Hun Sen. At the meeting, Gen. Xu said that his visit was to further promote Chinese and Cambodian relations and cooperation for mutual benefits, and to bolster military ties between the two countries, particularly in human resources development (*Global Times* 2014). Further, in November 2014, a delegation of 14 senior Cambodian military officers led by Gen. Pol visited China and met with Gen. Xu (Yao 2014). In May 2015, General Nem Sowath, Director General of General Department of Policy and Foreign Affairs, Ministry of National Defense of Cambodia, visited China and met with General Wang Guanzhong, Deputy Chief of General Staff of the Chinese People's Liberation

Army (PLA) (Yao 2015). In July 2015, Gen. Tea Banh, along with other 23 high-ranking military and civil officials, made a five-day visit to China. The purpose of this visit was to further enhance their bilateral ties and cooperation. In Beijing, Gen. Tea Banh was separately received by the Chinese Defense Minister Gen. Chang and CMC Vice-Chairman Gen. Xu. On this visit, the two sides also signed a number of agreements to enhance bilateral defence cooperation in which China would provide communication devices to Cambodia (Shen 2015; Parameswaran 2015).

In July 2016, Gen. Nem Sowath, Director General of General Department of Policy and Foreign Affairs, Ministry of National Defense of Cambodia, continuously visited China. At the meeting, Admiral Sun called China and Cambodia as 'good neighbors, good friends, good brothers and good partners' and firmly supported Cambodia taking a path of development suited to its own national conditions. He also stated his support for Cambodia's efforts to maintain sovereign independence, maintain stability and accelerate development (Shen 2015; Parameswaran 2015). At the same time, Sun also reiterated China's stance on the South China Sea arbitration and expressed his thanks to Cambodia for its support to China on the issue (*China Military Online* 2016). In January 2017, Gen. Khun Vuth, Undersecretary of State of the Cambodian Ministry of Defense, visited China and was received by Gen. Ma Yiming, Deputy Chief of Staff of the Joint Staff Department of the CMC. At the meeting, Ma stated that China and Cambodia were good neighbors, friends and partners and appreciated Cambodia's consistent and firm support for issues concerning China's core interests and declared that China was willing to work with Cambodia to exhance the military-to-military cooperation between the two sides (Yao 2017).

Along with a regular exchange of visits, China has continuously provided concessional loans and military equipment to the RCAF. In 2005, China handed over six patrol boats to Cambodia to help it combat maritime crimes. At the same time, it also helped the Cambodian naval forces to safeguard offshore oil sites associated with Chinese companies. In 2007, China provided another preferential loan to Cambodia for buying a further nine patrol vessels, worth US$600 billion (*Khmerisation* 2007). In 2013, Cambodia received a military equipment package from China including 12 Z-9 helicopters under a concessional loan of US$195 million (*Global Times* 2013). Out of them, there were four Harbin Z-9W helicopters aimed with machine guns, cannons, anti-tank missiles and 57 mm rocket launchers (*People's Daily Online* 2013). China accounted for 20 per cent of Cambodia's total purchased military equipment in 2012 and the figure increased to about 60 per cent of total purchases in 2013 (Becker 2017).

In February 2014, Cambodia received in addition 26 trucks and about 30,000 military uniforms for the RCAF from China (Belford and Thul 2015). In May 2015, China handed over Cambodia a military package in order to enhance military strength of the RCAF including 44 vehicles, including jeeps, rocket-launcher mounted trucks and at least a half-dozen anti-aircraft guns mounted on wheels. The inventory also included 20 forklifts, four mobile kitchens, and some 2,000 kg of unspecified chemicals and 10,000 kg worth of spare parts (Pheap 2015).

China's support for military training of the RCAF included assistance for running and management of training facilities. In 2009, there were about 200 military officials registered at a training course monitored by Chinese military advisors. All students here spent at least 6 weeks of training courses in Chinese military academies. In 2012, the Confucius Institute under the Royal Academy of Cambodia launched its fourth centre in the country to help Cambodian military personnel learn Chinese. The financial assistance and professional training courses given by China is an investment in Cambodian military leaders of the future. In May 2014, China announced that it would provide 400 scholarships to train military officials of Cambodia and from 2016 to 2018 a military package of nearly US$ 600 million would be given to Cambodia.

Chinese military ships have also made visits to Cambodian seaports. In 2013, a Chinese hospital ship *Peace Ark* called in at *Sihanoukville* port. According to Shen Hao, the mission commander, this visit was to provide medical service to the local people and militaries and conduct medical exchanges. At the same time, it was aimed at further developing mutual understanding and trust between the Chinese and Cambodian militaries (Li 2013). In February 2016, the 21st Chinese naval escort task force ended its navy duties against piracy in the Gulf of Aden and the Somali Sea and on the way back to China visited Sihanoukville. This was the fourth visit of the Chinese Navy to Cambodia over the past few years. During this five-day visit, the Chinese naval force also visited the Ream Naval Base of the Royal Cambodian Navy. Similarly, the warships of the 23rd Chinese naval escort taskforce too docked at Sihanoukville in October 2016 (Yao 2016).

By providing military assistance to Cambodia, China has been finding ways to influence Cambodia's foreign policy. On the Cambodian side, the enhancement of its relations with China, rather than with the United States, will help Cambodia to ignore pressure on democracy and human right issues. While aid packages from the USA are associated with political conditions, these packages from China including concessional loans, assistance or investment are not accompanied by any complicated conditions. As Phay Siphan, a secretary of state within Cambodia's Council of Ministers stated:

> 'In terms of money, China is the number one. The power of China is getting much bigger...we choose China because its investment does not come with conditions. A number of Western investments come with attachments...They say we have to be good in democracy. We have to be good in human rights. But in Cambodia we went through a civil war and we understand that if you have no food in your stomach, you cannot have human rights' (Kynge et al. 2016).

For this reason, Cambodia is willing to lean towards China rather than the USA but of course, Cambodia is also put under Chinese pressure in balancing its relations with Washington. For example, when China hosted the ASEAN Ministerial Meeting (AMM) in 2012, Phnom Penh had to support the position of China on the South China Sea issues contributing to the failure of ASEAN for the first time in 45 years to issue a final concluding statement.

Prospect for Bilateral Relations

Looking at the history of Sino-Cambodian relations from the past to the present, it is noted that the Chinese influence in Cambodia is strong and is deepening.

On the Cambodian side, in the past, Cambodia's Prime Minister Hun Sen had held a negative image of China because of its support to the Khmer Rouge. However, this perception has changed and the Hun Sen government has tried to strengthen its relations with China due to the Chinese support for Cambodia's economic development. At the same time, with the enhancement of bilateral ties, Hun Sen has also received great political support from China after the bloody coup d'état led by him to remove Prince Ranariddh in 1997. The strengthening of Cambodia's relations with China has helped Hun Sen consolidate his power while avoiding Chinese interference and support to opposition parties in the country as it had for the Khmer Rouge before.

From the geopolitical point of view, China has long been trying to access, engage and expand its influence in Cambodia. China always regards Cambodia as occupying an important strategic position in Southeast Asia. The access to the Sihanoukville port helps China easily enter the Gulf of Thailand and the Strait of Malacca. In the current situation, especially given the Chinese militarisation of the South China Sea, the enhancement of the Chinese engagement with Cambodia will help the PLA Navy to project its power, control the maritime lines in the region and expand its navy presence in the Pacific and Indian Oceans. In China's strategic calculations, the Sihanoukville port was even regarded as 'a pearl' in its 'string of pearls' strategy connecting Hong Kong with Sudan through the Indian Ocean. The enforcement of close relations with Cambodia also helps China access a number of air bases in Cambodia to serve its activities of refuelling Chinese surveillance flights in the South China Sea. Therefore, in the long term, bilateral ties will be continuously developed and expanded, and especially, ties between the navies of the two countries.

In the course of deploying its strategy toward the region, China needs political support from the ASEAN countries. China, therefore, has tried to draw Cambodia into its orbit of influence. Through military and economic assistance programmes, China has gradually influenced Cambodia's viewpoints and foreign policy on international and regional issues. In the past, Cambodia has strongly voiced its support for China at the United Nations. This political support has been very useful for Beijing since China has few major allies in the world. At the same time, Cambodia is also regarded as the weakest link of the chain in the ASEAN consensus on the South China Sea issues and has been subject to the Chinese 'strategy of divide and rule' toward the ASEAN. It is also important to note that besides military and economic aid, China also finds ways to influence Cambodian culture and language through the Chinese community to gradually achieve its long-term goals in the region. In the context of the highly strategic competition between the USA and China in the Southeast Asian region, the strengthening of China's relations with Cambodia aims to limit the American influence and to challenge or replace the US' leadership in the region.

Cambodia has used China as a counterweight to the US and avoided American pressure on democracy and human rights issues. A closer Sino-Cambodian relationship poses many challenges for US-Cambodia relations. When visiting Cambodia in November 2010, former US Secretary of State

Hillary Clinton also warned the government of Prime Minister Hun Sen not to depend too much on any one country, possibly referring to China (Pomfret 2010). Ties with China have also had impact on Cambodia's FDI from other countries such as the EU, Japan and other Western countries.

Finally, the strengthening of Cambodia's relations with China has also served Phnom Penh in using China as a counterweight to Vietnam. It is a fact that many Cambodians do not have a positive view of the Vietnamese military's entry into Cambodia to remove the Khmer Rougue regime. The opposition party in Cambodia is against the Vietnamese influence in Cambodia and regards the Hun Sen government as a 'puppet' of Vietnam. Hun Sen, therefore, has to consider the balance among interest groups inside his country and among political interest groups that believe in maintaining closer relations with the US or Vietnam. It is worth noting that in June 2015, the opposition party of Cambodia, the Cambodian National Rescue Party (CNRP), instigated a border violation with Vietnam (Sokchea and Turton 2015) and in 2016, a number of opposition personnel in the CNRP tried to distort the national map used for border demarcation between Vienam and Cambodia (*Reuters* 2016).

In the long term, the Chinese influence in Cambodia will not be reduced. Cambodia will also find a way to balance between China and the US, but is likely to lean heavily on China because of the potential benefits from economic, aid and military cooperation between the two sides. Furthermore, with Cambodia's national elections expected in 2018, Hun Sen's political prestige will be under test. If his Cambodian People's Party (CPP) continues to its standing and win, Cambdia is most likely to lean still further towards China. If the CPP fails, however, it will be a sign of future instability for Cambodia and a new Cambodian foreign policy will likely seek a new balance in ties with China and the US.

REFERENCES

Amaro, Yesenia. 2016. 'Cambodia to boost military ties to China', *The Phnom Penh Post*, 17 October, http://www.phnompenhpost.com/national/cambodia-boost-military-ties-china (accessed on 15 July 2017).

Baliga, Ananth and Vong Sokheng. 2016. 'Cambodia again blocks ASEAN statement on South China Sea', *The Phnom Penh Post*, 25 July, http://www.phnompenhpost.com/national/cambodia-again-blocks-asean-statement-south-china-sea (accessed on 15 July 2017).

BBC News. 2012. 'ASEAN nations fail to reach agreement on South China Sea', 13 July, http://www.bbc.com/news/world-asia-18825148 (accessed on 15 July 2017).

Becker, Jeffrey. 2017. 'What Is the PLA's Role in Promoting China-Cambodia Relations?', *The Diplomat*, 29 April, http://thediplomat.com/2017/04/what-is-the-plas-role-in-promoting-china-cambodia-relations/ (accessed on 15 July 2017).

Belford, Aubrey and Prak Chan Thul. 2015. 'Chinese influence in Cambodia grows with army school, aid', *Reuters*, 2 April, http://www.reuters.com/article/us-cambodia-china-military-idUSKBN0MT0SW20150402 (accessed on 15 July 2017).

Bopha, Phorn and Ben Woods. 2013. 'Tea Banh Jets to China on 'Imperative' Mission', *The Cambodia Daily*, 18 November, https://www.cambodiadaily.com/archives/tea-banh-jets-to-china-on-imperative-mission-47151/ (accessed on 15 July 2017).

Carmichael, Robert. 2010a. 'China and Cambodia grow closers', *Deutsche Welle (DW)*, 26 March, http://www.dw-world.de/dw/article/0,,5399830,00.html (accessed on 15 July 2017).

Carmichael, Robert.2010b. 'China-Cambodia ties grow tighter', *Voice of America*, 24 March, http://www1.voanews.com/english/news/asia/China-Cambodia-Ties-Grow-Tighter-88998402.html (accessed on 15 July 2017).

Chhoeun, Kongkea. 2017. 'The US–Cambodia debt stand-off', *East Asia Forum*, 14 April, http://www.eastasiaforum.org/2017/04/14/the-us-cambodia-debt-stand-off/ (accessed on 15 July 2017).

China Daily. 2017. 'Chinese companies to build world's tallest twin towers in Cambodia', 4 January, http://www.chinadaily.com.cn/business/2017-01/04/content_27857366.htm (accessed on 15 July 2017).

China Military Online. 2013. 'Chang Wanquan meets with Cambodian deputy prime minister and defense minister', *China Military Online*, 24 April, http://en.people.cn/90786/8220173.html (accessed on 15 July 2017).

China Military Online. 2014. 'Senior Chinese military official visits Cambodia on ties', 16 March, http://eng.chinamil.com.cn/news-channels/2014-03/16/content_5812820.htm (accessed on 15 July 2017).

China Military Online.2016. 'China, Cambodia boost bilateral military cooperation', *China Military Online*, 29 July, http://english.chinamil.com.cn/news-channels/china-military-news/2016-07/29/content_7180950.htm (accessed on 15 July 2017).

China News. 2009. 'Top Chinese political advisor meets Cambodian King', 21 February, http://en.people.cn/90001/90776/90883/6597876.html (accessed on 6 March 2010)

Council for the Development of Cambodia. 2012. *Cambodian Investment Guide*. Phnom Penh: Council for the Development of Cambodia

Council for the Development of Cambodia. 2015. *Investment Trend*, http://www.cambodiainvestment.gov.kh/investment-enviroment/investment-trend.html (accessed on 15 July 2017).

Global Times. 2013. '12 China-made helicopters delivered to Cambodia', 25 November, http://www.globaltimes.cn/content/827426.shtml (accessed on 15 July 2017).

Global Times. 2014. 'Cambodian PM meets with Xu Qiliang on ties', 8 May, http://www.globaltimes.cn/content/859224.shtml (accessed on 15 July 2017).

Gov.cn. 2006. 'Joint communique between Chinese, Cambodian govts', The Central People's Government of The National People's Congress, April 09, http://www.gov.cn/english/2006-04/09/content_249224.htm (accessed on 15 July 2017).

Haas, Michael. 1991. Cambodia, *Pol Pot, and the United States: the Faustian pact*. New York: Praeger Publishers.

Heder, Steve. 2007. 'Cambodia', in Andrew Simpson (ed.) *Language and National Identity in Asia*. Oxford: Oxford University Press, 288-311.

Hunt, Luke. 2011. 'What was China's Khmer Rouge Role?', *The Diplomat*, 17 December, http://thediplomat.com/2011/12/what-was-chinas-khmer-rouge-role/ (accessed on 15 July 2017).

Hutt, David. 2016. 'How China Came to Dominate Cambodia', *The Diplomat*, 1 September, http://thediplomat.com/2016/09/how-china-came-to-dominate-cambodia/ (accessed on 15 July 2017).

Khemara, Sok. 2014. 'Cambodian Opposition Criticizes Dependence on China Aid Money', *Voice of America*, 19 November, https://www.voanews.com/a/cambodian-opposition-criticizes-dependence-on-china-aid-money/2527010.html ((accessed on 6 July 2017).

Khmer Times. 2014. 'Cambodia Asks China to Provide Long-Term Training', 19 March, http://www.khmertimeskh.com/news/267/cambodia-asks-china-to-provide-long-term-training/ (accessed on 15 July 2017).

Khmerisation. 2007. 'China Handed Nine Patrol Boats to Cambodia', 7 November, https://khmerisation.wordpress.com/2007/11/07/china-handed-nine-patrol-boats-to-cambodia/ (accessed on 15 July 2017).

Kiernan, Ben. 1996. *The Pol Pot Regime: Race, Power, and Genocide in Cambodia Under the Khmer Rouge 1975-1979*. New York: Yale University Press.

Kosal, Long. 2009. 'Sino-Cambodia relations', CICP Working Paper, No. 28, Cambodian Institute for Cooperation and Peace: Phnom Penh.

Kotoski, Kali and Hor Kimsay. 2016. 'Coastal airport project gets nod', *The Phnom Penh Post*, 23 September, http://www.phnompenhpost.com/business/coastal-airport-project-gets-nod (accessed on 15 July 2017).

Kynge, James, Leila Haddou and Michael Peel. 2016. 'FT Investigation: How China bought its way into Cambodia', *Financial Times*, 9 September, https://www.ft.com/content/23968248-43a0-11e6-b22f-79eb4891c97d (accessed on 15 July 2017).

Li Hong. 2013. 'Chinese hospital ship arrives in Cambodia for goodwill visit', *China Central Television*, 24 September, http://english.cntv.cn/20130924/104726.shtml (accessed on 15 July 2017).

Li Hong. 2015. 'Cambodia inaugurates China-funded Mekong bridge, road', *Xinhua*, 1 April, http://news.xinhuanet.com/english/2015-04/01/c_134116289.htm (accessed on 15 July 2017).

Manet, Sum. 2016. 'China Gives US$2 Billion for Roads, Bridge', *Khmer Times*, 17 October, http://www.khmertimeskh.com/news/30849/china-gives—2-billion-for-roads—bridge/ (accessed on 15 July 2017).

Mishra, Rahul. 2016. 'Cambodia: China's Special Partner?', ICWA Viewpoint, 15 March, http://www.icwa.in/pdfs/VP/2014/CambodiaChinaSpecialPartnerVP14032016.pdf (accessed on 15 July 2017).

Naren, Kuch and Khy Sovuthy. 2015. 'PM Meets China's Xi, Receives US$150M Grant', *The Cambodia Daily*, 17 October, https://www.cambodiadaily.com/news/pm-meets-chinas-xi-receives-150m-grant-97440/ (accessed on 15 July 2017).

Ngamsangchaikitm, Wanwisa. 2017. 'Cambodia enjoys tourism growth', *TR Weekly*, 27 June, http://www.ttrweekly.com/site/2017/06/cambodia-enjoys-tourism-growth-2/ (accessed on 15 July 2017).

Parameswaran, Prashanth. 2015. 'Why is a Big Cambodia Military Delegation in China?', *The Diplomat*, 10 July, http://thediplomat.com/2015/07/why-is-a-big-cambodia-military-delegation-in-china/ (accessed on 15 July 2017).

People's Daily Online.2013. '12 China-made Z-9 helicopters delivered to Cambodia', *People's Daily Online*, 26 November, http://en.people.cn/90786/8467253.html (accessed on 15 July 2017).

Pheap, Aun. 2015. 'China Donates Heavy Weaponry to Military', *The Cambodia Daily*, 25May, https://www.cambodiadaily.com/archives/china-donates-heavy-weaponry-to-military-84249/ (accessed on 15 July 2017).

Pomfret, John. 2010. 'Clinton Urges Cambodia to Strike a Balance with China', *Washington Post*, 1 November, http://www.washingtonpost.com/wp-dyn/content/article/2010/11/01/AR2010110101460.html (accessed on 15 July 2017).

Reuters. 2013. 'China Pledges US$548 Million in Aid to Ally Cambodia', 10 April, http://in.reuters.com/article/cambodia-china-idINL3N0CXDAC20130410 (accessed on 15 July 2017).

Reuters. 2016. 'Cambodian opposition MP arrested over 'fake' border map on Facebook', 11 April, http://www.reuters.com/article/us-cambodia-politics-idUSKCN0X80HN (accessed on 31 July 2017).

Salidjanova, Nargiza. 2015. 'China's economic ties with ASEAN: A Country-By-Country Analysis', U.S-China Economic and Security Review Commission, 15 March. https://www.uscc.gov/sites/default/files/Research/China%27s%20Economic%20Ties%20with%20ASEAN.pdf (accessed on 15 July 2017)

Shen Qing. 2015. 'Cambodian Defense Minister to pay 5-day visit to China', *Xinhua*, 6 July, http://news.xinhuanet.com/english/2015-07/06/c_134386819.htm (accessed on 15 July 2017).

Sokchea, Meas and Shaun Turton. 2015. 'Hanoi slams "extremists", *The Phnom Penh Post*, 2 July, http://www.phnompenhpost.com/national/hanoi-slams-extremists(accessed on 31 July 2017).

Sophirom, Khan. 2013. 'Cambodia, China Reach a MOU on Military Human Resources Development', *Agency Kampuchea Press (AKP)*, 23 January, http://www.akp.gov.kh/?p=29498 (accessed on 15 July 2017).

Sovannara. 2014. 'Senior Chinese military official visits Cambodia on ties', *Global Times*, 17 March, http://www.globaltimes.cn/content/849077.shtml (accessed on 15 July 2017);

Strangio, Sebastian. 2009. 'Adjusting to life in China's shadow', *The Phnom Penh Post*, 6 October, http://www.phnompenhpost.com/national/adjusting-life-china%E2%80%99s-shadow (accessed on 15 July 2017).

The Economist. 2017. 'Why Cambodia has cosied up to China', 21 January, https://www.economist.com/news/asia/21715010-and-why-it-worries-cambodias-neighbours-why-cambodia-has-cosied-up-china (accessed on 15 July 2017).

The Phnom Penh Post. 2016. 'Chinese-Cambodian Ties Strengthen Day By Day', 1 December, http://www.phnompenhpost.com/post-plus/chinese-cambodian-ties-strengthen-day-day (accessed on 15 July 2017).

Titthara, May. 2012. 'China Reaps Concession Windfall', *The Phnom Penh Post*, 2 April, http://www.phnompenhpost.com/national/china-reaps-concession-windfalls (accessed on 15 July 2017).

Whitehead, James. 2016. 'Sihanoukville: The Next Boom Town', *Khmer Times*, 14 December, http://www.khmertimeskh.com/news/33142/sihanoukville—the-next-boom-town/ (accessed on 15 July 2017).

Xinhua. 2011. 'China leading investments in some fields in Cambodia: official', 5 April, http://news.xinhuanet.com/english2010/china/2011-04/05/c_13814075.htm (accessed on 15 July 2017).

Xinhua. 2013. 'Cambodia greets 333,900 Chinese tourists in 2012, up 35 pct', http://news.xinhuanet.com/english/travel/2013-02/12/c_132165732.htm(accessed on 15 July 2017).

XuRui. 2012. 'Cambodia's trade with China in 2011 up 73.5 pct', *ASEAN-China Center*, 10 February, http://www.asean-china-center.org/english/2012-02/10/c_131403060.htm (accessed on 15 July 2017)

Xue Lei and NguonSovan. 2016. 'Yearender: 2016 marks "new highs" in Sino-Cambodian ties: Cambodia officials, scholars', *Xinhua*, 6 December, http://news.xinhuanet.com/english/2016-12/06/c_135884349.htm (accessed on 15 July 2017).

Yao Jianing. 2014. 'China, Cambodia vow to deepen military ties', *Xinhua*, 18 November, http://eng.mod.gov.cn/TopNews/2014-11/18/content_4552254.htm (accessed on 15 July 2017).

Yao Jianing. 2015. 'China, Cambodian vow to cement bilateral military relations', *China Military Online*, 29 July, http://english.chinamil.com.cn/news-channels/china-military-news/2015-07/29/content_6605955.htm (accessed on 15 July 2017).

Yao Jianing. 2016. 'Chinese naval ships arrive in Cambodia for 4th port call', *China Military Online*, 17 October, http://eng.chinamil.com.cn/view/2016-10/17/content_7305388.htm (accessed on 15 July 2017).

Yao Jianing. 2017. 'Senior military leader meets with Cambodian military delegation', *China Military Online*, 18 January, http://eng.chinamil.com.cn/view/2017-01/18/content_7456896.htm (accessed on 15 July 2017).

12

China's Relations with Mongolia and Pakistan: The Current Situation and Some Comparisons

Nguyen Xuan Trung

China's relations with Pakistan and Mongolia form a pair of relations between a big power and two small neighboring countries. These relations were established many decades ago and saw stable development before being changed drastically in recent times when China adjusted its development strategy. Indeed, China's economic strategies have contributed to making significant changes in its regional and global positions and brought about changes in its relations with every country – be it a world power or a small regional country. Both Pakistan and Mongolia are characterised by an important geo-economic, geostrategic location, occupying a special place in China's foreign policies. Therefore, by looking at the current situation of China-Pakistan and China-Mongolia relations, it is possible for neigbouring countries to draw lessons in their relations with China. At the same time, through some comparative analysis of the similarities and differences in the relations of each country with China, it is possible to give certain assessments on the position and role of these countries in the region as well as characteristics of the cooperative and competitive trends in the world today.

China's Policy towards Pakistan and Mongolia under Xi Jinping

China's Policy Adjustments towards Pakistan

Its relationship with Pakistan is one of the rare cases of good foreign relations of the People's Republic of China since its foundation. Pakistan plays an increasingly important role in China's policies for some strategic benefits that it offers. China's objectives in its relations with Pakistan are now focused on several things.

First, there is the desire to replace the US as number one ally of Pakistan. Pakistan has been the key ally of the US during the war against terrorism, however, the two countries have also been deeply divided in this war. Flexibility is a characteristic of Pakistan's policy towards China and the US. Difficulties in its relations with the US will immediately turn Pakistan toward China to seek an alternative. China has taken advantage of this fact, using the discord between Pakistan and the US during the war against terrorism to drag Pakistan to its side. To demonstrate the nearly absolute support to Pakistan, China was the only country publicly expressing strong support for Pakistan following the assassination of Osama bin Laden in May 2011 (Buckley 2011). In the context of increasing suspicion about Pakistan's role in terrorism and Pakistan's relations with the US and many other countries suffering serious crises, the support of China has been very consistent. China has quickly moved from words to action. Many cooperative agreements were signed in May 2011. In recent years, China has surpassed the US in terms of both trade and investment in Pakistan. China-Pakistan trade reached US$16 billion in 2014, compared with US$5 billion of US-Pakistan trade. China's investments focus on improving the infrastructure and energy sectors of Pakistan. Particularly, in April 2015, Chinese President Xi Jinping came to Pakistan with the proposal of an investment package worth US$46 billion as part of a China-Pakistan Economic Corridor (CPEC). The Chinese aid to Pakistan is considered 'non-binding', i.e., there are no attached conditions as that of the US (Wake and Lavallee 2015). Therefore, despite a smaller amount compared to the US aid, it is nevertheless, highly appreciated. China also has an important voice in supporting Pakistan on the nuclear issue and in its disputes with India, which the US has always rejected so far.

All of this suggests that China is seeking to increase its influence and to become the number one partner of Pakistan. Tensions in US-Pakistan relations in the early 2010s created opportunities for Beijing to strengthen its deeper ties with Islamabad.

Second, China seeks to give more importance to the Pakistan factor in its strategy to contain India. India has deeply strained relations with Pakistan concerning territorial and other issues. Therefore, China sees that it will be very beneficial if Pakistan is used as a card to contain India. China believes that as long as India is kept busy on the western border with Pakistan, it will not create trouble on the eastern border with Tibet, where China and India also have territorial disputes (Kumar 2005). The Chinese believe that Pakistan is 'the last and the best card' to prevent the domination of India in South Asia, from the Persian Gulf to the Strait of Malacca (*Asian Warrior* 2013). Under Xi Jinping, the policy to use the Pakistan relationship to contain India continues to be promoted.

The most obvious manifestation of this scheme of China is the fact that Beijing has actively helped Pakistan modernise its armed forces. China has provided Pakistan with M-11 short-ranged missiles and helped Pakistan develop the Shaheen-1 ballistic missiles (Pant 2012). In the last two decades, the two countries have been engaged in a variety of arms manufacturing projects such as the JF-17 combat aircraft, which is capable of carrying nuclear weapons, radar systems and the Babur cruise missile. In addition, China also announced that it would sell eight submarines of the latest generation worth US$4-5 billion to Pakistan (*Dantri* 2015). Pakistan's possession of these submarines will make it difficult for India to blockade Karachi or Gwadar in a situation of conflict. There are also the economic benefits derived from the trade agreements in the defence sector with Pakistan.

China has also engaged in nuclear proliferation for Pakistan, helping it by designing and supplying heavy water reactors at the Khushab nuclear complex, and playing an important role in the production of plutonium. China also provided technical and financial support for the completion of the Chashma nuclear power reactors and the plutonium reprocessing facility built in the 1990s (Smith and Warrick 2009; Chang 2010). China continues to support Pakistan in its nuclear power development. In March 2013, China and Pakistan agreed to build the Chashma V nuclear power plant, following the four nuclear power plants at Chashma I, II, III and IV. In early 2014, China also agreed to provide US$6.5 billion in cash for Pakistan to build two nuclear power plants in the city of Karachi (*Nguoi Lao Dong* 2014).

However, it is also seen that the China-India relationship is both cooperative and competitive. In some aspects, especially in the economic aspect, China continues to consider India as an increasingly attractive economic opportunity for its trade and investments. Both China and India have benefited from the growth of their bilateral trade. China's annual exports to India easily outstrip its exports to Pakistan and the economic benefits in its relations with New Delhi make it imperative for Beijing to adopt a more subtle approach in the conflicts involving Pakistan.

Third, China is increasing its investments in infrastructure in Pakistan to bring about economic benefits but also to increase the latter's dependence on China. China's investments in Pakistan mainly focus on infrastructure and the energy sector through the CPEC with US$34 billion in energy projects and US$12 billion in infrastructure and transport projects announced during Xi's 2015 visit, which is more than double the total capital of foreign direct investment (FDI) to Pakistan since 2008, and significantly more than the entire aid from the US, the largest donor of Pakistan till now, since 2002 (*Baomoi* 2015).

In fact, China's focus on investment to expand the infrastructure of Pakistan is also a new approach to serve its hegemonic ambitions under the 'belt and road' or 'one belt, one road' initiative (BRI). The CPEC is considered an important stage of the 'belt', linking the Gwadar port in southwestern Pakistan with the Keshi (喀什, Kashgar) region of the Xinjiang Uyghur Autonomous Region of China, through a network of highways, railways and pipelines for oil and gas.

Through the CPEC, Beijing can also connect more easily with the Middle East and Africa, where thousands of Chinese enterprises with large numbers of workers are expanding their business operations. The CPEC also promises to help China expand its trade and influence throughout the Central and South Asian regions, competing with both the US and India. Fourth, there is a Chinese desire to turn Pakistan into a military 'backyard' in order to strengthen Beijing's position and to have an exit to the Indian Ocean. This serves the long-term goal of China to become a maritime power and expand Beijing's control to all the oceans. China is now paying attention to the Indian Ocean, which has so far been considered India's 'backyard'. China could pass through both Myanmar and Pakistan to enter the Indian Ocean, but the recent political changes in Myanmar have not been favourable for China, and thus, Pakistan becomes the main route to the Indian Ocean. After announcing the near completion of several artificial islands in the East Sea, all the signals show that China's next action will be to proceed to the Indian Ocean. In September 2014 and May 2015, Beijing consequently took submarines to the ports of Colombo in Sri Lanka and Karachi in Pakistan (Pandit 2015; Aneez and Sirilal 2014).

Pakistan's deepwater port of Gwadar plays a key role not only in the BRI of China, but importantly, also serves as a potential naval base for the Chinese military forces. It is considered an ideal location from which China can keep track of the US naval operations in the Persian Gulf, Indian operations in the Arabian Sea and the Indo-US maritime cooperation in the Indian Ocean. Along with a series of sea ports targeted for investment by China in Sri Lanka, Myanmar and in the near future, possibly also Bangladesh, Gwadar will be part of a 'string of pearls' for China and become one of the strategic naval bases for Beijing in its goal for reaching beyond its immediate waters (Chellaney 2015). The change in the functions of the ports will almost certainly happen when China and India begin competing more fiercely in the Indian Ocean.

The growing military dependence of Pakistan on China is also a relevant point. China's military support has long been focusing on building strength for Pakistan. For many decades, Beijing has been the sole reliable supplier of weapons for Pakistan. A SIPRI report shows that China has sold to Pakistan more than half of the weapons imported by Pakistan in the last five years before 2015 (*Small* 2015). Military technology transfer is especially seen as a real sign of China's intention of turning Pakistan into its military backyard. China has made important technology transfers to Pakistan, particularly in sensitive areas such as missile and nuclear weapons manufacturing, thereby creating credibility for as well as strengthening significantly Pakistan's military capabilities. In Pakistan, civilian and military leaders maintain a consensus in giving priority to a good relationship with China.

China's Policy Adjustments towards Mongolia

Mongolia is a country rich in natural resources and is a land of geopolitical importance. Mongolia is the strategic card that both Russia and China want to hold to have an upper hand vis-à-vis each other. Mongolia is also the target of US policy because, by having control of Mongolia, it can influence both Russia and China. In fact, the US has proposed the establishment of a permanent military base in Mongolia but the proposal has not been accepted (Tiezzi 2014). On the other hand, Mongolia also seeks to promote its relationship with the US to balance against Russia and China.

For its part, China is implementing an 'economic corridor' linking China with Central Asian and European countries via Mongolia within the framework of its Silk Road Economic Belt under the BRI. Mongolia will act as a gateway for China to enter a market of enormous potential, i.e., the European market, which will help liberate the investment forces and enhance China's economic and political influence in the international arena. Thus, in both economic and political terms, Mongolia is a land of special significance in Chinese strategy.

China's Objectives in its Policy towards Mongolia

China's first objective is to increase Mongolia's economic dependence on it. The Chinese government has encouraged the expansion of its business forces into the Mongolian market with a very large number of Chinese companies now engaged in building a Chinese 'empire' in this country. Chinese companies are actively engaged in building infrastructure to connect the major energy resource centres in the country and are also eyeing investments in mining projects (Li 2011; Stanway 2010). Currently, Mongolia's small and medium enterprises are increasingly under the control of China with offers also made for the construction of big factories in the country.

China's objective is to promote its own economy by supporting Mongolia's economic development. China has gradually become the number one investor in Mongolia with the figures increasing year by year. What is noteworthy is that China mainly invests in the industrial and mining sectors—the most profitable sectors—without paying attention to the consequences of environmental pollution. The situation is similar in the Chinese investment projects in infrastructure; most of the roads under construction lead to the mineral mines to be exploited. It can be said that Mongolia is 'using resources as capital' to attract investments from China. Due to this policy to attract investment, Mongolia's economy has increasingly become more imbalanced, focusing on mining and agriculture, in which mining is the pillar industry occupying 20 per cent of country's GDP and 80 per cent of exports (Muff et al 2016). The economic apparatus with a severely imbalanced structure operates mainly through foreign investments with a large part from China.

Second, China seeks to acquire Mongolian mineral resources. Although the Mongolian mining market is strongly engaged by powerful countries like the US, China, Russia, Japan and South Korea, overall however, it can be said that it is Russia and China that exert the greatest influence in Mongolia.

The US and Russia have made lots of efforts in promoting relations with Mongolia for a long time, but Mongolia has reasons to prefer China, which is willing to invest a significant amount to construct roads leading to the mines as mentioned above (Shishmishig 2009). China is also taking advantage of the lack of professional business practices in Mongolia to gradually monopolise the market. On the other hand, in a dependent situation due to the large amount of preferential credit loans received from China, Mongolia must always calculate so as not to offend its big friend. Beginning from 2005, the Chinese National Petroleum Corporation (CNPC) has conducted petroleum exploration in Mongolia, operating the Talmud Taga project, one of the largest Chinese investment projects in Mongolia. In June 2010, then Chinese Premier Wen Jiabao on a state visit to Ulan Bator pledged to give Mongolia US$500 preferential loan (Li and Lan 2011). These forms of largesse help soften the political climate in Mongolia whose parliament has factions divided into pro-US, pro-China and pro-Russia camps.

During the visit of the Chinese President Xi Jinping to Mongolia, the two sides witnessed the signing of a Memorandum of Understanding (MoU) between the representative of the Chinese National Petroleum Corporation and the head of the Department of Petroleum of Mongolia in order to strengthen cooperation in the petroleum sector to further deepen the oil and gas cooperation between the two countries (The Office of the President of Mongolia 2014). By gradually monopolising the mineral deposits in Mongolia, China has step by step occupied what is arguably the essence and most important factor of economic growth in that country. Mining operations by Chinese companies have caused serious environmental problems (Woods 2016), and at the same time contributed to the imbalanced growth of the economy, which has long-term consequences in the future.

A third Chinese objective is to have Mongolia as a part of the institutions headed by China. This scheme is a part of the long-term strategy of China to create a 'linking beam' to counter the US. Mongolia's participation in an alliance is encouraged to serve several purposes: firstly, it is to take the advantage of the collective strength to easily control Mongolia and to make Mongolia a loyal ally, and secondly, this also enhances the power of its economy.

China has brought Mongolia into the Silk Road Economic Belt Initiative through the Russian transcontinental railway system and a programme of building Mongolian steppe roads. On 12 September 2014, at the first Russia-

China-Mongolia Summit which took place within the framework of the 14th Summit of the Shanghai Cooperation Organization (SCO) in Dushanbe, Tajikistan, Xi along with the Russian President Vladimir Putin and the Mongolian President Tsakhiagiin Elbegdorj supported a proposal to set up an economic corridor linking the three neighbouring countries (Ministry of Foreign Affairs of People's Republic of China 2014).

China has also actively mobilised Mongolia to take part in economic organisations such as the Asian Cooperative Dialogue (ACD) and the Asian Infrastructure Investment Bank (AIIB) and supported Mongolia's observer status in the SCO. China has invited Mongolia to participate in the scheme to build the Silk Road, invited Ulan Bator to join the APEC (in 2014) and promised to lobby for Mongolia to become a permanent member of the forum (Ting 2014). Mongolia has also become a part in China's strategy to internationalise the reminbi. So far, the renminbi comprises 60 per cent of the currency in circulation in Mongolia (Wheatley 2013).

Fourth, China seeks to turn Mongolia into its political backyard. The Chinese economic policies contain within themselves political objectives. An easily discernable characteristic of the Chinese foreign policy under Xi is that China will not only use the economic card to put pressure on Mongolia but also strengthen its relations with this country through other diplomatic campaigns. Typically, Xi's visit to Mongolia on 21 August 2014 contributed to the elevation of the bilateral relations to a 'strategic partnership'. Called as a 'pin-point style diplomacy' (点穴式外交, *dianxueshi waijiao*), this visit strengthened bilateral cooperation and at the same time served the purpose of competing with the US and Japan in courting Mongolia and ensuring that the US and Japan could not use Mongolia as a 'card' to contain China. In addition, a closer cooperation with Mongolia will strengthen China's influence in the region.

Finally, there also appears to be an element of national assimilation for China. Old Russia's territorial acquisition policy by way of exporting labour surplus is now being implemented by Beijing in Mongolia. Chinese statistics show that in the first half of 2014, among the 22,400 people coming to Mongolia for work from 95 countries in the world, the Chinese people occupied 73 per cent (Economic and Commercial Counsellor's Office of the Embassy of the People's Republic of China in Mongolia 2014). This has created anxiety in Mongolia as the 'invasion' of the Chinese—an invasion without gunfire—

has the potential effect of subsuming the Mongolian national identity. Given just the experience of China's Inner Mongolian Autonomous Region where approximately four million Mongols are surrounded by more than 20 million Chinese (the Hans), it is possible to anticipate the risk of being assimilated.

Currently, China is seeking all possible ways to improve and promote its good image in Mongolia. The Chinese people are also actively constructing business centres and new buildings. China is implementing its policy of attracting Mongolian students and intellectuals to come to China by providing scholarships for their studies—the current number of Mongolian students in China is 8,000—and training Mongolian elites. In recent years, China has also supported funding for the establishment of over 30 schools in Mongolia, to promote research and teaching of the Chinese language (Enkhtsetseg 2014)

Outcomes of China's Relations with Mongolia and Pakistan: A Comparative Analysis

Depth of Cooperation

China's relations with Pakistan and Mongolia since Xi Jinping came to power have witnessed changes in a positive direction. With Pakistan, the two sides have upgraded their relations from a 'strategic partnership' to an 'all-weather strategic cooperation comprehensive strategic partnership' (Embassy of Pakistan, Chile 2015). With Mongolia, Xi's 2015 visit—the first visit of a high level leader to Mongolia in more than a decade—the two sides also upgraded the bilateral relations from a 'strategic partnership' (2011) (Bhattacharya 2014) to a 'comprehensive strategic partnership' (2014) (*Xinhua* 2014).

Chinese policy adjustments towards the two countries under Xi are part of a common trend visible with other neighbouring countries too. That said, the policy adjustment towards Mongolia is not as clear and strong as towards Pakistan. China's relationship with Pakistan is a close relationship in which China plays the role of a 'supporter'. Thus, Pakistan's dependence on China is understandable. Mongolia, though has long sought to get free from the influence of China, remains heavily dependent on China economically. Thus, it can be seen that the difference between Pakistan and Mongolia in their relationship with China is of political dependence. Mongolia is more politically independent of China, but economically, both countries are heavily dependent on China.

Broadly speaking, all small neighbouring countries of China are heavily dependent on China in economic terms at different levels, which do not follow the political wills of the countries in their relations with China.

Nature of Cooperation

While China's relations with Pakistan and Mongolia are basically mutually beneficial relations, there is also an element of mutually taking advantage of each other in the China-Pakistan relations. This usually occurs in relations which focus on political and security cooperation. For Mongolia, the relationship with China is more inclined to economic cooperation which focuses on economic interests, so the element of mutually taking advantage of each other is less evident. With Pakistan, it is evident that China takes the advantage of Pakistan's location and conflict with India, while Pakistan takes advantage of China to deal with India.

If we compare China's relations with Pakistan and Mongolia, we can recognise the similarities in Chinese policies to both countries, while the differences lie in the policy responses of each country towards China. This primarily stems from the two countries' awareness of the importance of China for their development strategies. Both countries consider China a very important partner, but the content and the level of importance are somewhat different. Though Mongolia is influenced by China in making decisions of national importance, it is also always conscious of the need to reduce its dependence on China and looks for support and investments from other powers. The China-Mongolia relationship is typical of a relationship between a world power and a dependent country. This kind of relationship is especially beneficial to China but causes imbalances in Mongolia's economic development, forcing this country to find ways to break the correlation between a big power and a small country. Ulan Bator seems to focus on economic development objectives, considering economic strength as a major driving force to get rid of Chinese influence.

For Pakistan, meanwhile, due to the benefits of its relationship with China and its disagreement with the US, it has a tendency of leaning towards China. The closer and deeper cooperative relationship between the two countries opens up future prospects that China may replace the US as the number one ally of Pakistan. On the other hand, compared to Mongolia, Pakistan has a certain voice in the region, and a relatively stable military potential backed by a partner stronger than China. These factors help Pakistan avoid being 'swallowed up' by its partner. The relationship between the two countries is not a kind of relationship between a big power and a small dependent country, but a mutually beneficial relationship. Compared to Mongolia, Pakistan's relations with China seem to be more balanced. There is a relative balance in the position of the two countries including balance in the two main areas of cooperation, i.e. economy and military, and balance in the influence of the major powers. It is this balance that will allow the China-Pakistan cooperation continue its sustainable development in the near future.

Another noticeable feature is that China's relations with the two countries, no matter how good they are, whether it is 'alliance' or 'comprehensive strategic partnership', are still unequal in nature. It is China that dominates the relationship, not these two countries, and China uses economic instruments to mould the bilateral relationships.

Major Fields of Cooperation

In diplomatic and political relations, China's relations with Pakistan and Mongolia have improved markedly. With Mongolia, China was soon aware of the role and the importance of Mongolia to its national security, so it has put great importance on promoting the relationship with Mongolia, such as through inviting Mongolian participation in the SCO and the establishment of a 'strategic' and later 'comprehensive strategic' partnership. Compared to Mongolia, Pakistan and China have more cultural and religious differences, but their bilateral relations have developed quite stably for many decades. There have also been some adjustments in China-Pakistan relations. Previously, they focused on issues of security and defence, but recently they have expanded to the economic field as well.

Security and military relations are an important and very sensitive issue because they are directly related to the issue of territory and national security of each country. For Pakistan, security and military are the main issues that not only China but also Pakistan tries to focus on. While supporting Pakistan in issues of defence and security, China also takes advantage of the diplomatic relations and the geographical location of Pakistan to strengthen its military power and security in the Tibet and Xinjiang areas. This relationship has an invaluable geostrategic role in combating perceived threats from India and Russia. For Mongolia, the bilateral security—military cooperation with China is not as close as that of Pakistan. The main reason is that Mongolia's national security is no perception of threat from a third country as in the case of Pakistan vis-à-vis India. On the other hand, Mongolia's good relations with the US and its calls for American presence on its soil have worried China. Therefore, China has to promote its cooperation with Mongolia in order to prevent space for the US. Mongolia's geographic location is extremely important to the national security of China as its territory lies deeply inside Chinese territory. While Mongolia is in fear of 'being assimilated' and of becoming a part of China, security and defence cooperation with China will not help Mongolia solve any problem. It is for this reason that China has increased its influence in Mongolia through economic rather than national defence and security means.

The other major field of cooperation is in economic relations. The outstanding common feature in China's relations with both Pakistan and Mongolia is that China is the largest economic partner of both countries, and China's role seems to grow bigger day by day. However, the trade relations of the two countries with China are insignificant compared to the total international trade of China. Moreover, the growth rate of the China-Pakistan bilateral trade has been constant from 2009 to the present, while China-Mongolia trade relations in 2013 decreased, compared to the previous two years and only saw an increase again in 2014 (Fig. 1).

Figure 1: China's Total Trade in Goods with Pakistan and Mongolia (in billion US$)

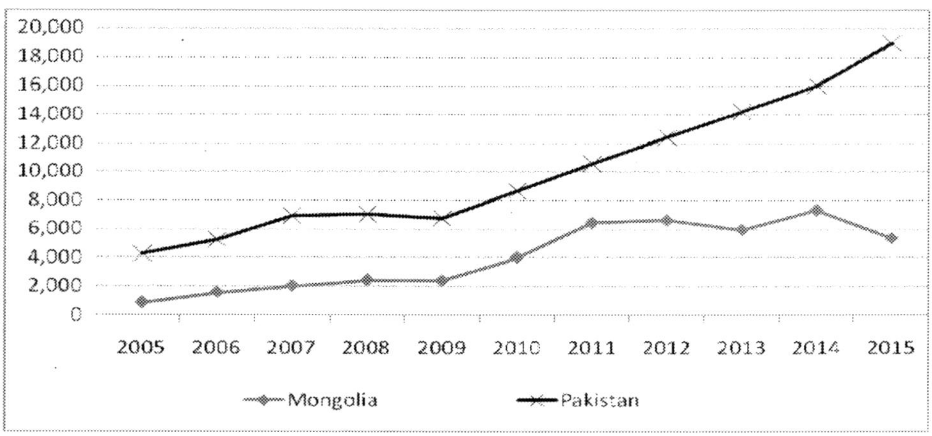

Source: Calculated from the data of the International Trade Center, 2017.

China's economic relations with the two countries are a natural need because they are neighbouring countries. However, the level of economic relations of China with the two countries is quite different. This is largely due to the differences in the natural conditions and social situation of each country or, in other words, the differences in comparative advantages of each country with China. Moreover, the economic relations of Pakistan and Mongolia with China while not important as a whole to China are particularly important to the Chinese border provinces neighbouring these countries. Thus, economic relations depend also on the level of development and the characteristics of China's localities adjacent to these neighbouring countries.

Socio-cultural relations are another aspect for comparison. Historically, the neighbouring countries have been more or less subject to the invasion of Chinese culture in a natural way. In this regard, Mongolia is clearly affected, but Pakistan is different because it is separated from China by unfavourable terrain and Pakistan itself was strongly influenced by culture and religion from its west. In today's context, with deliberate cultural propagation by China, the cultural exchange activities between China and the two neighbouring countries—Pakistan and Mongolia—have gained certain traction contributing to building political trust, enhancing economic linkages and placing their bilateral relations in a good setting. However, there remain many limitations in the cultural exchanges between China and Pakistan and between China and Mongolia such as the lack of comprehensive cooperation mechanisms and of the adequate participation of ordinary people in official cultural activities and so on.

Degree of Impact on Pakistan and Mongolia

China's policy with both Pakistan and Mongolia has been built with the purpose of making the most of the benefits that the cooperation with these two countries offers, without paying too much attention to the damages that may be incurred by them.

The partnership with China has helped rejuvenate the economies of Mongolia and Pakistan for the time being. China has launched several new initiatives related directly to the neighboring countries, such as the BRI and the AIIB. Mongolia and Pakistan, which are two out of the 57 co-founding members of the AIIB, have the right to negotiate the institutional issues of the organisation and have easier access to its capital. However, it must be confirmed that the more they cooperate with China, the more difficult it is for them to compete with China in their own domestic markets because the Chinese goods are more competitive in terms of price.

In addition, most of China's investment packages in the neighbouring countries are to implement infrastructure projects connected with China, and bring it many strategic benefits both economically and militarily. China always stands at the central position, and therefore, although these packages bring much economic benefits to the countries involved, they also inevitably cause more dependence of these countries on China. China has neither directed its partners towards sustainable development nor built a better image in the region. In Mongolia, China's mining projects have caused a serious impact on natural resources and the environment, leading to an unsustainable development of the economy, while in Pakistan, the 'implicit consent' of China to the nuclear plans of the country shows that China has not paid much attention to the practical benefits of these countries. China appears to wants to assert its position as a world power but has not properly fulfilled the responsibilities of a world power on important regional and international issues.

Conclusion

It is important to note that Chinese policies show the great importance Beijing has attached to its neighbours and this brings about good opportunities for both Mongolia and Pakistan. However, it is also a challenge because China is rising and looking outward with these neighbouring countries considered only as starting points. In addition, increasing opportunities for economic cooperation also mean that these countries will see increased dependence on China if they do not diversify their economic partners.

Moreover, China's relations with Mongolia and Pakistan are those between a big power and smaller countries. These pairs of relationships not only showcase mutual benefits but also mutual advantage-taking. In a way, Pakistan is used as a tool in the implementation of China's policy towards India. Unless the competition between China and India disappears, the importance of Pakistan for China cannot be reduced. Therefore, Pakistan finds it very difficult to escape from 'the game' of China when Pakistan's destiny is sometimes not decided by itself. The difficult relationship between India and Pakistan serves China's highest national interests.

It appears very difficult for Pakistan and Mongolia to escape the influence of China; rather, as things stand it is very easy for them to be trapped in their relationship with their bigger neighbour.

REFERENCES

Aneez, Shihar and Sirilal Ranga. 2014. 'Chinese submarine docks in Sri Lanka despite Indian concerns', *Reuters,* 2 November, http://in.reuters.com/article/sri-lanka-china-submarine-idINKBN0IM0LU20141102 (accessed on 21 January 2017).

Asian Warrior. 2013. 'Why Pakistan is so important to China?' 20 June, http://www.asianwarrior.com/2013/06/why-pakistan-is-so-important-to-china.html#.VRKYzPysVl8 (accessed on 7 October 2015).

Baomoi.com 2015. 'Trung Quoc duoc gi tu hanh lang kinh te noi toi Pakistan' [What China gains from the China-Pakistan Economic Corridor], http://www.baomoi.com/Trung-Quoc-duoc-gi-tu-hanh-lang-kinh-te-noi-toi-Pakistan/c/17217718.epi, (accessed on 07 August 2015).

Bhattacharya, Abanti. 2014. 'China and Mongolia: Realising a 'Comprehensive Strategic Partnership'' *IPCS*, 29 August, http://www.ipcs.org/article/china/china-and-mongolia-realising-a-comprehensive-strategic-partnership-4632.html (accessed on 21 January 2017)

Buckley, Chris. 2011. 'China hails death of bin Laden, defends partner Pakistan', *Reuters*, 3 May, http://www.reuters.com/article/us-binladen-china-idUSTRE7421O020110503 (accessed on 21 January 2017)

Chellaney, Brahma. 2015. 'A Silk Glove for China's Iron Fist', *Project Syndicate*, 4 March. https://www.project-syndicate.org/commentary/china-silk-road-dominance-by-brahma-chellaney-2015-03?barrier=accessreg (accessed on 21 January 2017)

Dantri. 2015. 'Trung Quoc ban 110 chien dau co tthan sam cho Pakistan' [China sold 110 JF-17 Thunder fighter jets to Pakistan], http://dantri.com.vn/the-gioi/trung-quoc-ban-110-chien-dau-co-than-sam-jf-17-cho-pakistan-1430871100.htm (accessed on 18 September 2015).

Economic and Commercial Counsellor's Office of the Embassy of the People's Republic of China in Mongolia. 2014. 'Mengguguo 2014 nian shang bannian zongti jingji yunxing zhuangkuang' (蒙古国 2014 年上半年总体经济运行状况) [A Panorama of the Mongolian Economy in the first half of 2014], 27 August, http://mn.mofcom.gov.cn/article/ztdy/201408/20140800712493.shtml (accessed on 21 January 2017).

Embassy of Pakistan, Chile. 2015. 'Joint Statement between the Islamic Republic of Pakistan and the People's Republic of China on Establishing the All-Weather Strategic Cooperative Partnership', 20 April, http://www.mofa.gov.pk/chile/pr-details.php?prID=2733 (accessed on 25 September 2017).

International Trade Center, 2017. 'Trade map: Trade Statistics for International Business Development', http://trademap.org/Bilateral_TS.aspx (accessed on 30 July 2017).

Kumar, R. 2005. *Making Peace with Partition.* New Delhi: Penguin Books.

Li Xiaokun and Lan Lan. 2011. 'Mongolian pact called 'milestone'', *China Daily*, 17 June, http://www.chinadaily.com.cn/cndy/2011-06/17/content_12719188.htm (accessed on 21 January 2017)

Li, Justin. 2011. 'Chinese investment in Magnolia: An uneasy courtship between Goliath and David', *East Asia Forum*, 2 February, http://www.eastasiaforum.org/2011/02/02/chinese-investment-in-mongolia-an-uneasy-courtship-between-goliath-and-david/ (accessed 21 January 2017)

Ministry of Foreign Affairs of People's Republic of China. 2014. 'Xi Jinping Attends Meeting of the Three Heads of State of China, Russia and Mongolia', 11 September, http://www.fmprc.gov.cn/mfa_eng/topics_665678/zjpcxshzzcygyslshdsschybdtjkstmedfsllkydjxgsfw/t1191093.shtml (accessed on 21 January 2017)

Muff, R., Otgonbaatar, A., Bolormaa, B. and Batsukh, E . 2016. *Annual Bulletin of the Geology and Mining Sector of Mongolia.* Ulaanbaatar; Mineral Resources Authority of Mongolia, https://www.bgr.bund.de/EN/Themen/Zusammenarbeit/TechnZusammenarb/Downloads/mongolei_MRAM_AnnualBulletin2016.pdf?__blob=publicationFile&v=2 (accessed on 21 January 2017).

Nguoi Lao Dong. 2014. 'Trung Quoc cho Pakistan vay 6,5 ti USD xay nha may dien hat nhan' [China commits $6,5 billion for Pakistani nuclear project]', http://nld.com.vn/thoi-su-quoc-te/trung-quoc-cho-pakistan-vay-65-ti-usd-xay-nha-may-dien-hat-nhan-20140103093030718.htm, (accessed on 21 January 2017).

Pandit, Rajat. 2015. 'Chinese submarine in Karachi, India alarmed', *The Times of India,* 27 June, http://timesofindia.indiatimes.com/india/Chinese-submarine-in-Karachi-India-alarmed/articleshow/47845930.cms (accessed on 21 January 2017)

Pant, Harsh V. 2012. 'The Pakistan Thorn in China-India-U.S. Relations', *The Washington Quarterly,* Vol. 35, No.1, 83-95.

Shishmishig, J. 2009. 'Current situation of Mongolia-China trade and economic cooperation and further trends', Welcome address, Joint Dissemination Workshop on the Study of Zamyn-Uud, Erlian Border Development Program, 14 April, http://www.carecprogram.org/uploads/events/2009/Joint-PRC-MON-Dissemination/Joint-Dissemination-Session1-Mongolia-PRC-Cooperation-notes.pdf

Small, Andrew. 2015. *The China–Pakistan Axis: Asia's New Geopolitics.* New York: Oxford University Press.

Smith, Jeffrey and Joby Warrick. 2009. 'Pakistani nuclear scientist's accounts tell of Chinese proliferation', *Washington Post.* 13 November, http://www.washingtonpost.com/wp-dyn/content/article/2009/11/12/AR2009111211060.html (accessed on 21 January 2017)

Stanway, David. 2010. 'Doing business in Mangolia a tightrope walk', *Reuters,* 27 May, http://www.reuters.com/article/us-frontiers-mongolia-idUSTRE64Q08M20100527 (accessed 21 January 2017)

The Office of the President of Mongolia. 2014. 'Mongolia and China Sighed Documents', 21 August, http://www.president.mn/eng/newsCenter/viewNews.php?newsId=1245 (accessed on 21 January).

Tiezzi, Shannon. 2014. 'US Promises Increase in Military Aid to Mongolia', *The Diplomat,* 11 April, http://thediplomat.com/2014/04/us-promises-increase-in-military-aid-to-mongolia/ (accessed on 22 January)

Ting Shi. 2014. 'Xi Upgrades Mongolia Relationship as Bilateral Trade Grows', *Bloomberg.* 22 August, http://www.bloomberg.com/news/articles/2014-08-22/china-s-xi-upgrades-mongolia-relationship-as-trade-links-deepen (accessed on 9 October 2015).

Tserendorj Enkhtsetseg. 2014. 'Mengguguo zhong-xiaoxue Hanyu jiaoxue xianzhuang diaocha - yi Wulanbatuo xiwang Hanyu xuexiao weili' (蒙古国中小学汉语教学现状调查--以乌兰巴托希望汉语学校为例, 硕士论文) [A Survey of Chinese Language Teaching in Mongolian Primary and Secondary Schools: A Case Study of Schools in Ulan Bator], MA Thesis, Hebei University, 27 August, http://cdmd.cnki.com.cn/Article/CDMD-10075-1014040742.htm (accessed on 9 October 2015).

Wake, Damon and Guillaume Lavalle. 2015. 'China's Xi Jinping calls this $46 billion China-Pakistan corridor project a 'historic development opportunity'', *Business Insider.* 21 April, http://www.businessinsider.com/afp-security-fears-for-china-pakistan-corridor-as-xi-ends-visit-2015-4 (accessed on 3 November 2015).

Wheatley, Alan. 2013. 'The pretenders to the dollar's crown', in Alan Wheatley, *The Power of Currencies and Currencies of Power.* Adelphi Series, 45-74.

Woods, Lucy. 2016. 'Mining threatens Mongolia's fragile environmental balance', *Chinadialogue,* 25 April, https://www.chinadialogue.net/article/show/single/en/8849-Mining-threatens-Mongolia-s-fragile-environmental-balance%20 (accessed on 21 January 2017).

Xinhua. 2014. 'China, Mongolia upgrade ties to comprehensive strategic partnership', http://www.chinadaily.com.cn/world/2014xivisitmongolia/201408/21/content_18465053.htm (accessed on 7 August 2016).

13

China-Vietnam Interactions on the Mekong: Institutional Arrangements, National Priorities and Regional Implications

Panchali Saikia and Mirza Zulfiqur Rahman

The Mekong River has its origin and headwaters in the southeastern Himalayan mountains of the Tibetan Autonomous Region of China, from where the Mekong flows to the south and east on its way, before emptying into the South China Sea. The Mekong flows through six nations—China, Myanmar, Laos, Thailand, Cambodia, Vietnam—and is considered to be the hydrological backbone of mainland Southeast Asia (Jacobs 2002), being its largest river, and binding all the six co-riparian countries in a complex and a tightly woven web of interdependencies (Lauridsen 2004). The Mekong River is known as a 'boundary river', as it flows through China's southwestern province of Yunnan for almost half of its length, subsequently entering the 'Golden Triangle' region of Southeast Asia, forming the boundary between Myanmar and Laos, and then the boundary between Laos and Thailand, before flowing eastward into Laos; and after turning south within Laos, the Mekong River again forms the boundary between Laos and Thailand, and then flows into Cambodia. In Cambodia, the Tonle Sap River connects the Mekong with Cambodia's Tonle Sap lake, which is also known as the 'Great Lake'; during the wet season, the Tonle Sap River carries high flows away from the Mekong to the Tonle Sap lake, which subsequently expands to the north and west, while during the dry season, the Tonle Sap River reverses its flow and carries waters from the Tonle Sap lake back to the Mekong River. Below Phnom Penh, the Mekong splits into two rivers, with the main stem of the Mekong being the eastern branch, and the western branch being the Bassac River; both the rivers then flow into the Mekong Delta of Vietnam, finally entering the South China Sea.

The 1995 Mekong Agreement, which established the Mekong River Commission (MRC) is regarded as a milestone in international water resource management treaties among co-riparian countries, due to its emphasis on the joint development of the river basin and its resources, ecological protection and a dynamic process of trans-boundary water allocation. However, the MRC has also been struggling to balance varied interests within the basin and in persuading China to address the priorities and concerns of the downstream countries. A major hurdle comes from the fact that China is not an active member of any of the institutional arrangements on the Mekong River cooperation, including the MRC, and so is not bound by any legal mechanisms. Second, China's priority in the Mekong is driven by its energy demand growth with increased interest in economic integration and dam development as a strategic option rather than as a normative commitment. This stands in contrast to the larger priorities of plugging gaps in the regulation of river development activities and livelihood concerns of the lower riparians.

This paper analyses the trajectory of conflict and cooperation between China and the MRC countries of Thailand, Laos, Cambodia and Vietnam, and examines to what extent the current institutional regimes governing trans-boundary water in Southeast Asia have been successful in contributing towards collective action, addressing the interests, threat perceptions and concerns of the co-riparian states. The most critical ramification of the Chinese interventions in upstream Mekong will be felt the furthest downstream of the Mekong basin in Vietnam, and this paper will, therefore, examine Vietnam's responses in particular. This is particularly so in the context of Vietnam's concerns over the flow-depleted Mekong Delta being severely affected by saltwater entering from the South China Sea, and China's increasing water discharge from its Jinghong Dam operating since 2008 (Miao et al. 2015) The cascades of dams operating in Lancang (i.e. Jinhe, Gongguoquiao, Xiaowan, Manwan, Dachaoshan,

Nuozhadu and Jinghong), with the ones in the lower stretches of the Mekong such as the Xayaburi hydropower project in Laos, among others, along with the climate change impacts on the river basin, will further exacerbate the downstream flow regime of the Mekong Delta, which is critically significant for its local livelihoods (International Rivers 2013; Miao et al. 2015).

Mekong Cooperation and Development Agenda in the Post-Cold War Context

The foundation of the Mekong cooperation was laid in the hostile environment of the Cold War, when the Committee for Coordination of Investigations of the Lower Mekong Basin, known as the Mekong Committee, was initiated in 1957. The geopolitical influence of the United States in the Southeast Asian region had a major role in establishing this formalised cooperation; it was the United States Bureau of Reclamation and the United Nations (UN) that urged the formation of an international river basin organisation towards the development of irrigation and hydropower in the Lower Mekong Countries (LMC) of Thailand, Cambodia, Laos and Vietnam (then South Vietnam). The Mekong Committee was the product of the US efforts at containing China's influence in the region by uniting the LMC against the spread of communism (in North Vietnam and China), which resulted in non-participation of these communist countries in the committee. Also, as China and Myanmar were not members of the UN at that point of time, and with the UN being the main funder of the MC, these countries were not invited to participate (Lauridsen 2004).

China was not incorporated in the Mekong regime for a long time despite being the influential and crucial upper riparian stakeholder in the basin. This arrangement was altered with the shift in the geopolitical order in Southeast Asia soon after the end of the Cold War, with China emerging as the most important regional power in the new regional order through its economic development initiative in the Mekong region (Keskinen et al. 2008; Makim 2002). Alongside China's policy shift, moving from a Cold War superpower competition to building beneficial relations with the LMC and its hydropower development initiatives in the Mekong River basin, created major dilemmas in the lower basin area on recognising and opening up to China in the Mekong regime. Disagreements among the lower basin countries continued on whether to continue with the Mekong committee framework or to develop a new framework by incorporating China (Keskinen et al. 2008). It was finally only in the late 1990s that China and LMC began discussions on water resource management and river basin development cooperation.

For the lower basin countries, water management of the Mekong River had never featured in their discourse on China, except from the point of view of China's dam-building initiatives, the first being the Manwan Dam in Yunnan province, constructed in 1995 (Summers 2008). The 1995 agreement on Cooperation for the Sustainable Development of the Mekong River Basin that established the MRC (MRC 1995), was a major breakthrough as it incorporated China even if only as an observer member in 1996 along with Myanmar. This agreement is regarded as a milestone in international water resource management treaties among co-riparian countries, bringing in new development initiatives with a formalised institution working on joint development of the river basin and its resources, along with ecological protection and a dynamic process of trans-boundary water allocation and sharing (Lauridsen 2004). There are also member agencies, the National Mekong Committees (NMCs), established at country-level, to strengthen the link between the MRC and the national governments and to engage with civil society and local populations at the national level (Dore and Lazarus 2009).

The water-related events and processes in the post-Cold War period in the Mekong River basin form the basis of the upstream–downstream riparian relations in the new regionalism context and perspective, which swept Southeast Asia and East Asia in the 1990s. It is from this lens that we can explain the hegemonic tendencies in the overall Mekong River basin, and how hegemonic leadership roles have been acquired in China in the Upper Mekong basin, and in Thailand and Vietnam in the Lower Mekong basin.

River Regionalism: Locating the Mekong in China-MRC Relations

The Mekong can be referred to as a truly 'regional river', encompassing the high plateaus and hilly regions of southwestern China, passing by Myanmar, constituting almost all the water resources of Laos, the northeastern part of Thailand, Cambodia and irrigating the extensive Vietnamese rice production areas of the Mekong Delta. Borrowing from Dent's definition of 'political regionalism' (Dent 2002), the concept of 'river regionalism' refers to integral formations of transnational government and policy networks, the expression of shared political, economic and development interests among the basin riparians and stakeholders, advancement in policy coordination and policy enterprises, and the creation of regional level institutions to manage the common 'river basin interest'. Dosch and Hensengerth (2005) point out that the sub-regional cooperation in the Mekong Basin falls in the category of 'positive type' regionalism, a classification borrowed from Taga's two-fold typology of post-Cold War regionalism—defensive type regionalism and positive type regionalism (Taga 1994)—emerging from the debate on regional bloc-building.

If we look at the trajectory of relations between China and the MRC countries particularly on Mekong cooperation, the strategy of counterbalancing a rising China by the MRC countries forming a group, with Vietnam and Thailand taking leadership roles within that group, seems unable to explain the complex and dynamic relationship of the countries involved (Bobekova et al. 2013). Rather, it is an institutionalist approach that better explains China's role in Mekong basin politics with the MRC countries and development dynamics (Bobekova et al. 2013).

Institutional cooperation over sharing and management of water resources of the Mekong River basin has often been cited as one of the successful arrangements of riparian cooperation and basin development (Phillips et al. 2006). Even at times of strained relations and during conflicts, cooperation on the Mekong River has remained resilient. For example, during the Vietnam War, the Mekong Committee continued exchanging water data and information among its member countries (Wolf et al. 2005). The Mekong has seen remarkably few conflicts over water, and when these have occurred, they have had the form of political tensions rather than involving violent confrontation between riparian countries. It is likely that the early foundation of the Mekong Committee has played an important role in facilitating cooperation rather than violent conflict in river basin politics and experts often refer to a special 'Mekong Spirit' of cooperation when writing the history of regional hydro-politics (Lauridsen 2004). The concept of benefits beyond the river (Sadoff and Grey 2002) from basin-wide cooperation, in the case of the Mekong, has been the driving principle right from the emergence of the Mekong cooperation and this economic rationale still holds strong, as has been highlighted by the intensification of institutional initiatives.

What limits the effective operation of the MRC is that, the two upstream countries, China and Myanmar, are not its members and are not bound by any legal agreements keeping open their avenues for unilateral actions upstream

(Backer 2007). The Mekong 'river regionalism' dynamics is integral to understanding the upstream-downstream basin development debates, and how that has promoted regional peace and economic prosperity among the Mekong basin riparians.

Regionalism, Institutions and Securitisation in the Mekong River Basin

Over the past decades, there have been multiple levels of regional cooperation arrangements that have facilitated water cooperation and basin development of the Mekong River. These include the MRC and the ASEAN-Mekong Basin Development Cooperation (AMBDC) arrangements, which were introduced for a joint development of the river basin and its resources. The MRC remains the central institution promoting cooperation and looking after the water resource management of the Mekong River, now running numerous development and integrated water resource management initiatives (Sunchindah 2013). Complementing these are other regional structures such as the Association of Southeast Asian Nations (ASEAN) formed in 1967 and the Greater Mekong Sub-region Economic Cooperation (GMS-ECP) initiated in 1992 with the objective of promoting sub-regional economic connectivity and infrastructural development, and others such as Golden Quadrangle or the Quadripartite Economic Cooperation (QEC), the Lower Mekong Initiative (LMI), etc. (Lu 2016). The lack of coordination among these multiple institutions dealing with almost similar issues but with different approaches suggests that instead of working towards inclusive growth and regional development, countries are promoting their own individual interests (Keskinen et al. 2008; Hirsch et al. 2006).

A new addition to this multifaceted arrangement is China's parallel initiative to the GMS-ECP and MRC, namely, the Lancang-Mekong Cooperation Mechanism (LMCM) introduced in 2015 (MOFA 2016; Biba 2016). Whether the LMCM would facilitate better cooperation and trust among the riparians or increase the risk of tension and confrontation among them, is too early to be answered but, it is crucial as it is the first sub-regional cooperation arrangement agreed upon by all the six riparian countries. China's behaviour and engagement with the various institutional forums relating to cooperation on the Mekong has been described as 'forum shopping', where Beijing picks and chooses forums, or creates new ones which are conducive to its interests, and in the process, bypassing existing institutions, such as the MRC and its legally binding rules (Hensengerth 2009). The formation of the LMCM and the symbolic gesture by China of accommodating lower riparian Vietnam's concerns of releasing more water is indicative of China's forum shopping behaviour.

China's hydropower development on the Lancang River or the Mekong River might be securitised in a number of ways (Goh 2004; Biba 2014; Ho 2014). First, China's potential control over vital water flows to the lower riparian states may be framed as a challenge to the sovereignty and autonomy of the lower riparian states, which are also the members of the MRC. Second, the possible large-scale and adverse impacts on communities within each of these lower riparian states might affect the popularity and stability of the governing national or local regime, for example, as seen in a growing community mobilization challenging the central government's policies and priorities in Thailand. Third, expected problems with demand, supply and pricing, particularly, if affected by the reduced lifespan of dams or the impact of environmental factors on electricity supply, when the regional power grid is in place, may lead to diplomatic tension between the riparian states. Finally, the negative impacts on regional livelihoods and food supply may be substantial in terms of the number of people affected, particularly in the absence of effective alternatives amidst increased empowerment of communities, which may lead to migration and other socio-political instabilities which may be securitised at the national level in the lower riparian countries; such securitisation has in fact, occurred in Vietnam, with it arguing in various multilateral negotiation platforms for tighter control over water utilization of the Mekong through prior consultation measures, in order to safeguard the livelihood and food security of its people dependent on fisheries and agriculture (Mirumachi 2015).

China's Behaviour in the Mekong River Basin

China's performance in international negotiations over water as well as in the regional Mekong regime reveals Beijing's understanding of transboundary cooperation as being more of a strategic option than a normative commitment. This also suggests that alliances confronted with the impacts of Chinese water policy should focus on strategies of counterbalancing rather than criticizing or ignoring Chinese ambitions (Menniken 2007). China being in a dominant position hydrologically and politically, a second strategy for such alliances would be 'issue linkage', by offering incentives in non-water fields in return for the cooperative management of shared water resources (Menniken 2007), and an important part of this can be regional economic development cooperation. Indeed, this explains the present character of the China-MRC relations.

The fact that China is not a member of the MRC is seen by some as a source of potential weakness of the Commission itself, with lower riparian countries such as Cambodia and Vietnam seeing upstream dams constructed by China as a threat to the 'flood pulse' of the river and the livelihoods it sustains (UNDP 2006). Moore (2009) points out that the Mekong River system presents particular challenges for China's security, as relations between China and its downstream neighbours in the Mekong basin have long been fragile, and this situation is likely to be exacerbated by the construction of several dams in the Chinese province of Yunnan, restricting flow to the downstream nations. Further, as climate models suggest, if the transboundary water flow to the Mekong becomes more variable under climate change, China's 'asymmetric' control of the river's headwaters will become an issue of even greater concern to the Southeast Asian nations (Moore 2009), especially Vietnam, where floods and droughts occur almost every year, with an average of 1.7-1.8 flood and 0.14-0.24 droughts per year (MRC 2012).

Along with these complexities, the increasing saline intrusion and reduced nutrient-rich alluvial deposits in its delta has largely affected the agricultural production and food security (Miao et al. 2015). The worst of the floods in Vietnam occurred successively between 1999 and 2002, and in 2006, which largely impacted the Cuu Long Delta and in 2008 that affected the eastern highlands of the country (Nguyen et al 2007, MRC 2012). Severe droughts have occurred over the period 1998–2005, with the worst and prolonged drought experienced in 1998, which continued for five months. The UNDP report, 'Vietnam: Drought and Saltwater Intrusion Situation Update' notes that Vietnam's 2016 drought induced by the El Nino—the climatic cycle in the Pacific Ocean—was one of the worst droughts that has affected the country's southern Mekong Delta, the main rice-growing region. This drought has affected nearly 1.75 million people, with a loss of 477,113 hectares of land, 470,256 hectares of crops, and 6,857 hectares of aquaculture and fisheries (UNDP 2016). Vietnamese officials time and again have stressed that these prolonged droughts occurring in the Mekong Delta are not just the result of natural phenomena such as the El Nino but also due to the Chinese hydropower dams operating upstream (Zhou 2016).

China's relations with the MRC must be seen as a function of Chinese foreign policy, and Chinese foreign policy at the time of the conclusion of the 1995 Agreement was resistant in general to regional multilateral initiatives; until the mid-1990s, Beijing was an adamant 'bilateralist', on issues both central and peripheral to its interests (Hirsch et al. 2006). At about the same time period as it did not join the MRC, for example, it rejected other initiatives by the Southeast Asian countries to multilateralise the South China Sea, and had initially resisted broader initiatives for consultative arrangements such as the ASEAN Regional Forum (ARF), which it finally agreed to with great reluctance (Hirsch et al. 2006).

The most critical political ramification of China's hydropower development on the Mekong is that China will be able to control the quantity of water released to the lower riparian countries, with the worst-affected states being those furthest downstream—Vietnam and Cambodia. And, the lack of any formal treaty agreements, even of the minimum kind found in the Mekong Agreement for the lower basin which obliges co-riparian states to consult with or to inform the others in the case of any hydrological projects, means that there are no adequate safeguards in place (Goh 2004). The Chinese government however, has all along been saying that it remains committed to the integral and comprehensive development of the Mekong River basin in the light of greater China-ASEAN integration, and to ensuring that Chinese activities in the upper Mekong River will not be carried out at the cost of the riparian countries in the lower reaches (Tang 2002), and this theme is demonstrated in subsequent Chinese official pronouncements, for example in the 2010 Hua Hin Declaration (MRC 2010a) and the 2016 Sanya Declaration; the latter was also the occasion for the formation of the LMCM.

Furthermore, downplaying its hydropower dams' affecting the downstream flow regime, Beijing has switched towards a 'damage control' strategy (Storey 2010). For instance, in 2010, China invited the LMC officials to visit its Jinghong Dam for inspection as a goodwill gesture (Biba 2016). In 2013, China and the lower riparian countries renewed the 2002 agreement on hydrological data sharing during the annual flood seasons, and China agreed to expand the period of data sharing from four to five months (June to October) and the frequency of data sent from once to twice a day (MRC 2016). China had indicated its willingness to share data during the dry season from the hydro-meteorological stations at Jinghong and Manwan, limited to only emergency conditions (MRC 2010b; MRC 2013). However, there are no agreements for the sharing of data during the dry seasons, which is critical for the LMC to prevent droughts (Biba 2016). China's uncertain behaviour and signaling on the Mekong cooperation agenda thus directly affects the lower riparian interests.

Locating China-Vietnam Relations in Mekong River Basin Cooperation

The meandering maze of Vietnam's deltaic region, considered to be its rice bowl and fish basket, is under threat from an increasing saltwater intrusion into the Mekong estuary from the South China Sea, and the primary reason for this is the erratic and reduced flows of the various tributaries of the Mekong, owing to interventions on the river upstream by China. Prior to the Sanya Declaration in March 2016, there were incidents of saltwater intrusion, which were causing damage to fisheries and rice cultivation in the lower reaches of the Vietnamese delta, and following concerns voiced by Vietnam, China decided to release excess water from its upstream Jinghong Hydropower Station in Yunnan. This move created a cascade effect, which allowed midstream Laos to release more water from its dams to replenish the lower reaches of the Mekong in Vietnam.

The common assumption of unilaterist behaviour by upstream China in relation to the MRC countries (Waterbury 2002) is seen as shifting towards looking at China being open to cooperating with the lower riparian countries, and especially with Vietnam, which is the most vulnerable in the Mekong River basin. Although there are other bilateral disagreements, such as over the South China Sea issue, the realignments of China-Vietnam relations on the Mekong River is seen by the region as a positive sum interaction dynamic, and the base of which is the economic and infrastructural development of the region (Zhu 2010, Lu 2016). It is in the joint interests of both China and Vietnam to take forward Mekong cooperation, and to achieve a leadership role in such joint and regional commitments, towards benefiting their relatively underdeveloped border provinces, China's southwest and Vietnam's north (MMN and AMC 2013).

The southwestern provinces of China, namely Yunnan and Guangxi, border Vietnam's northern land border, and it is the development and connectivity of this expanse of mountainous region linking both the countries which holds priority for Beijing and Hanoi. China's Western Development Strategy has been directed at pushing economic development zones and connectivity corridors linking Yunnan and Guangxi with the northern provinces of Vietnam, such as the Lang Son and Quang Ninh as well as the cities of Hanoi and Haiphong (MMN and AMC 2013). Such connectivity and opening up are expected to benefit both China and Vietnam, enabling access to markets for Chinese and Vietnamese consumer products in larger Southeast Asia (ASEAN 2011, Ho 2014).

Cooperation on the Mekong and joint investments on critical infrastructural projects on developing the water resources and the watercourse of the Mekong River basin, by both China and Vietnam, has uniquely positioned them to take forward their respective national development goals. The spillover effects of Mekong cooperation can be seen in Beijing and Hanoi allocating greater resources to their southwestern and northern provinces, respectively. Such collective action can be seen as being benefits beyond the river as put forward by Sadoff and Grey (2002) and Bobekova et al. (2013), in their explanation of types of cooperative river basins, enabling socioeconomic and livelihood development and political stability in the region. In terms of hydropower development on the Mekong River basin, China sells electricity through the GMS power grid to Vietnam, and Vietnam also has investments in hydropower projects upstream in Laos and Cambodia, in addition to the ones it is developing in its central highlands (Bobekova et al. 2013). Schmeier (2009) points out that Vietnam indirectly supports the same hydropower projects that it suffers from eventually, and this signifies the complex interlinkages of national and regional priorities in the Mekong.

Conclusion

The Mekong has witnessed a surge of water-related events in the past 15 years, which have corresponded with important political events, be it bilateral or multilateral in nature, within the region. The land boundary dispute between China and Vietnam was successfully resolved in 2000, a time period which also marked the beginning of China's shift in stance on providing critical hydrological data to the Mekong basin riparians, and moving from an upstream hegemonic unilateralist to showing signs of engagement on a multilateral platform. The economic rationale of Mekong cooperation has seen China behaving as a donor to many hydroelectric projects in the Lower Mekong region, and this has also brought Vietnamese support and investment in such projects, given the huge demand for electricity in the region. Hydropower generation and economic development seem to be the primary driving forces behind inter-state cooperation in the Mekong region, and the cooperation between China and Vietnam on the Mekong also falls under the same broad context.

The nature of such cooperation is multi-scalar and bears a host of interlinkages from upstream arrangements and priorities to downstream rearrangements and priorities. The politics of position within the Mekong River basin and the assumption of hegemonic leadership roles by China and Vietnam in the Upper Mekong and the Lower Mekong, respectively, will largely determine whether institutional forums have any efficacy or role to play in intensifying the Mekong cooperation process. The benefits accrued from the new forums such as the LMCM for the riparian stakeholders of the Lower Mekong basin will determine the success and validity of Chinese engagement in the region. Vietnam's participation and engagement has been critical in bringing about the six-party development consensus through the LMCM.

There is definitely a sense of caution among the MRC countries on the 'dominant role' of China in the LMCM at present while in the past external donors to the MRC such as the United States and Japan have been critical of China's branding and rebranding of institutional regimes in the Mekong basin (Hensengerth 2009). This reprioritizing of regional calculations in the Mekong basin cooperation, given the six-party consensus on the Chinese-led LMCM, comes in the backdrop of China's ambitious 'one belt, one road' or 'belt and road' initiative infrastructure development goals in the larger region, of which the MRC countries and Southeast Asia form an integral part (Lu 2016). Regional cooperation and solidarity as emphasized by China through the LMCM process is directed to spin off strategic benefits for the 'belt and road' initiative, and Vietnam's participation and engagement is of particular importance, given the maritime contestations in the South China Sea, which have remained unsolved. Concessions among the riparians on important livelihood concerns such as agricultural production and fisheries' sustainability and development and other core environmental services, will translate into a sense of goodwill, which will spillover to other issue areas, and this has been the prime driver of China's current engagement with Cambodia and Vietnam.

The relationship between China and Vietnam on the Mekong can be contextualized in the frame of the river as a site of production, located among layers of differing national priorities, one of hydrological development and electricity generation, and the other of agricultural production and fisheries, the 'river as a powerhouse site' and the 'river as a rice-bowl and fish farming site'. It is the cooperative calibration of livelihood sustainability and the economic development aspirations of the people living in the Mekong basin that both China and Vietnam need to move towards. It remains to be seen how the old and new regimes achieve this for the Mekong.

REFERENCES

Association of Southeast Asian Nations (ASEAN). 2011. *Master Plan on ASEAN Connectivity*. ASEAN Secretariat.

Backer, E. B. 2007. 'The Mekong River Commission: Does it work, and how does the Mekong basin's geography influence its effectiveness', *Journal of Current Southeast Asian Affairs*, Vol. 26, No. 4, 32-56.

Biba, S. 2014. 'Desecuritization in China's Behavior towards its Transboundary Rivers: the Mekong River, the Brahmaputra River and the Irtysh and the Ili Rivers', *Journal of Contemporary China*, Vol. 23, No. 85, 21-43.

Biba, S. 2016. 'China drives water cooperation with Mekong countries'. *The Third Pole*, https://www.thethirdpole.net/2016/02/01/china-drives-water-cooperation-with-mekong-countries/ (accessed on 5 July 2016).

Bobekova, E., Scott Pearse-Smith and Isak Svensson. 2013. 'Rivers of Peace: Institutionalised Mekong River Cooperation and the East Asian Peace', *European Journal of East Asian Studies*, Vol. 12, 7-34.

Dent, Christopher M. 2002. 'Introduction: Northeast Asia—a region in search of regionalism?', in Christopher M. Dent and David W. F. Huang (eds). *Northeast Asian Regionalism, Learning from the European Experiences* (Routledge-Curzon Press: London and New York).

Dosch, J. and Oliver Hensengerth. 2005. 'Sub-Regional Co-operation in Southeast Asia: The Mekong Basin', *European Journal of East Asian Studies*, Vol. 4, No. 2, 263-85.

Dore, J. and K. Lazarus. 2009. 'De-marginalizing the Mekong river commission', in Molle, F., Foran, T. and Kakonen, M., (eds), *Contested waterscapes in the Mekong region: Hydropower, livelihoods and governance* (Routledge: London).

Goh, Evelyn. 2004. 'China in the Mekong River Basin: The Regional Security Implications of Resource Development on the Lancang Jiang', Working Paper No. 69, Institute of Defence and Strategic Studies, Nanyang Technological University, Singapore, https://www.rsis.edu.sg/wp-content/uploads/rsis-pubs/WP69.pdf (accessed on 9 February 2016).

Hensengerth, O. 2009. 'Transboundary River Cooperation and the Regional Public Good: The Case of the Mekong River', *Contemporary Southeast Asia*, Vol. 31, No. 2, 326-49.

Hirsch, P., K. M. Jensen, N. Carrard, S. FitzGerald and R. Lyster. 2006. 'National Interests and Transboundary Water Governance in the Mekong', Australian Mekong Resource Centre in collaboration with Danish International Development Assistance. The University of Sydney, http://sydney.edu.au/mekong/documents/mekwatgov_mainreport.pdf (accessed on 9 February 2016).

Ho, S. 2014. 'China's policies in the Mekong and the Brahmaputra in comparative perspective', *Journal of Contemporary China*, Vol. 23, No. 85, 1-20.

International Rivers. August 2013. 'Lancang River Dams: Threatening the Flow of the Lower Mekong', https://www.internationalrivers.org/files/attached-files/ir_lacang_dams_2013_5.pdf (accessed on 4 July 2016).

Jacobs, Jeffrey W. 2002. 'The Mekong River Commission: transboundary water resources planning and regional security', *The Geographical Journal*, Vol. 168, No. 4, 354-364.

Keskinen, M., K. Mehtonen and O. Varis. 2008. 'Transboundary cooperation vs. internal ambitions: The role of China and Cambodia in the Mekong region', *International water security: domestic threats and opportunities*, 79-109, http://lib.tkk.fi/Diss/2010/isbn9789526032344/article1.pdf (accessed on 13 April 2016).

Lauridsen, Poul Erik. 2004. 'Transboundary Water Management in the Mekong: River of Controversy or River of Promise?', in Jannik Boesen and Helle Munk Ravnborg (eds) *From Water 'Wars' to Water 'Riots'?: Lessons from Transboundary Water Management*, Proceedings of the International Conference, December 2003, DIIS, Copenhagen, Copenhagen: Danish Institute for International Studies, http://diis.inforce.dk/graphics/Publications/WP2004/jbo_hmr_water.pdf#page=51 (accessed on 20 April 2016).

Lu, Guangsheng. 2016. 'China Seeks to Improve Mekong Sub-Regional Cooperation: Causes and Policies', *Policy Report*, S. Rajaratnam School of International Studies, Nanyang Technological University Nanyang Technological University, Singapore, February, https://www.rsis.edu.sg/wp-content/uploads/2016/02/PR160225_China-Seeks-to-Improve-Mekong.pdf (accessed on 20 April 2016).

Makim, A. 2002. 'The changing face of Mekong resource politics in the post-Cold War era: re-negotiating arrangements for water resource management in the Lower Mekong River Basin (1991-1995)', Working Paper No. 6, Australian Mekong Resource Center.

Mekong Migration Network (MMN) and Asian Migrant Centre (AMC). 2013. 'Migration in the Greater Mekong Subregion, Resource Book, In-depth Study: Border Economic Zones and Migration', January, http://www.mekongmigration.org/finalised%20BEZ%20pdf% 20file.pdf (accessed on 5 July 2016).

Mekong River Commission (MRC). 1995. Agreement on the cooperation for the sustainable development of the Mekong river basin. Mekong River Commission, Chiang Rai, http://www.mrcmekong.org/assets/Publications/policies/agreement-Apr95.pdf (accessed on 4 July 2016).

Mekong River Commission (MRC). 2010a. Hua Hin Declaration, 'Meeting the Needs, Keeping the Balance: Towards Sustainable Development of the Mekong River Basin', http://www.mrcmekong.org/assets/Publications/Events/MRCSummit2010/MRC-Hua-Hin-Declaration-05-Apr-10.pdf (accessed on 20 April 2016).

Mekong River Commission (MRC). 2010b. 'China ready to share data on Mekong water levels ahead of regional river summit', http://www.mrcmekong.org/news-and-events/news/china-ready-to-share-data-on-mekong-water-levels-ahead-of-regional-river-summit/ (accessed on 4 July 2016).

Mekong River Commission (MRC). 2012. 'The Impact & Management of Floods and Droughts in the Lower Mekong Basin and the Implications of Possible Climate Change', *Working Paper* (2011-2015), March, http://www.mrcmekong.org/assets/Publications/basin-reports/FMMP-working-paper-110820.pdf (accessed on 4 July 2016).

Mekong River Commission (MRC). 2013. 'Mekong River Commission and China boost water data exchange', August, http://www.mrcmekong.org/news-and-events/news/mekong-river-commission-and-china-boost-water-data-exchange/ (accessed on 4 July 2016).

Mekong River Commission (MRC). 2016. 20 Years of Cooperation, 1995-2015, January, http://www.mrcmekong.org/assets/Publications/20th-year-MRC-2016-.pdf (accessed on 20 April 2016).

Menniken, Timo. 2007. 'China's Performance in International Resource Politics: Lessons from the Mekong', *Contemporary Southeast Asia*, Vol. 29, No. 1, 97-120.

Miao, C., A. G. Borthwick, H. Liu and J. Liu., 2015. China's policy on dams at the crossroads: removal or further construction? *Water*, Vol. 7, No. 5, 2349-2357.

Ministry of Foreign Affairs of People's Republic of China (MOFA). 23 March 2016. 'Sanya Declaration of the First Lancang-Mekong Cooperation (LMC) Leaders' Meeting: For a Community of Shared Future of Peace and Prosperity among Lancang-Mekong Countries', http://www.fmprc.gov.cn/mfa_eng/zxxx_662805/t1350039.shtml (accessed on 20 April 2016).

Mirumachi, N. 2015. *Transboundary water politics in the developing world.* Routledge. Abingdon, Oxon, UK.

Moore, Scott. 2009. 'Climate Change, Water and China's National Interest', *China Security*. Vol. 5, No.3, 25-39.

Nguyen H.N., Vu K.T. and Nguyen X.N. 2007. 'Flooding in Mekong River Delta', in *Vietnam Human Development Report, 2008* (Hanoi).

Phillips, D., M. Daoudy, S. McCaffrey, J. Öjendal, and A. Turton. 2006. 'Trans-boundary water co-operation as a tool for conflict prevention and broader benefit sharing', https://lwrg.files.wordpress.com/2014/12/phillips-et-al-benefit-sharing-smfa-2006.pdf (accessed on 20 April 2016).

Sadoff, Claudia W. and David Grey. 2002. 'Beyond the river: the benefits of cooperation on international rivers', *Water Policy*, No. 4, 389-403.

Schmeier, S. 2009. 'Regional Cooperation Efforts in the Mekong River Basin: Mitigating river-related security threats and promoting regional development', *Current Research on South-East Asia Series*, Vol. 2, No. 2.

Storey, Ian. 2010. 'China's "Charm Offensive" Loses Momentum in Southeast Asia [Part II]', *China Brief*, Vol. 10, Issue 10, http://www.jamestown.org/programs/chinabrief/single/?tx_ttnews%5Btt_news%5D=36372&cHash=95a6ce07ea#.V34fB7h96M9 (accessed on 4 July 2016).

Summers, T. 2008. 'China and the Mekong Region', *China Perspectives*, No. 3, 68.

Sunchindah, A. 2013. The Lancang-Mekong River Basin: Reflections on cooperation mechanisms pertaining to a shared watercourse. RSIS Centre for Non-Traditional Security Studies No. PO13–01, http://econpapers.repec.org/paper/esswpaper/id_3a5287.htm (accessed on 4 July 2016).

Taga, H. 1994. International networks among local cities: the first step towards regional development. In F. Gipouloux (ed.), *Regional Economic Strategies in East Asia: A Comparative Perspective* (Maison Franco-Japonaise: Tokyo).

Tang Jiaxuan. 2002. Speech by Foreign Minister Tang Jiaxuan at the ASEAN-China Dialogue at Bandar Seri Begawan, Ministry of Foreign Affairs of the People's Republic of China, http://www.fmprc.gov.cn/mfa_eng/wjb_663304/zzjg_663340/gjs_665170/gjzzyhy_665174/2612_665212/2614_665216/t15321.shtml (accessed on 9 February 2016).

United Nations Development Programme (UNDP). 2006. *Human Development Report 2006*. Palgrave Macmillan: New York.

United Nations Development Programme (UNDP). June 2016. Report on Vietnam: Drought and Saltwater Intrusion Situation Update No. 3,

http://www.un.org.vn/images/stories/pub_trans/Viet_Nam_Drought_and_Saltwater_Intrusion_SitRep_3_-_15_June_2016.pdf (accessed on 4 July 2016).

Waterbury, J. 2002. Between Unilaterism and Comprehensive Accords: Modest Steps toward Cooperation in International River Basins. *Water Resources Development*, Vol. 13, No.3, 279-89.

Wolf, A.T., A. Kramer, A. Carius, and G.D. Dabelko. 2005. 'Managing water conflict and cooperation', in *State of the World 2005: Redefining Global Security*, The Worldwatch Institute, 80-95, http://transboundarywater.geo.orst.edu/publications/abst_docs/wolf_sow_2005.pdf (accessed on 4 July 2016).

Zhou, Margaret. 2016. 'China and the Mekong Delta: Water Savior or Water Tyrant?', *The Diplomat*, 23 March, http://thediplomat.com/2016/03/china-and-the-mekong-delta-water-savior-or-water-tyrant/ (accessed on 4 July 2016).

Zhu, Zhenming. 2010. Mekong Development and China's (Yunnan) Participation in the Greater Mekong Subregion Cooperation. *Ritsumeikan International Affairs*, No. 8, 1-16.

Index

*